TRAVERS, Stephen

The Miami
Showband massacre

THE MIAMI SHOWBAND MASSACRE

A Survivor's Search for the Truth

Stephen Travers

&

Neil Fetherstonhaugh

HACHETTE
BOOKS
IRELAND

Copyright © 2007 Stephen Travers and Neil Fetherstonhaugh

First published in paperback in 2008 by Hodder Headline Ireland

1

A CIP catalogue record for this title is available from the British Library.

ISBN 978 0340 937 94 5

Typeset in Adobe Garamond by Hachette Books Ireland
Cover design by Anú Design, Tara
Printed and bound in Great Britain by Clays Ltd, St Ives, plc

Hodder Headline Ireland's policy is to use papers that are natural,
renewable and recyclable products and made from wood grown in sus-
tainable forests. The logging and manufacturing processes are expected
to conform to the environmental regulations of the
country of origin.

Hachette Books Ireland
8 Castlecourt Centre, Castleknock, Dublin 15, Ireland

A division of Hachette Livre, 338 Euston Road, London
NW1 3BH, England

Contents

To Tony, Fran and Brian

Prologue

County Down, March 2006

There is nothing remarkable about the journey south from the small Northern Ireland town of Banbridge to its larger neighbour, Newry, least of all this small, shaded section of dual-carriageway near Buskhill. Located in County Down on the busy A1 motorway, it is used by thousands of motorists everyday, most of whom are probably oblivious to its terrible significance in recent Irish history. For it was here, on a beautiful summer's night, that one of the most notorious acts of savagery ever committed during Northern Ireland's Troubles took place. In the early hours of 31 July 1975, a minibus carrying five of the six members of The Miami Showband was stopped at this exact spot, at what they thought was a routine British army checkpoint. It wasn't.

My companion on this journey today, Stephen Travers, was one of those travelling on that minibus just over thirty years ago. As he turns the car and stops at the side of the road, I think I can recognise the scene from the media footage I have viewed so many times: the twisted remains of a tour bus, police sifting through debris, the poignancy of a pair of stage platform boots lying to one side. I may be just imagining it, but, yes, that tree, the bend in the road, how it slopes off slightly downhill towards the south, makes it all feel somehow familiar; as if I've been here before.

I glance over at Stephen as he stops the car and I wonder what he is thinking. His face is set hard as he stares straight ahead. He doesn't look at me as I ask him some questions about what happened that night.

We get out of the car and I follow him the few short steps to where a small bus shelter now stands, at the exact location where the Miami Showband stopped their minibus after being flagged down by a torch-waving soldier on the dark road. For four of the five young men in the vehicle that night – guitarist Tony Geraghty (twenty-three), singer and keyboardist Fran O'Toole (twenty-nine), trumpeter Brian McCoy (thirty-two) and sax player Des McAlea (thirty) – being pulled over was not unusual. They had travelled the length and breadth of the country with the Miami, consolidating their position at the very top of the Irish pop-music scene. By 1975, the bitter sectarian conflict that had afflicted the North for generations was being waged openly across its towns and fields. As the security situation continued to deteriorate, the band had become used to the minor inconvenience of suddenly encountering British forces as they crisscrossed the border separating the Irish Republic and Northern Ireland, on their way to or from another sold-out show.

For twenty-four-year-old bassist Stephen Travers, however, it wasn't so normal. It was part of a very steep learning curve. As the most recent member to join the group, this was just his sixth week as a Miami musician, army checkpoints in the dead of night were another fascinating aspect of his big adventure: 'I was the bass guitarist in one of Ireland's most popular bands, playing to thousands of people every night. And to come across a checkpoint in the middle of the night was like being in a movie. For someone who had rarely been stopped, even by the police, never mind armed soldiers, it was an exciting experience.'

Usually there would be a cursory glance into the vehicle, a quick check of identification and the occasional request for an autograph from a bemused soldier who suddenly realised he was pointing his gun at celebrities. 'Invariably, the next thing would be, "Hey, it's the Miami. How did it go tonight, lads?" And we'd return the banter; ask how it was going for them. Quite often they were young, about the same age as us, sometimes even younger, and would speak with English accents. It was great to be recognised, you know? Celebrity requires recognition, and friendly recognition is a stamp of approval.'

That night, however, things were very different. The Miami were told to step out of their van, and in a few terrifying minutes this seemingly random checkpoint changed into something that would devastate not just those present but an entire country, with repercussions that are still being felt to this day.

'I felt no concern, no worry at all,' Stephen is saying, almost to himself, as we stand beside the bus shelter, looking down into the ditch. 'We were lined up outside our minibus, facing this field. I stood where I'm standing now. One of the soldiers jokingly said something like, "Bet you'd rather be tucked up at home in bed than out here", and Fran, always the quick-wit, replied, "Bet you'd rather be anywhere else but lying in a ditch." When I think back on it now, it is difficult to understand how men could be so casual and jocular knowing full well the carnage, savagery and slaughter they were about to unleash.'

He goes quiet and starts to walk slowly along the edge of the ditch to where it meets a side road a few paces away. He stops and stares into the field. I start to follow, to ask a few more questions, but decide to leave him alone for a moment. Instead, I take some notes, and wonder what it must be like to revisit a place where your friends died in such a brutal way. Is it all coming back to him now that he has returned to this bleak spot? Maybe, over the years, it is possible to leave something so terrible behind and get on with your life without thinking about it every minute of every day. But what happens when you come back? Does it stir up the memories and awaken the ghosts?

I shake myself out of my reverie. It's getting cold and the sun is starting to set. It's time for us to leave. As we get back into the car and prepare for the drive back to Dublin, Stephen is silent. It is at times like this that the usual journalistic enquiry seems flat, hollow and inappropriate. 'How do you feel?' sounds inane and useless. How would I feel? How would you feel? And what about those who stopped the minibus that night and unleashed terror on those inside – how did they feel?

Night has fallen and it's dark as we cross the border, watching Northern Ireland and its many unanswered questions fading in our rear-view mirror.

*

Three weeks have passed since I stood on the side of that cold roadside with Stephen. Three short weeks, but already the difference in the weather is amazing. Today, it is a beautiful spring day, one that makes you think that perhaps we're in for a good summer.

Once I hit the motorway, I put a tape in the car stereo. It's an old recording and the sound quality isn't great, there are crackles and hisses before the song comes on. 'I didn't even know your name … and it didn't even matter …' Fran O'Toole belts out the lyrics to one of his greatest hits. It's good, notwithstanding the quality of mid-1970s recording techniques. I tap my fingers on the steering wheel.

It will be another hour before I reach Cork city and I settle back to enjoy the journey. On the seat beside me are newspaper cuttings. I glance at the headline on one, 'Three Dead in Horror Gun Attack – Showbiz World Unites in Grief', and think back to the last time I saw Stephen, on that windswept March day, by the side of the road where his friends had died.

*

On the way home from the North that day, he had been subdued. After a few miles driving in silence, I eventually asked if he was okay. He had assured me that he was fine, but I could see that the day had taken it out of him. It had been a long one and we were both tired. Stephen was driving. I leaned back in my seat and closed my eyes, and that's when he started to speak, slowly revealing his motivation in reliving the story he had suppressed for over thirty years. I reached over and quietly pressed the record button on my dictaphone. Now, I root around and find the tape recorder buried under the newspapers. I turn off the car stereo and press play.

'For a long time, and for many reasons, I couldn't talk about what happened. I resented the fact that I was even associated with it. It was called an atrocity – "the Miami Showband massacre" – but I call it "the incident". You know, I rationalised it with self-coined clichés like, it was "not personal". It was just something that happened simply because I was in the wrong place at the wrong time. Eventually, if it was ever mentioned, it felt like I was talking about someone else. Perhaps it's a strategy that worked to a certain extent because you're led to believe that you should be devastated or even destroyed by an experience like that. I wasn't. I survived. I got on with my life.'

He went on to reveal how the cracks in this coping mechanism had started to appear exactly twenty years later.

'On the twentieth anniversary of the incident, I flew into Dublin from my home in London. I wanted to get as much done as possible during the course of that day. I needed to fill it up so there wouldn't be a moment to spare where an uncontrollable thought might sneak in, like a sliver of dark light. I hired the biggest, fastest car possible. I drove to the spot where it all happened and stared without thinking or remembering. I stopped in the centre of Banbridge and, as if in a fit of bravado, I asked an armed policeman if a particular building had once been called The Castle Ballroom. He answered casually, "Yes, sir, I believe it was."

'I visited Daisy Hill Hospital. It had changed since the manic night I was brought there. As I left, I glanced sharply at a sign that said 'Mortuary', where the lads had been laid out after they were brought in – a cold bed I might have shared with them had the aim of evil men been half-an-inch to one side or the other. A cold chill returned to freeze me even then, twenty years later. I continued towards Dublin and on to Bray in County Wicklow, where Fran is buried. Silently, I thanked him for his faith in me. Finally, I made my way to Mount Jerome where Tony was laid to rest, but I couldn't find his grave. I was frustrated. I thought it would be easy just to walk in and remember where it was, but that place is so big I was soon alone and lost among the broken angels, headstones and uninvited memories.'

His carefully planned strategy had faltered just long enough to let in the ghosts he had intended to finally bury. He recalled how a psychiatrist had once assured him that he had seen more than he appeared to remember about that night.

'They suggested that, years later, I could be walking down a road and suddenly everything would come flooding back. They considered giving me sodium pentothal, the truth drug, to get it all out in a controlled environment so it wouldn't unexpectedly hit me like a ton of bricks. But they eventually decided that this wasn't necessary. They said I had dealt with it naturally.

'But who can confidently say that I have? Who can know for certain that I won't see it all again? I don't know if I have really dealt with all of the horrors. Are these terrible images and dreadful memories hidden away, locked in some deep cavern of my mind, awaiting release or escape? It was a beautiful moonlit night and, while I was in that field after the bomb had exploded, I did see my friends. Our handsome front man Fran must have been in a dreadful state. But part of my mind closed down, allowing me only to recall what it feels I can bear. I am apprehensive that this book, this journey we are about to take, might turn out to be the key that releases a renewed terror. I am fearful. Have I really exorcised the demons or have I just locked them away? Are they really gone forever? I don't know. But I have to take that chance.'

I turn off the tape. As he had driven on into the darkness, Stephen had mentioned that he was anxious to pay tribute to his friends, to ensure that their story, already secured a place in history, was told truthfully and accurately. I assured him that that was exactly what I wanted to help him achieve.

Then he revealed another motivation. He said it was time to shine a light into the dark corners. When I asked what he meant by that, he said he wanted to meet those who had tried to kill him.

I press Forward on the dictaphone. The speeded-up voices whirr past. Stop. Play.

'I need to know what motivated young men of my own generation to take up positions on a dark country road and ambush a minibus full of innocent musicians. I can tell you all I know about Tony, Fran and Brian – and I'm sure that their families would be willing to share their memories of them – but, on the other hand, we know relatively little about their killers.

'When I contemplate how much we must have had in common, at many stages of our lives, I am compelled to find out what brought us together on that fateful night … I would like to understand how children who played the same games, teenagers who liked the same music and young adults, perhaps aspiring to many of the same goals, could meet under such shocking circumstances. These people will certainly need to feature in our book. But I do not wish to draw them, or those they claim to represent or their cause, with simplistic broad brush-strokes … We should try to meet them.'

This is a big undertaking, and I'm not sure if it is what I had in mind. For some reason, the prospect of meeting murderers hadn't occurred to me when I approached Stephen with the idea of writing about his experiences with the Miami, but I have to admit, I am intrigued by the notion. Here is a man who, despite the terrible pain inflicted on him, after seeing his friends suffer the cruellest of deaths, has been able to forgive. I, on the other hand, find it difficult to understand how anyone could genuinely feel for somebody who tried to take away their life.

'I've prayed at my bedside for those men every night before going to sleep,' Stephen continues. 'I see them as the victims of the atrocity, too. I want to make sense of it all and show a curious world how those, who might ultimately reveal themselves as just ordinary people under extraordinary circumstances, can arrive at such a position.'

I cannot see how sitting down and talking to people whose business is killing is going to convince anyone that they are just 'ordinary people'. Murder is murder. But, then, who am I to judge? I have resolved to make this journey with Stephen Travers and I am going to do just that, wherever it might lead us.

Part I
BEGINNINGS

Chapter 1

I pull up outside the house in one of the leafy suburbs of Cork where Stephen lives with his wife, Anne, and their fourteen-year-old daugher, Sean. We greet each other warmly on the step and go inside for a cup of tea. We sit and chat, then head back out to the car to start our seventy-mile journey to Stephen's hometown, where he was born and grew up – Carrick-on-Suir in south Tipperary. It is a relaxing drive through some of the most striking countryside in the southeast of Ireland. Along the way, Stephen talks about his life before the Miami, and how he became a member of one of the most popular bands in Ireland.

The road sweeps round and suddenly the seaside town of Dungarvan lies beneath us, nestled behind a thin shoreline before a calm, glittering sea. It's then a short but glorious journey through the Comeragh Mountains and on to Carrick-on-Suir, where Stephen was born on 12 January 1951 in Carrick Beg, or 'Little Carrick', which lies on the south bank of the River Suir. This part of the river also divides two great Irish counties – the southside of the town is located in County Waterford, but across the river, where Stephen lived from the age of four, is County Tipperary.

The town of Carrick-on-Suir stands in a beautiful valley overlooked by Sliabh Na mBan to the north and the Comeragh Mountains to the south. Now a busy modern town, back in the 1950s it was a quiet, quaint backwater, one of Ireland's hidden gems. It provides quite a backdrop for Stephen's memories of his boyhood. As we arrive in the town, he points out the large green spaces, with their clusters of trees, which had been their Sherwood Forest, their lookout posts and jungle lairs. We pass a place they used to call 'Humpty's', which provided a safe area to circle the wagons when imaginary red Indians appeared on the horizon. A railway crossing runs past the outskirts of the town, and it was here the local children gathered when they heard the approach of the Limerick–Rosslare boat-train.

On his way to and from school, Stephen would pass one of the mysterious 'fairy rings' that dot the country-side around here. In the evenings, after school, Stephen would gather with his friends at the bottom of New Street to await the arrival of the post-office mailman, Tommy McCormack. When he came into sight with his hand-held cart, they would help him push it from the town park to the railway station. For the ageing man, a gang of kids who were only too happy to help lever a heavy load up the steep hill at the bottom of Cregg Road must have been a godsend; for the kids, it was just another game.

The mighty River Suir flows through the veins of all Carrick folk, it is the lifeline of the town. Stephen's late father, Patrick, was one of many townsmen who owned a locally produced flat-bottom boat called a cot, examples of which can still be seen moored along the riverbank today. He proudly took his eldest son on many fly-fishing expeditions and taught him how to make artificial flies, solemnly initiating him into the secrets of how the different colours and shapes would fool the fat trout and salmon that inhabited the river.

To Stephen, his father was a hero. 'He was a spiritual man, dignified, kind, loving, strong-willed, intelligent, fair and gentle.' While his job at the local Miloko plant, or 'chocolate factory' as it was known in Carrick, provided a regular wage, it was one that could just about keep the family's heads above water in tougher times. However, unlike many men of the town, he never drank, so the family was spared some of the harshness that alcohol inflicted on other homes.

We have stopped at the graveyard where Stephen's

parents are buried and we enter to pay our respects. Patrick Joseph Travers died in 1973 of a sudden heart attack at the age of fifty-six. Beside him lies his beloved wife, Mary, who survived her husband and best friend for many years until she died in 2001, aged eighty-six. They met in London, at the end of the Second World War. They married and had a daughter, Patricia, before returning to Ireland, where Stephen Thomas Travers was born in 1951. When a third child, Michael, was born three years later, the Travers family was complete and they settled down to a quiet and peaceful life in the small town at the edge of the great river.

Stephen's parents were devout Catholics. Their faith was staunch and unquestioning, and religion was an influential force in young Stephen's life. 'They were active participants and encouraged the same devotion in their children as they themselves had,' he remembers. Stephen, his sister and brother attended Mass every morning before school and the whole family would kneel together every night to recite the Rosary before bed.

Religion also played a huge role in education in Ireland. As we walk past St Nicholas' Church on William Street, Stephen points out the old Presentation Convent School where he was enrolled at the age of four. Three years later he attended The Green School, run by the Christian Brothers, who are credited with bringing education to the masses in Ireland. Sadly, they could also enforce discipline with a harshness that would later be considered unacceptable. Corporal punishment was an everyday event and was meted out on a regular basis during class, its arbitrary nature creating an atmosphere of fear and brutality. 'Some of them were frustrated, misguided, dedicated fanatics who expected unquestioning respect, but who rarely earned it,' Stephen recalls. 'Favouritism could be shown to some kids while others suffered at the hands of Brothers who simply did not like them. The teaching staff was augmented by lay teachers, who also had their fair share of bullying thugs among their ranks.'

As a quiet child, thin and fair-haired, Stephen avoided the worst excesses of the more brutal teachers and Brothers. While he didn't have a great interest in sports and didn't join any of the school teams, he had many friends and could hold his own against the bullies who roamed the schoolyards. Academically, he was lazy, paying attention only to those subjects in which he was interested, but he was clever enough to get by in other classes.

Like most families at that time, Stephen's listened avidly to the wireless. In a rural setting, radio provided one of the few methods of connecting with the outside world. An entire family would gather around a radio set and tune in to Radio Éireann for the news and entertainment, presented by household names such as Paddy Crosbie and Eamonn Andrews. The Travers family was no different. They had a huge radiogram – a shiny piece of furniture that was both a radio set and a record player. When bought new, the family was offered three free records as part of the deal.

'My sister Patsy was three years older than me and had developed a taste for popular music so she was allowed to choose two of the records. My father was a great music lover and among his favourites were Brendan O'Dowda singing Percy French, and Mario Lanza, the famous "voice of the century". I remember his choice was an EP record by Fr Sidney McEwan. One of the records my sister chose was 'It's Now or Never' by Elvis Presley. I liked it and I would sing along whenever she put it on. But it was the B-side that really caught my attention – it was called 'Rock-a-Hula Baby' and it sounded so different to the A-side. I loved it. It had been released in 1962 and was a number-one hit in Ireland that April. I was eleven years of age and I had discovered rock 'n' roll for the first time.'

One day, his parents brought home a huge black-and-white television set. This was an extraordinary development in the lives of people who, until then, had only the written or spoken word to keep them entertained and informed.

When television was introduced into parts of rural Ireland in the early 1960s, it switched on a very bright light and the country woke up, rubbing its eyes in amazement. It transformed rural communities from insular, tight-knit villages and towns to a mass that gazed in astonishment at images that may as well have been from another world. RTÉ's first broadcast to the nation, on New Year's Eve 1961, was a televised gala celebration from the Gresham Hotel in Dublin, hosted by broadcasting legend Eamonn Andrews. 'It was really astounding,' Stephen says. 'We were among the first families in our neighbourhood to own a television set. When it was switched on, we gathered with our neighbours' children to watch. In the daytime all we got was the test card, but the kids sat around watching even that for hours, fascinated.'

Early programmes that Stephen can remember include grainy cartoons, such as a sort of Irish version of Donald Duck called Daithi Lacha, and a show called *Rescue Eight*. Saturday night in the Travers' household was TV night and there was much excitement as the children, having had their baths and laid out clean clothes and polished shoes for early morning mass, sat in their pyjamas to watch old movies.

'I remember they showed the horror film *Nosferatu*, that scared the living daylights out of me, but our family favourite was a variety Sunday evening show called *Curtain Up* that featured, among others, comedienne Maureen Potter and the girls' favourite Cordovox player, Jackie Farn.'

The variety shows also featured broadcasts from the burgeoning showband scene and figures who would go on to become legends made their first appearances on this new, far-reaching medium. 'Of course we were accustomed to watching international artists like Elvis Presley in his movies at the local cinema,' Stephen recalls, 'but when TV came along, we suddenly had our own talent beamed into our homes. Home-grown entertainers may have been emulating the likes of Elvis, but they were stars in their own right.'

One of these exciting new performers was a young man from neighbouring Waterford. His name was Brendan Bowyer, a former choirboy who would score the biggest Irish hit of the 1960s with 'The Hucklebuck', a song he had heard on an album in the USA and which became the anthem of the showband scene. It even charted in England – a dream accomplishment for Bowyer, who had an ambition to break into the English and American charts since his early days with The Royal Showband, the undisputed kings of the Irish showband scene in the early 1960s.

'The Hucklebuck' went into the Irish charts in January 1965 and stayed there for twelve weeks. It became the signature tune for RTÉ's *The Showband Show*. Stephen first saw it performed on that show by the Royal, with Bowyer singing along with his trademark flailing of limbs and backed up by the Hucklebuck dancers, and it made a big impression on the young boy from Carrick-on-Suir.

'I wasn't old enough to get to see the bands performing in the dancehalls, so my first real experience of them was on television. However, later I did have the opportunity to meet some of the great showband musicians who came to the Ormond Ballroom in Carrick-on-Suir. Me and my friends would patiently wait for the bands to arrive before the performance to set up their equipment. We were allowed to help carry the band gear from the van to the ballroom stage, where we would then pester the musicians to show us the latest guitar riff or chord sequence to some popular hit. Among the most obliging of these showband stars was Henry McCullough, who later went on to accompany Joe Cocker at Woodstock before becoming the lead guitarist with Paul McCartney's Wings.

'Showbands are often criticised for covering popular songs rather than performing their own material, but the reality was that the audience demanded to hear instantly recognisable music. The musicians faced the choice of acquiescing to public demand or taking up alternative employment. To them, playing covers was the lesser of two evils. The positive outcome of playing everything that entered the pop charts was that Irish showband musicians were among the most versatile and accomplished in the world. They had to play material as diverse as The Beach Boys, The Beatles, Glen Miller and Blood, Sweat and Tears. Sadly, there is no such training ground any more and music is much the poorer for it.

'The Checkers was one of two resident bands on *The Showband Show*. One of them had a twin-neck guitar, which was very impressive indeed. The other was a rock 'n' roll outfit called The Greenbeats and they featured a great pianist named John Keogh, who was Ireland's answer to 'The Killer', Jerry Lee Lewis. Big names like Dickie Rock, who fronted The Miami Showband for many years, Brendan O'Brien and The Dixies, Butch Moore and The Capitol Showband and Joe Dolan and The Drifters were star attractions. But it was Brendan Bowyer who had all the moves. As far as we were concerned, he was our very own Elvis Presley and, like everyone else, I took up a brush handle and pretended I was him.'

While television provided a medium for home-grown talent, it was also a window into the huge cultural explosion that catapulted the 1960s into the history books as the decade of change. In the United States, the Kennedys were in office, trailing power and glamour wherever they went. The June 1963 state visit by John F. Kennedy to Ireland was one of the first big international stories covered by RTÉ.

'It was a renaissance,' Stephen declares, 'but, for me, the 1960s really started in 1963 when The Beatles came back as seasoned musicians from Germany. They, just like the showbands, had played covers and honed their skills by listening to and copying the styles of greats, such as Chuck Berry, Bo Diddley and Little Richard. All of a sudden, they were on our TV screens, playing ground-breaking songs like 'I Feel Fine', 'Help!' and 'She Loves You'. They created a massive chasm between our parents and us. Suddenly, there was a marked difference between what they liked and what we liked. The showbands had taken the country through its all-important musical transition period, but now there were the beat groups. Every generation strives to define itself and it was The Beatles who labelled mine. We could relate to them, we were the first generation of post-war babies and were indulged, in as much as was possible then, by our parents.'

By the time The Beatles arrived in Dublin in November 1963, on the Irish leg of their first inter-national tour, Beatlemania had taken over the country and thousands gathered outside the Adelphi Cinema on O'Connell Street to catch one of the two shows they performed. As the crowds streamed out of the theatre after the first show, they clashed with the throng waiting impatiently outside for the second concert. Police were called to break up what turned into a mini riot and dozens were arrested. The four young men who were at the centre of it all were forced to crouch down in a newspaper van, which smuggled them over to the relatively safe confines of the Gresham Hotel.

The scenes that greeted The Beatles' arrival in Dublin were practically unheard-of in Ireland at that time and for Stephen Travers, watching the events on television, it was a defining moment. Something clicked inside him, and although he didn't know it at the time, the excitement generated by the images would eventually change his life. Nothing would ever be the same again.

Chapter 2

In Catholic Ireland, there was no better way of guaranteeing a place in Heaven than by joining the priesthood. When a boy was selected for one of the strict training colleges, it was considered a great honour and a blessing on his family. So, naturally, there was a surge of pride in Carrick when a handful of the local children were accepted by the Christian Brothers' recruitment officer, Brother O'Brien. In a moment of misplaced enthusiasm, Stephen decided the Church was for him, too. It was 1964 and he was just thirteen years of age.

'Everyone seemed very proud that our school had been selected to sacrifice some of its finest for such a noble cause. I suggested to my parents that perhaps I might like to join the following year, when I was old enough. I was only toying with the idea and I was too young anyway to really know what I was doing but they were absolutely over the moon. My parents had a great faith in the Catholic Church and suffered from what I would describe as a frightening innocence in their wholehearted, unquestioning acceptance of Church dogma. I was carried on the tide of euphoria and pride they had in me and I was happy to go along with it. It had certainly made them proud and if I ever hinted at backing out, they appeared to be hurt. I tried to convince myself that I had a genuine vocation but, deep down, I knew that wasn't really the case. I tried not to think about it but by the summer 1965, when my time had run out, I knew I had made a dreadful mistake. But, by then, a black suit had been tailored, and white shirts and black ties had been bought at great expense. Before I knew it, everyone was waving their white handkerchiefs as the black car whisked me off to a new life among the men of God.'

Stephen's travelling companion was a big lad from his class named Michael Kelly, who tried to calm his fears. By the time they reached Wynn's Hotel in Dublin, where they were met by the Carrick-on-Suir Brother Superior, Stephen felt a little bit better about his decision. 'As we made the short drive to the training college at Carriglea Park, Dún Laoghaire, on that rainy afternoon, I looked out the window and my spirits fell. I questioned my sanity for the first time in my life. We were met on the steps at the front of the college by the Brother Superior, a fat monk with a jolly face and a well-rehearsed attitude. He smiled and told me I was a good-looking boy.'

Stephen was led to a cramped, Spartan cubicle in the college dormitory, where he tried to settle down to his new life. 'Strangely, unlike the other boys, I didn't cry myself to sleep that first night,' he remembers. 'Most of them were upset as they were far away from home but, for me, it only really started to sink in after a few weeks. By then, I was the one who was crying.'

Buckling down to a life of early-morning prayers and silent communal eating didn't prove easy and within a few weeks he was wondering aloud why he was there. 'I didn't settle into the strict regime and I knew I didn't have a true vocation. As the Christmas holidays approached, the Brothers realised this too and the Brother Superior solemnly informed me that I would not be welcome back after the break. I tried to appear disappointed, but my heart was jumping for joy. It was one of the happiest days of my life. I had planned to break the news gently to my parents but on arrival at the train station in Carrick, I just blurted it out. They were very understanding and said they were proud of me for trying. I suspect that they were secretly relieved to have me back home again.'

The timing was perfect – his new-found freedom coincided with his own coming-of-age and as he hit his teenage years, he developed interests outside those of cowboys and Indians and schoolbooks. Suddenly, girls existed and, like the other young lads around town, he was curious how he could attract their attention. He had never shone at school or dazzled on the playing field, but now he was beginning to think there might be another way to impress the girls who strolled nonchalantly along Main Street or on the riverbank, during the long summer holidays from school.

The highlight of every school term was a play, or an operetta, staged by the children before the Christmas break. These were huge events, attracting not only the proud parents of the participants but also the whole community. Near the end of his primary schooling, Stephen was at one of these performances in which a classmate, Jim Power, had taken an active part in the proceedings. 'Jim's mother was the choreographer of the school show. With her classically trained flautist husband, she had encouraged her son to take drum lessons. Now he was tasked with keeping the beat for the various marchers and singers during rehearsals. His party-piece was the snare-drum accompaniment to 'The March of The Toy Soldiers'.

In Stephen's eyes, Jim was transformed from another ordinary kid into a minor celebrity. He attracted the attention of the girls and drew admiration and envy from his classmates. Stephen was fascinated by his friend's talent, which had earned him this new respect and popularity. 'I also loved the sound he produced. It added to the fantasies already dancing in my head.' Stephen immediately became firm friends with Jim, a friendship that endures to this day. And this new alliance sowed the seeds of what would become Stephen's true vocation – a life dedicated to music.

Not long after the school show, Jim revealed that he had joined a young local band put together by a teenage entrepreneur, Noel Carroll, who had surrounded himself with other bright kids who displayed an artistic ability, lads like David Prim, Gay Brazel and Robert O'Connell. Robert, who sat beside Stephen in class for many years, is a nephew of the Clancy Brothers, a locally produced act that enjoyed massive international success. Jim asked Stephen if he would like to drop down to where the band rehearsed in a big storeroom at the back of McGrath's pub, which was owned by David Prim's mother.

When he stepped out of the sunlight and into the dark confines of the pub storeroom that afternoon, Stephen walked through the doors of another world. The fledgling musicians were standing on a stage built out of empty beer crates on a flat sheet of timber. Old, dyed bedsheets were draped from the roof to provide stage curtains and a backdrop. They were rehearsing some Shadows' and Beatles' songs. Stephen watched spellbound as they faithfully reproduced the Mersey sound. 'This was a whole new thing for me. I had never experienced anything like it before and it instantly snapped me to attention. When I saw these kids playing together I thought, that's it, this is what I want to do for the rest of my life.'

On his way home that day, his head was ringing with possibilities. What if he could do what they did? What if he could become a musician? He ran the rest of the way home with an idea.

'Recently, I was reading an interview with Jack Bruce of the rock band Cream in which he said that his first instrument was an old four-string plastic guitar that was called an Elvis Presley model because it had a picture of The King on the headstock. When I read it, I nearly fell off my chair because that too was my first instrument. I had the same old four-string guitar at home that had been lying around for years, an unwanted toy. Now, after watching Dave Prim and Gay Brazel produce these sounds, I wondered if it might be possible to copy them on my old Elvis Presley guitar. When I got back, I dug it out from under a pile of other stuff lying in a cupboard and started fumbling on one string. By moving one finger along the neck I thought I was able to copy part of a tune I'd heard them play. From that day on, I carried this little plastic guitar around, tormenting anyone who would listen to my one song and announcing to my parents and neighbours that I was a guitar player.'

Of course, strumming a plastic Elvis guitar and playing in a band were two opposite ends of the musical spectrum. Although he had found a new interest, he had nowhere to express it. 'I wanted to join these guys, but I didn't have any skills or developed talent. I had nothing to offer them in those terms, but they let me hang out with them anyway, perhaps because they saw something in me that convinced them that we had something in common. They'd encourage me to come down and watch them rehearse and afterwards we'd talk about music and art.'

In the meantime, the band had taken on a bass player called Michael Kerwick, an older brother of Stephen's childhood friend, Frannie Kerwick. 'I clearly remember him practising a bass line from a Wayne Fontana and The Mindbenders' hit called 'The Game of Love'. I was fascinated by it and in my head I thought, I could do that! I could be a bass player.'

Stephen finally got a break when he heard that Chelsea Power, the bass player with another local band, Jesse Walsh and The Web, had quit. Chelsea was selling his guitar for £5 and when Stephen expressed an interest in buying it, Jesse offered to cough up half if he came up with the rest.

'I asked my dad for the other £2.50 and he obliged, even though he hardly knew what an electric bass guitar was. True to their word, the lads paid the balance and now I had a real guitar. I brought it home where I stared and stared at it. I thought it was beautiful. It was a shiny red Egmund bass guitar, not much more than a block of wood really, but I loved it. I brought it to a car mechanic's paint shop and had it sprayed a very light blue. Because I didn't have an amplifier, I would push the headstock against a bedroom door to amplify the sound.'

In between hanging out with his new band-mates, Stephen practised at home with another neighbour and well-respected guitarist in the town, Noel Kelly. Together they learned to play Beatles' numbers by listening to their albums, and soon he was experimenting and discovering how to put his own stamp on songs copied from the radio. Within a few weeks, he had built up the confidence to play his first show in front of a live audience.

'A lady called Mrs Carton was trying to raise money to build a swimming pool in the town and she gave us our first gig in the Forresters' Hall in Carrick. It was on a Sunday afternoon and the place was packed solid with noisy boys and girls. The very talented vocalist Jesse Walsh, guitarist John 'Bear' Griffin, Noel Kelly, drummer Tom White and I imagined we were the Rolling Stones. Although I was playing mostly nonsense, the others, who had been together for some months, said I had great potential. For me, it had the added benefit of local celebrity which, of course, attracted the attention of the girls.'

The band could only afford to hire a small PA system from local baker Pete Walsh and they plugged everything into it, including the bass. The powerful low frequencies of the bass guitar naturally drove the little speakers to distortion and had them almost bouncing off the wall on which they were suspended. At half-past five in the afternoon, an appointed lookout announced that Pete was on his way to retrieve his gear and the bass was quickly unplugged. It meant Stephen's first stage show ended prematurely, but the die had been cast.

'From that day on, we told everyone how well the band was progressing. To be honest, we spent as much time that summer rehearsing with the girls as with our band. I think we were more concerned with our hairstyles than the music. But we managed to convince not only quite a few of the local girls but also ourselves that the big time was just around the corner.'

Chapter 3

By now, music was the main force in the lives of Stephen and his friends and their talk was dominated by the charts and debates about which pop group was the best. For Stephen, schoolwork was only an occasional distraction from the serious business of rehearsing with his band and hanging out. 'By 1967, everyone was raving about the new Miami Showband. There was something special about the Miami that had not been seen in Ireland before. The Miami had been a hugely successful showband, but they were now experimenting with some of the best young beat-group musicians that the country had to offer.'

Occasionally, other exciting home-grown acts that were about to become massive stars would come to play in Carrick. 'Thanks to Seamus Finn, a budding promoter, we got to see and hear some of the finest beat groups on the scene. A big stir was caused when up-and-coming

Irish band Thin Lizzy made an appearance at the local Forrester's Hall. The rock band's impressive front man, Phil Lynott, cut an exotic figure in the country town, 6 feet tall and every inch a star.'

A group of eager youngsters gathered after the gig and the band found time to hang around and sign autographs. 'Phil talked to us afterwards about being a musician and it just burned a greater desire in me to make music my life. As a bass player, I felt a connection with this man and that day will live in my memory forever.' Later, Phil Lynott, a great friend of Fran O'Toole, would turn up regularly at Miami gigs, especially when they played at the Showbiz Night Out in Dublin's TV Club.

Stephen was starting to realise that there was a whole world of adventure beyond Carrick waiting to be discovered. The restrictions of living in a rural town started to curtail his youthful aspirations. With an average Leaving Certificate result under his belt, Stephen had fewer ties keeping him in Carrick and, in his own words, he became a bit wild.

'I suppose the breaking point came during the summer of 1968 when I had finished school and was riding around on a motorbike I had borrowed from a friend. One day, I was racing a car along the winding narrow roads above the town when I lost control of the bike and it crashed into the wall of the local golf club. I damaged my knee. It wasn't a bad injury, but I think it was when my parents finally realised they couldn't talk sense into me. It was time for a compromise.'

Just across the Irish Sea, the booming, swinging city of London had become the epitome of cool, the centre of the universe for fashion and music.

'I had always been aware of the bigger picture, as it were, and there was no greater magnet than London at that time – it was quite simply where it was at. Whenever I think about London, the song 'Sunshine of Your Love' pops into my mind because Cream, whom I loved, was there. In fact, all the bands and musicians I was into had made London their base. With my dreams of becoming a pop star, I set my sights outside Ireland and I could see that London was the place to be. All I had to do was convince my parents. They had never really pushed me one way or the other about what I should do with my life but, for obvious reasons, they were concerned at the prospect of letting their son go so far away. They finally agreed, on condition that I report to my Uncle Mick, who lived there. I suppose, in retrospect, their personal experiences of travel – my father had served as part of General Montgomery's Eighth Army during the Second World War and my mother had worked with the French Resistance – she even evaded execution when she escaped from the Germans – probably swung the decision in my favour, but I had to promise that I would try to get a decent job and make something of myself.'

Emigration was an accepted way of life in Ireland, so the structures were already in place to assist young people seeking a new life abroad. Stephen's family talked to the local priest, who contacted the Catholic Society at Quex Road in London. They provided addresses for lodgings and also helped by setting up job interviews for those fresh off the boat. Not for the first time in his young life, Stephen waved goodbye to his family. He boarded the boat-train from Carrick-on-Suir to Rosslare, from where he caught the 'emigrant' ship to Britain.

'It was very emotional to leave my family and Ireland, but I was excited too. I remember, just before we arrived at Paddington Station, I changed from my travelling clothes into my hippest gear to let London know I had arrived. But nobody noticed. Everyone on the train was fast asleep while I was wide-eyed with excitement. But it didn't matter, I was here and I was going to be a rock star.'

The winter of 1969 was one of the coldest in recent records and the snow was thick on the ground when Stephen met his uncle at the station on 4 February. After catching up on family gossip, Stephen was escorted to his new accommodation in Kilburn, an area famous as a home from home for the young Irish arriving in London for the first time. His uncle gave him a telephone number and told him to call it if he ever needed any help. Stephen was shown to his room, then left to his own devices. 'The landlady told me to take one of the three beds in the room. Then she gave me some pots and pans and said I could borrow them until I got my own. I looked at her as if she was completely mad. This was not the welcome I had envisaged. I was expecting everything to be laid on for me, like it had been at home. But, of course, the longer I sat there, the hungrier I got.'

Stephen decided to try the famous London fish-and-chip supper and went out through the snow again that first evening. 'It was a letdown because by the time I got to back to my digs, my food was cold. This was definitely not the introduction to the London of my imagination. It was starting to dawn on me that I was on my own here.'

A few days later, armed with an introductory letter from the Catholic Society, Stephen arrived at the offices of the Horse Race Totalisators Board, near Ludgate Circus. He was told to come back and start work on Monday in the legal department.

The following morning, he was unceremoniously shaken awake by the landlady, who wanted to allocate the spare beds in his room to two very large and much older Irish construction workers. 'This was a shock to realise that I was to have room-mates. I had always had my own space at home and now I was going to have to share with two strangers. I thought, I have to get out of here.' He fled back to another uncle's house, where he stayed until he had earned enough money to rent his own place.

Eventually, he was able to move into a tiny bedsit in Queen's Park Road with another young Irishman, who showed him the ropes.

'I had been one of these typical Irish sons who had been mollycoddled at home. Everything had been picked up after me. If I drank a cup of tea, my mother would follow behind, ready to wash the cup. When I went to live with Pat 'Bugsy' O'Reilly from Waterford, I soon learned that things were going to be different. He was having none of it. It was like living with a sergeant major. When we got up in the morning, his bed would be neat and tidy and he warned me that he wanted to look over at the other side of the room and see mine exactly the same. He would bring me down Portobello Road to the markets, where we would buy fresh vegetables and meat with our shared money, which was an eye-opener for someone who could barely boil an egg. In the evenings, we would talk about music. He was very intelligent, a walking encyclopaedia of modern music, even though he wasn't a musician. He introduced me to bands that were not in the mainstream. I learned a lot from Bugsy.'

Stephen was beginning to enjoy his new lifestyle, away from the constraints of his parents and small-town Ireland. London was an exciting place, always abuzz with life, sights and sounds that were a far cry from those of Carrick-on-Suir.

'I used to go and sit under The Monument which

commemorated the Great Fire of London, or on the steps of St Paul's Cathedral, with a lad from work, and listen to the lunch-time concerts by the military bands. I regularly visited the Tower of London. I was fascinated at being in the centre of what had been one of the greatest empires in the history of the world. The city was full of treasures. I grudgingly respected the fact that this small country had once ruled three-quarters of the planet, and even though I was not politically aware, I remember thinking that it was such a pity that this great nation had been so cruel to my own.'

Despite the occasional excitement going on outside the window, the job in the Horse Race Totalisators Board didn't suit Stephen's temperament and he lasted only a few weeks before finding another job as a trainee at Price Forbes, brokers for Lloyd's. 'This was a major insurance company in the City of London, which made my parents very proud.'

While it paid well and he was in a better position, it was still just a temporary solution— he was marking time until he got his big break, in a band. 'I had been holding down these jobs, but I was disastrously bad at them. There were other people happily working there, young fellows, who were career-minded and who saw this as their future. My parents were happy to see I had a white-collar job with a regular income, but it wasn't for me.'

Stephen was in London just a few weeks when St

Patrick's Day came around. He decided to visit a cousin, who was unwell, and her daughter in north London.

'It was a great opportunity to get a free home-cooked meal, and after a fine dinner I was invited to a St Patrick's Day dance that evening at The 32 Club in Harlsden. I went along and, when we arrived, there was a support band on before the main act. They were called Hank Jackson and the Green Shades. I was always on the lookout for a chance to get back into music so, after they came off stage, I knocked on the door of the band room and introduced myself.

'I told them that while they were very good, they badly needed a bass player. They said, "I suppose you play?" and I said, "Well, as a matter of fact I do." They took this precocious kid in and put a guitar in his hands and said, "There ya go, let's see what you got." I played a popular Irish tune called 'The March Hare' and, when I finished, I got the distinct impression that it was a case of don't call us, we'll call you. I gave them my address anyway and told them to call me if they decided to give me a try. I was thinking as I walked out the door, well, that's the end of that. But the following Saturday morning, there was a knock on my door and there they were, offering me a job. I told them that I didn't have a bass and with that they produced this magnificent, top-of-the-range Fender Precision bass and said I could use it.

'I was absolutely delighted. At last, I had found a way

to play music and with a great bunch of guys. Two of them, Peter 'Hank' Jackson and guitarist Michael Roe were from Waterford and they treated me like an old friend. There is a great sense of being Irish when you are abroad. Wherever we played in London, people from back home would come and support us.'

Stephen managed to get through his day job, but his heart belonged to the nights, which were spent on a stage, playing covers of songs by the Rolling Stones and The Beatles to crowds of eager music fans. Still, for the ambitious young bass player, playing with The Green Shades was just a stepping stone to the bigger and better things he was still convinced were just around the corner.

'We were very busy and played on a regular basis. On a Saturday we had two gigs, at The Prince of Wales on Harrow Road and later at The 32 Club. It was great fun and I was making a bit of money on the side, too. I remember playing one night and I realised that more and more people were coming back to our shows. This particular group of fans became regulars and they would sit up in the front row. We got chatting one night after a gig and it turned out they were Portuguese. They invited me out to show their appreciation, as they put it, and we had a great night at a wonderful Spanish nightclub. Before we left to go home, they asked if they could call around to my house later with a little gift. The following day, they presented me with a lovely Suzuki motorbike, simply because they liked my playing! London was great for that. There was always room for talent and if you stood out, people showed their appreciation. If you were good, you got noticed.'

One Sunday evening, as he was leaving the Prince of Wales pub, Stephen heard footsteps behind him and he turned to face an intimidating figure in a long leather coat, who walked right up to him.

'He said, "I've been watching you all night", and I thought, Jesus, what's this all about? But he introduced himself as Gerry Walsh and said he was with a band called The News. He said, "I want you to play bass with us." I pointed out that I was already in a band and he said they would pay double whatever I was getting.

'I was intrigued by this character, so I decided to check them out. I went up to meet the rest of the band for lunch and they introduced me to their manager, Frank Hannon. Frank was impressive, always immaculately dressed and he drove a Rolls Royce. He was also the landlord of a famous music pub called the Rising Sun in Sudbury Hill, near Harrow.

'The deal was that The News played his club every Sunday and Tuesday night and he sponsored them. He had set them up as a full-time travelling showband and had bought them a new van and suits so they could play all over the country.

'What could I say? I was offered much more money than I was getting in the day job so I decided to quit and join The News. When I told my parents, my mother was horrified. I was packing in a good job with a reputable company to go on the road with some band!

'We were so busy with gigs around Christmas and the New Year that I didn't get a chance to go home and spend Christmas with my family. That had a very bad effect on me. Christmas had always been a special time for us growing up and even though Joe Carroll, my best friend in the band, and his wife Doreen gave me a great Christmas at their home in Northolt, I became seriously homesick. I played out a few gigs into the New Year and then, without another word, I simply walked off stage one night, went home, packed my bags and caught the next boat to Ireland.'

Chapter 4

When he returned to Carrick, Stephen caught up with his old friends Billy Byrne and Gay Brazel, who had turned professional and were now touring Ireland with a country-and-western band called The Cowboys. He watched them play at a few shows and their popularity convinced him that the music scene in Ireland had changed while he had been away. It was an exciting time to be a musician in Ireland. Every weekend, thousands danced their cares away in the 'ballrooms of romance'. From the Arcadia in Cork to the Stardust in Derry, there was glamour and excitement as Dickie Rock launched into 'Simon Says' or The Dixies sang 'Little Arrows' to exuberant crowds of as many as 4,000 fans.

Stephen joined The Cowboys, who were benefiting from the latest music craze. Country-and-western music had arrived and stolen the limelight, and the likes of Big Tom and The Mainliners, Larry Cunningham and The Mighty Avons, Margo and The Countryfolk, The Smokey Mountain Ramblers, and The Cotton Mill Boys were taking their places in the charts beside the showbands and British beat groups. The Cowboys had loyal followers all round the south – Limerick, Cork, Tipperary, Waterford, Kilkenny and Wexford. Whenever they played in those areas, and even in the National Ballroom in Dublin, they were always guaranteed a full house. This was still a boom-time for Ireland's music scene in venues of every description all over the country – from the huge, exotic dance halls in the larger towns to big marquees erected temporarily in every townland and village during the summer.

'Even though there were literally hundreds of bands touring up and down the country, there was enough going on to provide work for everyone,' Stephen says. 'We were constantly playing. It was a great time for live entertainment in Ireland.'

One night, while enjoying a rare night off at the cinema in Clonmel, Stephen got a tap on the shoulder. 'I looked around and there was a chap standing there, a very fine guitarist called Martin Hennessy, who I knew, and he said, "T.J. Byrne wants to see you straight away."'

Nobody in the music industry in Ireland at that time needed to be told who T.J. Byrne was. A larger-than-life character from Carlow, he had managed The Royal Showband, which he had transformed from a bunch of amateur part-time musicians in Waterford into one of Ireland's first truly successful international acts. Brendan Bowyer and Tom Dunphy were the local heroes of the band, now performing in legendary venues such as The Stardust in Las Vegas. At one stage in their early career, The Beatles had played support to The Royal Showband in Liverpool. Bowyer told a young Paul McCartney that if the four Liverpool lads could stick together, they would do well. Both Bowyer and Dunphy were pioneers of the showband era and had become superstars in every sense of the word. In 1971, however, despite a string of hits and international fame, they both quit the Royal and set up The Big 8, with T.J. Byrne once again at the helm.

Stephen had met Bowyer years before in Waterford, when the famous front man was home on holiday from Las Vegas. 'Even though they were massive stars, Brendan still stayed at his family home in South Parade when he wasn't touring. I knew where he lived, so it was simply a case of walking up to the house and knocking on the front door. I was sixteen years of age and I wanted to give him a tape of a song I had written. Together with his lovely wife, Stella, he brought me into his house and gave me some lemonade and biscuits. I don't think he was taking me all that seriously, but he was very nice and promised that he would listen to my tape. On the way out, I bumped into Tom Dunphy, who was on his way in, and I boldly introduced myself. I told him I was a fellow bass player and asked him to keep an eye out and let me know if any gigs came up. He said he would, but I think that Tom, like Brendan, was just a little bit bemused by this cocky kid. He very graciously asked that I keep my voice down, as he didn't want to lose his job to me.'

Years later, Tom Dunphy would unknowingly fulfil his promise to the sixteen-year-old.

'The night Martin Hennessy told me T.J. Byrne wanted to see me, Tom had fallen ill and The Big 8 was playing at The Arcadia in Cahir, County Tipperary. T.J. was in a panic to find a bass player who might be capable of standing in at the last minute. My name was mentioned and Byrne quickly gathered a posse and sent them on a manhunt to find me and bring me back to Cahir.

'I got into my car and started driving the ten miles to Cahir, thinking the whole way that this was all too surreal. When I got to The Arcadia, I had to fight my way through the crowds that had gathered outside. Standing there, instantly recognisable, was T.J. Byrne himself. He spotted me, approached my Fiat 124 and tapped on the window. I rolled it down and he said, "Are you young Travers?" I was flabbergasted that this was all happening, but I recovered my wits and said, "Yes, Mr Byrne, I am."

'He snapped his fingers and a guy appeared who

parked my car. I was ushered in through the stage door and brought to the side of the stage, where I met bandleader Paddy Cole. T.J. introduced me as the stand-in bass player and we quickly shook hands. The gig had already started and the band was getting ready to launch into their next number. As I walked across the stage to pick up Tom Dunphy's Fender bass, I looked out on this sea of adoring fans and was totally taken aback. I asked if I could stand behind the bass amplifier, out of sight, but the band was having none of it. They insisted that I stand right out in front with them. I had been quietly relaxing on a night off at the cinema and now I was getting ready to play with The Big 8, one of the great Irish super bands of the time. I was standing on the same stage as Paddy Cole, perhaps one of the most famous saxophone players and band leaders in the country, with Twink on vocals, Mickey O'Neill on drums, Dave Coady from Waterford, a fabulous singer and trumpet player, Jimmy Conway on guitar and Michael Keane on keyboards.

'And there, in centre stage, under the glare of the spotlight was Ireland's very own king, Brendan Bowyer. He glanced over at me, winked and turned his collar up. This was a signal to the band to launch into an electrifying medley of Elvis Presley hits. A shudder went down my spine. They were sensational. I will remember it for the rest of my life.'

Back on the road with The Cowboys, Stephen was

enjoying all that life as a twenty-year-old guitar player in a reasonably successful band offered. He had enjoyed the attention that musicians inevitably attracted from some of the female admirers in the crowd. While he admits he had 'an eye for a nice-looking girl', the last thing he had in mind was settling down. But that would all change the night before Christmas Eve 1971.

'We were playing at a dance when I spotted this girl with long red hair dancing away and the thought occurred to me, If I was ever to get married, I would marry a girl like her. I couldn't take my eyes off her for the rest of the night. At the end of the show, fans would approach the band and ask us to sign photos. Like everyone else, this girl, accompanied by her sister, came up to the stage. When it was my turn to sign her band card, I tried my best to talk to her. She would hardly look at me, but I persisted. She reluctantly told me her name was Anne. I asked if she and her sister needed a lift home, but they said they had a taxi waiting outside. As quick as I could, I packed my guitar and got around to the front of the venue to catch up with them before they left. I eventually convinced them to allow me to drive them home as there was a long queue at the taxi rank. They both got into the back seat. The entire way to her house, I tried to make a date with her for the next time we would be in town, but I dropped them off with no guarantee that I would ever see her again.

'Two weeks later, we were back playing a gig and I craned my neck all night to see if she was there. I spotted her in the crowd and, this time, I got to speak to her alone after the gig. She agreed to go out on a date with me. Even though she was still very young, not quite seventeen, the girl with the long red hair who I knew I would marry when I first set eyes on her, would later become my wife. The great love of my life.'

Chapter 5

In 1972, Stephen left The Cowboys to join the Mick Delahunty Jnr Orchestra, a dance band set up by Mick's father, a veteran performer who had achieved fame all over the world. In his twilight years, he had stopped touring and swapped the red carpet that had been rolled out for him at New York's Carnegie Hall for a legendary residency in Cruise's Hotel, Limerick. Trained in the very best tradition of showbusiness, his son, Michael, took up the baton and formed a super-showband to pick up where his dad had left off, bringing with him the cream of the talent from the old line-up. He recruited Paddy Byrne on trumpet, Harry Doherty on sax and his first cousin, Maxi Delahunty, on drums. Pat Fitzgerald fronted the band – a singer of astonishing ability, often compared to Tom Jones – and Gerry Fitzgibbon on guitar.

It was a humbling experience to play with such musical royalty, but for Stephen it was also a fertile learning ground. His time with Mick Delahunty Jnr proved to be a quantum leap in his development as a musician. Unfortunately, the vagaries of working for a man like Delahunty, who could be quite eccentric, soon played against him. He quickly learned that the tempestuous band leader would fall out with various members of his band on a whim. Stephen was almost fired for cutting his long hair without permission; a sackable offence because part of Stephen's job, as Delahunty saw it, was to appeal to the younger members of the audience.

In 1973, Stephen left to branch out once again with his old sparring partner, David Prim. It was a casual arrangement that allowed them to play where and when they wanted. They gave a young James Delaney his first job before the pianist became one of Ireland's most celebrated keyboard players with folk-rock group Clannad. Stephen and David's reputations as top guitarists grew steadily through their progressive rock playing, but the partnership was a rambling affair that never made money. This was now becoming an issue because Stephen's romance with Anne had led to talk of marriage. For Stephen, it was time to admit that he needed to move on and earn some real money.

It was a tearful goodbye, but a necessary one. Once again, he was looking for work and toying with the idea of returning to London. But his life changed in an instant when he received the news that his beloved father, Patrick, had died suddenly. It was a massive blow and it sent Stephen, and his family, reeling.

'I thought he would live forever. He was always very religious and would go to mass every morning before work, and on the first Friday of every month, he would attend evening services. It was at one of these Friday masses that he suddenly felt unwell and went outside for some fresh air. Our neighbour, Paddy Daly, offered to bring him to the hospital and he agreed, which was unusual for a man who believed in his own strength.'

When the Travers family arrived at the hospital, Patrick assured them that he was all right. His doctor said he had suffered a mild heart attack and would recover, but added that it was a warning sign. The following day, Patrick assured Stephen that he was fine and convinced him to travel to Cork, where he was going to visit Anne.

About a week previously, Anne had dreamt of her upcoming wedding, but in her dream everyone was dressed in black. Patrick Travers was missing from the gathering and could not be found. She was disturbed by the image and admitted to her mother that she had an awful feeling that Stephen's dad would not live to see the wedding. On his arrival in Cork, Anne insisted they both go to a local church to pray for his father. After visiting the church, Anne suddenly turned to Stephen and told him he must go home immediately. Frightened, he left at once. He was almost back in Carrick, just passing the factory where his father had worked for so many years, when, out of nowhere, what looked like a beautiful, multicoloured orb appeared on the bonnet of his car and then, almost instantaneously, burst into millions of incredibly bright, tiny stars.

'It was one of the most beautiful things I've ever seen in my life. It lit up the road for a second and then it was gone. I was astounded. I'd never seen anything like it. Six minutes later I turned the key in my mother's door and my sister was standing there. She just said, "He's gone." I cannot explain what happened, but perhaps it was a sign that my dad had passed away. That night was the very first time in my life that I could not sleep. It was one of the worst things that ever happened to me.

'It stopped everything in its tracks. Anne suggested that we put off our wedding, planned for July 1974, for at least another year, but I said I couldn't do that. I knew I had found my soulmate. I saw marrying Anne as my salvation and I was absolutely right. It was the best decision I ever made and we married exactly twelve months after my father died.'

In the aftermath of his father's death, Stephen became disillusioned with music. The difficult intervening months were spent drifting in and out of a series of uninteresting jobs. Eventually, he took up an office job in Clonmel to help pay the bills. Occasionally, people from the music business approached him with offers to work with professional bands. While he took up the chance to play a night here and there, a full-time life on the road just did not appeal to him.

'Gerry Walsh, whom I had worked with in The Cowboys, told me there was a gig going with The Morris Mulcahy Orchestra, an outfit similar to The Delahunty Orchestra, based in Mitchelstown, County Cork. They were well established and were offering good wages, about £80 a week, which was huge at the time. I agreed to help until they found a permanent bassist.

'They were playing in Cavan on my first night with the band and I met the band bus in Durrow, County Kilkenny. I got into the van expecting the usual camaraderie of a showband on the road, but we travelled almost the entire journey in silence. Nobody spoke, nobody welcomed me aboard and everyone just sat doing their own thing. One guy who was sitting across from me took out a big bag of sweets and ate one after the other, never once offering them around. We went on stage, played and walked off. I thought it was the worst thing that could ever happen to a bunch of musicians, doing it just for the money.

'When we were dropped off later that night, Joe Mulcahy, the band leader, came around the back of the van as I was taking out my guitar and said, "Right, you've got the job." I asked, "What job?" and he said, "The bass job, head, you're our new bass player." I told him I didn't want it and he was astounded. Nobody turned down such well-paid work in those days, but I just walked away.'

While his heart wasn't into playing full-time, Stephen still needed an escape from the mundane world of the nine-to-five office routine. He approached some local musicians in Carrick with the intention of setting up a part-time band, and this is when he recruited an old friend, Liam O' Dwyer, as front man. With Liam on vocals and Andy Burroughs on guitar, the new band was almost complete. There was just one more musician he had his eye on, and when his old Cowboys' pal Paul O'Keefe returned from abroad, he immediately hired him as their drummer. 'It was a strange set-up,' Stephen recalls. 'A mix and mash of personalities, but although it was a crazy concoction, it worked.'

They practised in a bar just outside the town, but it was a pub on Kickham Street, known as the Kickham Inn, that would become their home from home. At the time, it was a dull, empty and unpopular place but when The Sinners became the house band in 1974, the place underwent something of a metamorphosis. Soon people were travelling from across the countryside as word got out that there was a hot new band at the Kickham. One night, the crowd was four-deep trying to get in to see The Sinners, despite the fact that the top band in Ireland,

Bagatelle, was playing in the town in another venue on the same night.

'It's that hard to believe that an unknown band would get such support,' Liam reflects. 'We were a local pheno- menon. We only played venues within a twenty-mile radius of Carrick, but we packed them out. Our nearest rival was an excellent band called Simon. They were a Waterford band and played generally in the urban venues. Between us, we carved up the southeast.'

An early indication of their popularity came one evening when they left at 7.00pm to travel to a gig in Mothel, outside Carrick. They were scheduled to do a live rehearsal before the performance. O'Dwyer remembers it well. 'The mile-and-a-half stretch of road back from Paddy Mansfield's venue was packed with cars. I turned around to the lads and said, "We have a problem here, it must be double-booked with some big band." I thought that maybe it was a funeral wake and I wondered why the owner hadn't informed us. It took over an hour to find parking. We walked in and the place was mobbed. When we found the owner, he was delighted. He said the crowd had been waiting for us for two-and-a-half hours before the gig.'

It was not very long before The Sinners attracted the attentions of scouts, who were on the lookout for talent. Stephen was almost tempted by one offer. 'Louis Walsh offered me a job with the excellent pop band Chips and I agreed to meet them at a marquee in Wexford, but I didn't show up. On reflection, I was sorry I didn't go. I wanted to meet up with them as they were popular and I respected them as a great outfit, but I just couldn't do it. I had convinced myself that this wasn't really the life for a newly married man, getting home at all hours after travelling across the country from gig to gig.'

The pressures to pay the bills were mounting and it was becoming increasingly difficult to ignore the financial responsibilities of married life and the costs of the new house he had just built in Carrick. 'Now and again, I would jam with some band, but I didn't like leaving Anne behind. I had turned down a number of jobs until she told me that if another full-time offer came along, then perhaps I should seriously consider it. She said she had married a musician and was prepared to live with the lifestyle. She saw that I wasn't very happy working in a nine-to-five and she selflessly insisted that I should pursue music as a career because she knew how much I loved it.'

It was at this moment that fate stepped in. And once again it was helped along by a former band-mate. Gay Brazel, the guitarist from The Cowboys, was now gigging with a rock band called Tweed, who were managed by Top-Line Promotions, based at Parnell Square in Dublin. This was also the head office of a band that was already very famous.

'One of the directors had asked Gay if he knew

anybody good enough to replace Johnny Brown, a bass player, who was leaving the Miami. Gay told him he knew the right man, but added that I might be reluctant because I had only recently married. He said he'd try and when he came to my house to tell me about the offer, I listened curiously. I wasn't a big fan of the Miami when they were still a showband but, by that time, they had changed beyond recognition from their original incarnation. By 1975 they were very much a modern pop group. The management had even dropped the word 'showband' from the name.'

Formed in 1961, the original Miami Showband had split up in 1967 after a huge run of success that included singer Dickie Rock's appearance at the 1966 Eurovision Song Contest. While some of the members left to form The Sands, Rock and Tom Doherty, the manager, cleverly recruited the best of the beat-group musicians and singers on the Dublin scene to fill the gaps. They hand-picked the cream of the rock crop of the day and reformed the Miami as a pop group that had discarded most of its showband roots.

The youngsters who completed the new line-up were considered to be some of the most gifted musicians in the country. Along with Dickie Rock, there was Paul Ashford on bass, Pat McCarthy on trombone, original Miami drummer Tony Bogan, saxophonist Des McAlea from Belfast and the exceptionally gifted Fran O'Toole on keyboards and vocals. They scored a series of top-ten hits with Dickie as the front man, singing songs like 'Simon Says' in May 1968 and 'Christmas Time and You' in December of that same year. In spite of their success, a simmering dissatisfaction with his earnings led Rock to leave in 1972 to form his own band. Following some experiments with replacements, Fran stepped up to the mic and quickly established his own sensational style as a soul and rock singer-songwriter.

In 1974, 'Clap Your Hands, Stamp Your Feet' was a massive hit for the Miami. Although they were still playing other artists' material, they quickly became an original act, writing and performing their own songs. They pursued success relentlessly, and it was taken for granted that these young stars were destined for great things. By the summer of 1975, having gone through more personnel changes, the Miami had become one of the most popular bands in Ireland. The line-up now included Tony Geraghty, one of the country's most respected guitarists, and new drummer Ray Millar. The excitement generated whenever they played the massive ballroom circuit throughout the country was phenomenal.

The sudden departure of Johnny Brown threw a spanner in the works, however. Before they could renew their assault on the charts, the band needed to find a replacement who would be capable of filling the role of bass player. Intrigued as to what might be on offer with a band whose talent hinted at further untapped potential, Stephen agreed to meet them. He travelled to Ennis, where they were due to play, and they had a quick jam before the band went on stage.

'I got on really well with them. So when I got a letter from their head office a few days later stating that the lads had been impressed, I was happily surprised. The letter went on to offer me the job but then I noticed it was not the one that I expected.

'Bass player Dave Monks had moved over to guitar when Johnny Brown joined on bass. Now that Johnny was leaving, Monks insisted that he get back his old job on bass. They were now looking for a guitarist rather than a bass player, and this was the position they offered me. They reasoned that if I was half as good on guitar as I was on bass, then I could consider the job mine. But I wasn't sold on the idea. I was a bass guitarist after all, so it looked like it was all going to come to nothing. To be honest, it was a relief rather than a disappointment because I was still debating the merits of life on the road and this seemed to take the decision out of my hands.'

As far as Stephen was concerned, that was the end of the matter. Then, a few months later, he got a call from Tony Bogan, one of the band's business directors, who told him that Monks was leaving to go to South Africa and the bass job was once again up for grabs.

'He asked me to meet the lads again and to bring my

instrument along. The meeting was scheduled for the George Hotel off Parnell Square in Dublin. I assumed that I already had this job. I drove there thinking that I would have a quick jam with them, sort out my wages and that would be that.

'I pulled up in front of the National Ballroom where Tony Bogan saw me arrive, and when I got out he asked me if I was the young fellow from the country. This set me back a bit. I didn't expect the red-carpet treatment, but I had at least thought that he would know who I was. He said, "Look, head" – as all showband people referred to each other – "there's been such interest in this job that all the top players have decided to audition." I was taken aback. "What audition?" I asked him. I had considered the job mine, but now I was being told that I would have to take my chances against some of the best bass guitarists in the land. I walked over to where the band had set up their gear and even a quick glance around the room was enough to tell me that the top brass had turned up. Two of the original members of the band, Tony Bogan and Joe Tyrell, the band's original keyboard player, were now directors. Sitting in the middle of them was Tom Doherty, the manager and managing director of the company that ran the Miami. This showed the level of interest in the proceedings.

'I joined the line of musicians auditioning for the job. There were quite a number of guitarists there I instantly recognised – some were the best bass players of their day. They were standing around talking and smoking with their guitar cases at their feet. Tony Bogan must have seen my expression because he said, "Look, head, at least it will be good experience. It will stand to you in the future." From his manner, I knew instantly that he didn't even consider me in the running.

'I looked around and saw faces that would have been on TV shows and in *Spotlight* magazine every week and I thought, This guy is probably right. There were about ten bass guitarists there from the best beat groups in the country and each of them would have been good enough to get the job. I was so impressed that I thought I would just sit and watch them perform. It would be a rare treat.

'I watched these guys get up one by one and go through their paces. As each one finished, I felt my confidence grow. As impressive as they were, none of them did anything that I couldn't do. When it came to my turn, Bogan looked surprised that I was still there. He asked if I felt like giving it a go. So I strapped on my Dan Armstrong Plexiglas bass – a striking instrument that stood out among all the Fenders of the other musicians. As I stood up, Fran noticed me and he gave me a big smile and a wave of encouragement and said, "Okay, Steve, what do you want to do?" I had nothing to lose so I just said, "Let's jam and loosen up." Fran started playing this up-tempo soul riff and I just went with it. The rest of the band gradually joined in and we were only jamming for a couple of minutes when Fran stopped the song, stood up at his keyboards, pointed over at me and said to the guys in the suits and ties, "This is the man I want." I looked over and Tony Geraghty had his back to me, facing the line of managers. With his hands raised he said just two words, "No contest." As he was leaving, a highly respected bass player walked over to me and said, "Where the f**k did you come from?"

'I was still standing there, wondering what had just happened, when Tom Doherty approached me and said, "I have never seen or heard the Miami play like that." Fran told me afterwards that if he had known I was there, they wouldn't have bothered with the audition. As I put away my guitar, I looked around and realised the room had emptied – the other players had all packed up and gone.

'The manager invited me down to the Parnell Mooney pub, across the road, to talk about money. I was offered fifty punts a night for three nights and an extra ten for each additional night. It was great money but, because I had had to endure the auditioning process, I demanded just a little bit more as a mild form of protest. Tom Doherty agreed and nodded his head. I was in the Miami.'

Stephen had mixed feelings about telling Anne because they both knew what life on the road entailed. 'But from the day I met her, Anne has never stood in the way of the music. She has always understood. Joining the Miami gave me a steady income. We were paying for the house in Carrick, so the money was definitely a factor.'

Finally, it came time to say goodbye to Carrick and prepare for life with Ireland's biggest pop band. There were exciting times ahead and Stephen had a feeling that his life would never be the same again. 'I told the rest of the lads in The Sinners and they wished me well. They accepted that it was a great opportunity for me.'

Liam recalls that they decided to play a farewell gig for Stephen at their usual haunt, the Kickham Inn. 'At the end of our last song, we played the national anthem, as usual,' Liam remembers. 'Then I announced from the stage that it would be our last gig as Stephen was leaving to join the Miami. I'm not joking when I say there was a standing ovation for ten minutes. The goodwill in the place was overwhelming.'

'Here I was,' Stephen adds, 'a local lad who had done well, and they had given me the best send-off to the big time. What more could a young man wish for?'

Part II
THE MIAMI

Chapter 6

Today, there is no obvious border between the Republic of Ireland and Northern Ireland. Where once there were army checkpoints and customs posts, now there is just a series of billboards and road signs to indicate that you have entered the United Kingdom.

On our journey north, Stephen and I have left the M1 at the border, where it becomes the A1, and are driving towards Banbridge. On the hills surrounding the road, the British army observation towers that silently stand guard over the valleys hint that we are now in a country that, until a few years ago, was an active war zone. As we enter Banbridge, we hear a low-flying helicopter pass over the town. We stop to ask directions and an old man points us back in the direction from which we have come. He tells us to look out for a building that is now a bingo hall. Stephen spots it along the main street and we pull over to the kerb, outside Lucky's Bingo Hall. In the 1970s, this was the Castle Ballroom, a popular venue owned by Cecil Thompson, a well-known local businessman. It was the last place the Miami ever played.

We go through the front door and climb the steps leading to the foyer. As we glance inside the hall, a woman asks us if we need any help. When we explain who we are, she greets us warmly and invites us to have a look around. She explains that the building had been a nightclub for many years, before a fire almost completely destroyed it. It had also been heavily damaged by a huge car bomb that exploded in Banbridge town centre in 1998, injuring thirty-three people. She says there is still a significant crack along one of the back walls from the blast. It was converted into Lucky's four years ago and while there was some work carried out to accommodate the latest incarnation, the basic structure has remained the same.

She guides us through a brightly lit hall, packed with ranks of bingo tables, and down a side passage to steps that lead to the stage.

Stephen walks slowly up the steps and across the platform to the far side, to the place where he had stood on the night of 30 July 1975. He indicates where Fran had sat at his keyboard and where the rest of the lads had been positioned. He asks about the kitchen, where the band had their last meal. 'I'll always remember we were fed a bowl of Irish stew. It stands out in my mind because we had never been offered that before. Sometimes it might have been a burger and chips and more often than not it would have been sandwiches. This was the only place that we had ever been offered Irish stew and we relished it. It was lovely.'

After another quick look around, we thank the woman for her time and get back into the car. As we pull away, Stephen recalls his roller-coaster six weeks as the Miami's latest star attraction, culminating in that last performance at the Castle Ballroom.

'It was an utterly manic, magical time. The first time I played with them, the screams from the crowd were so loud that I could only sync up by watching the others' hand positions on their instruments. This was pure adulation. I had played in all these other bands, but I had never seen such a reaction before. The Big 8 were superstars, The Cowboys had their strengths and The Sinners were local heroes, but those first few gigs with the Miami were something else.'

For a start, there was the female element. Whenever the Miami launched into 'Clap Your Hands, Stamp Your Feet', which was their biggest hit, the music would be all but drowned out by the wild noise of the hundreds of girls thronged in front of the stage. They knew all the words and when it came to the chorus, the thousands of stomping feet would send a tremor through the floor. While many of the other showbands attracted a mixed audience, the Miami had a massive female fanbase. With cherubic lead singer Fran O'Toole fronting the band, it was always going to prove a particular favourite with the ladies.

'Fran was very good looking,' Stephen remembers with a smile. 'He always had women around him, but the attention never fazed him. He couldn't have been less interested, married as he was to Valerie. In fact, it went right over his head. He was always polite and very approachable, but that's as far as it went for Fran. He just loved playing the songs. He was the perennial performer; born to be on the stage.'

For the other young musicians in the band, who had been playing together for a number of years, this sort of reaction was hardly new. As Stephen puts it, they had grown in to this while he, on the other hand, felt thrown in at the deep end.

'I had been so blasé about joining the Miami that I hadn't even bothered to learn their set list. When I joined, we were brought out to St Anne's Park in north Dublin for a photo shoot. They did this every time there was a new member. When we were finished, Fran handed me a reel-to-reel tape with a recording of one of their shows on it. They were going off on a short break and Fran asked me to listen to it so I'd know the songs by the time they came back. I threw the tape onto the backseat of my car, where it was promptly forgotten.'

On the eve of his first gig, in Blackrock, outside Dundalk, Stephen met the band's road manager, Brian Maguire. On the way to the gig in Maguire's van, it occurred to Stephen that perhaps he had been too relaxed in his preparations.

'I started to get a bit nervous and by the time we got there, I was really worried that I was going to foul up. My anxiety was not helped by the fact that, when we arrived, the first thing I could hear was this almighty noise as we got out of the van. There were hundreds of people outside the venue trying to get in. We were getting ready back-stage and we could hear them chanting to the tune of the old Al Johnson number 'Mammy', except they were roaring "Miami, Miami, I'd walk a million miles for one of your smiles, Miami."

'As we were preparing to go on, I peeked through the curtains and saw hundreds of girls waving their scarves and their hands in the air. As I said, the other guys were used to this, but for me, it was almost overwhelming. When we walked on stage, I was stunned by the roar of the crowd. I tried to remain inconspicuous but Fran, like Bowyer, was a showman and he grabbed me around the waist with one arm and pushed me up to the front.'

This gesture was Stephen's introduction to the audience and a signal that he was now part of the Miami.

After that he loosened up a bit and started to enjoy himself. 'I was in awe of these guys though. Fran's voice was absolutely fantastic. He had this ability to sing both rock and soul. When I looked over at the guitarist, Tony Geraghty, I thought, Wow, this guy is world class. Yet here he was, laughing and smiling away, having a great time, making his guitar sing. When it came to the last song of the evening and Fran introduced 'Clap Your Hands, Stamp Your Feet', the hairs stood up on the back of my neck. I couldn't hear a note we were playing as the whole place, hundreds of people, clapped their hands and stomped their feet in unison. It was absolutely incredible.'

Stephen got through the gig and backstage his new band-mates congratulated him on his performance.

'I can't remember coming off the stage – I must have been flying with adrenaline – but I had survived and the lads gathered around to say well done. Fran put his arm around me and asked where I had got a particular bass line from, which I had played during 'Reach Out, I'll Be There'. I didn't know what he was talking about. I told him I had just made it up and he said, "Well hold on to it, it's a great line."

'To get that sort of credit from these guys gave me a real sense of pride and boosted my confidence. I was struck by their professionalism. To watch them go through their paces, doing their thing out front and working the crowd to get them going, you know, they had all the moves and all the steps. I was thinking, these guys are real stars and I was over the moon to be in their company and be part of it.'

Stephen had little or no time to sit back and enjoy his achievement, however, because he was propelled headlong into a punishing schedule of gigs. The Miami were re-mounting their attack on the charts plus it was coming into summer, which is always the busiest period for the music industry. There was very little opportunity for rehearsals, never mind producing new material. One show could be many miles away from the next and that meant bands spent long hours crossing the country overnight to make it to their next gig.

The Miami was successful and popular enough for the management to ensure a reasonable schedule. They would plan their route and work their way down through the country, playing each major venue along the way. Still, it was a gruelling workload. Generally, they would perform five nights every week, sometimes six. Monday night was traditionally the night when most musicians rested between shows, but the Miami would often play the TV Club in Dublin to an audience of their peers.

'We travelled all over the country,' Stephen recalls. 'We had a separate personal vehicle, a Volkswagen van, and it suited the image. The band would arrive like stars, you know, in their own vehicle. It was a great adventure and we had many fun-filled times in that van.'

The long hours spent in the minibus touring the country gave Stephen a chance to get to know the five guys with whom he was now spending most of his time.

'Des McAlea, Fran and Brian McCoy were the old guard, if you like. To me they were like well-known movie stars. They had been recruited by Dickie Rock when the original Miami split around 1967 and were well used to the success and the adulation by the time I came along. Tony Geraghty and Ray Millar, the drummer, had joined up later and I saw them and myself almost as the junior members. We were never made to feel like that but whenever we played together, I used to admire how professional the senior lads were. I sensed how much I could learn from them.'

Of the old guard, Stephen had less in common with Des McAlea (whose stage name was Des Lee), the saxophone player from Belfast. 'When I first joined, I felt that Des was perhaps the least approachable. He was the one I felt least close to. Having said that, he was a professional musician who took his work very seriously and he could be utterly relied upon when you were on stage.'

Brian McCoy had also joined the Miami soon after it had reformed under Rock and manager Tom Doherty. He had been the trumpeter with a well-established Belfast band called The Secrets. However, his extraordinary stage presence and excellent voice had pushed him into centrestage to take up vocal duties before he left to join the Miami. 'Brian was a real gentleman. He was a father figure to the newer guys. He came across as much older than the others even though he was only thirty-two. He was the sensible one. Soft-spoken and dignified, he had a lovely, gentle way about him. If there was somebody I wanted to ask for advice on a personal matter – like what car I should buy, or what insurance I should get – I'd ask Brian.'

Of the new guard, Stephen immediately hit it off, and would become best friends, with the band's lead guitarist, Dubliner Tony Geraghty. Tony was one of the country's most exciting guitarists, with many people comparing him to Gary Moore. He came from a credible rock background with Adolf J. Rag and had brought an edgier rock sound to the Miami's music. He was, in Stephen's opinion, destined for great things. 'Tony was my buddy. We were soul-mates. From day one, we were interested in the same things. There was huge mutual respect – he was an incredibly gifted player, world class, and it was great to listen to him play. Between shows, perhaps in a hotel room or backstage somewhere, we would experiment with some blues or jazz. He'd bring along some written parts for the great jazz standards. We were into that in a big way. Tony and I secretly intended to leave the Miami and form our own rock group as soon as it was financially viable.'

Drummer Ray Millar, from Antrim, was the link between the old Miami Showband and the new pop group, which the band simply referred to as 'The Miami'. 'Ray was scatty. He was everyone's pal and was just out for a laugh. He was from a wealthy background in the North, so he was less concerned about making money or the pay structures than the rest of us, but he loved being part of top-flight Irish showbiz. He saw himself as a Miami man and the band as his career.'

Stephen had less day-to-day dealings with the managers and directors of the Miami. It was usual for former band members to become involved in the business side of the music industry once they had stopped performing. This was certainly the case with Tony Bogan and Joe Tyrell, who had played the drums and keyboards respectively with the band and who now, together with director and manager Tom Doherty, operated the Miami as a business enterprise. They hired and fired musicians, paid their wages and booked the gigs.

Every one of the Miami musicians was respected in his own right and each had a solid grounding in the art of showbusiness. Nonetheless, the undoubted star of the show was Fran O'Toole, the handsome lead singer. The quality and range of his voice is still obvious today, and in the occasional archive footage that exists it is easy to discern the unique quality that set him apart from other front men. If fate had not interrupted he would have gone on to even bigger things than the Miami, and just a few days after Stephen joined the band, Fran outlined that dream future to him.

'There are many versatile musicians who can cover a multitude of styles, but the important ones are those who will leave their own instantly recognisable footprint. These are the people who, when they play their instrument or sing their songs, you know immediately who they are. Fran O'Toole was one of those people. He had a very distinctive voice and a particularly impressive aura.

'I had only been on the road with the Miami a few days when he said, "You know, they're grooming me for America and when that happens, I want you to come with me." I was astonished. Apparently, the management had other ideas for Fran. They wanted to promote him as a solo performer in the US, playing the hugely lucrative hotel cabaret circuit. This was a common progression. When a performer showed enough promise, they would bring him to the States. Bowyer had set the standard when he went there with The Royal Showband and later with The Big 8. When the time came for these solo performers to record their own songs, they were usually saddled with a bunch of session musicians. It was a common fault due to the shortsightedness of management. They would insist on bringing in these guys because studio time was so expensive. The rationale was to get in and out in the shortest time possible with players who churned out the backing tracks in a quick and clinical manner. The singer would go in, add his vocals and walk out again. As a consequence, recordings made in the 1960s or 1970s quite often had no soul. To me, records from back then can sound a bit dead. Perhaps, in retrospect, when Fran got his chance he wanted to take me with him to retain something of the natural feel of the band. Whatever his reasoning, I still get a thrill today to think that he asked. It was kudos, a mark of respect and I took it as a massive compliment.'

Stephen's enduring memory of Fran is that, regardless of his massive talent and how focused he was on his career, he was also a great practical joker who didn't take himself too seriously.

'Driving from gig to gig, I would sit in the middle seat with Fran and he would start all these games that drove everyone else mad. Childish games like I Spy With My Little Eye and all that wonderful nonsense. It was hilarious. Here was a pop star who had all the girls in Ireland chasing after him and all the men envious, nudging me in the side saying, "Come on, Steve, you're the only one who will play this with me. I spy with my little eye ..." I was happy to go along with it. I didn't mind. He was a lovely guy and I'd always be happy to play his games. He also had a sweet tooth. He would stop at a shop and buy a big bag of sweets, liquorish Allsorts and black jacks. There would be nothing in the bag individually worth more than a few pennies. Everyone else bought one or two things, like a chocolate bar or a bottle of Coke or whatever. Fran was like a big kid. He was very childlike, very innocent in that way. But he was great fun to be with and he had a fantastic sense of humour. He loved playing jokes on people.

'When I first met him he was driving a very powerful purple Ford Capri with a raised bonnet. He'd pull over and call me as if he had something urgent to say. As soon as I got to the window, he would slowly move two or three feet away and say, "Oops, sorry, my foot slipped", so I'd have to walk up to his window again, where he would repeat the procedure. This was his way of having a laugh. He also had a radio-cassette recorder on which he would record a phrase over and over, like "get up, ya old eejit". Then, he would press play and hang it on a door handle in the hotel to rouse the night porter. He would get the rest of the band to hide around the corner and watch the poor man scratch his head in frustration.'

Musically, the members of the Miami were one thing on stage and quite another once they stepped off it. They understood that their appeal lay in their ability to recreate the hits of the day, but they knew instinctively that their futures lay elsewhere.

'Because Fran was such a powerful singer, we would play covers that other bands might baulk at, like Motown and soul numbers and hits by artists, such as The Four

Tops, Percy Sledge and James Brown. However, even though we played the popular music of the time, we still considered ourselves children of the flower-power generation. During rehearsals, we would be playing Hendrix and Cream, but the minute the lights went out, we were The Beach Boys, playing surf music. Sometimes, we were The Bay City Rollers or whoever the punters wanted us to be, but we knew we were only acting out a role. It was an image that the management had created. It was all contrived. That's the way they wanted it because that's what worked and that's what made money. It was a huge industry and a massive social phenomenon, which played a very important part in the musical development of this country.'

For now, this formula was working. Wherever the Miami played, they were greeted with the same astonishing reaction reserved for the biggest bands of the day. Along with the popularity came the inevitable fame. From the relative obscurity of performing as a jobbing musician, where he was a sideman in a number of popular bands, Stephen found himself elevated to the world of celebrity. People asked for his autograph in the street, journalists wanted interviews and his picture appeared in the newspapers.

'Here was the novelty factor of fame and at the very start those first whiffs are very seductive. That's part of why you pick up a guitar in the first place, so everyone will think you're wonderful. Ireland was creating its own stars and making heroes of these young men. We were as high as you could climb on the showbiz ladder in Ireland and it didn't get much better than this.'

Things were moving fast. Stephen and Anne had to make some quick decisions. As the Miami was based in Parnell Square in Dublin, they decided to move to the capital. They got the chance to move to a house in Clondalkin, not far from the city, which had the added benefit of belonging to Billy Byrne, a band leader friend of Stephen's who would later become the music director of the Garda Band.

As Stephen was loath to leave his new wife alone night after night, it was a comfort to know she now had the company of Billy, his wife Maria and their daughter Ruth. 'Here she was, a beautiful young girl, just married and her husband away all the time. It brought home to me how hard it must have been. Anne is a very generous person and she just wanted me to be happy, but it is not a good life for any married couple. That's why, if I was offered a fortune today to do a lengthy tour, I would refuse. I don't want to lose another second with my family. No money and no amount of fame could ever amount to a hill of beans compared to them.'

In the meantime, the hard touring continued. Day after day the band was driven from one sold-out gig to another. Every night, another delirious audience screamed at them throughout the set while they launched into the hits of the day. Then it was back in the van, with Brian McCoy at the wheel, while Brian Maguire headed off separately in the equipment van.

'Often, the rest would be sleeping in the back of the minibus, so I'd sit up front with Brian on the long journeys. He would tell me stories of his early days with the Miami, when Dickie Rock was the front man. He told me about the special Miami train, packed with hundreds of fans, that travelled down the country to events such as the Kilkenny Beer Festival. We knew the halcyon days of the showbands were over. The Miami had successfully transformed into a modern pop group with a younger pop/rock appeal more suited to the times. Large crowds still attended dances, but increasingly the gigs took on more of a concert atmosphere. However, if the house full sign was not up before the support band finished, we would be worried. I remember once asking Brian if the heady days of the showband era would ever return. He said that it would never happen.'

For now, the diary was full and there was little or no respite from the schedule. The Miami were booked through the rest of 1975 and beyond. On Monday, 28 July, during the packed Galway Races Festival, they kicked off two sold-out nights at the massive Seapoint complex in Salthill. Just as they were preparing to go on stage for the second night, they were rocked to the core with the news

no sectarianism in the ballrooms. It was left at
The young people, from both sides of the
ty, wanted a good night out and we were more
by to oblige.'

has been made of the fact that the Miami
represented a cross-section of people living in
that time, being made up of Catholics and
s from both sides of the border, but the truth is
Miami themselves were completely unaware of
le impact they were having on the situation in
. Religion was not a factor in the band and it
difference to them as individuals. 'When I
band, I didn't know what religion anybody
as never an issue. I didn't know, nor did I care,
Protestant and who was Catholic.'

own to them, they posed a threat to those who
division. Somewhere in that twisted, shadowy
tit-for-tat, a plot was hatched to smash the one
promoted harmony and non-sectarianism, and
at the band that crossed boundaries and united
ise divided community became a target.

rowds were thinning out, and small groups of
their way home along the quiet streets of
. The Miami left the Castle Ballroom and waved
to drummer Ray Millar, who was driving to
spend the night with his parents. The rest of the
into the blue-and-white Volkswagen minibus for

of the sudden death of Irish superstar Tom Dunphy, who was killed in a car accident. He was forty years old.

Dunphy was considered a grandee of the showband scene. Along with Brendan Bowyer in The Royal Showband, he had conquered the Irish music scene before achieving similar acclaim with The Big 8 in the USA. The band had just returned to Ireland for a series of one-night stands, having completed a six-month stint at the Stardust in Las Vegas. Dunphy and fellow band member Noel Ryan were travelling from Waterford to a festival when their car collided with a truck at a bend on the Carrick-on-Shannon–Longford road. Dunphy had been a role model for the young Stephen Travers, and his death affected him and the Miami deeply.

'We were still in Galway when we were told that Tom Dunphy had been killed. We were devastated. Dunphy was setting the scene and writing modern Irish entertainment history while we were still only kids. Standing in for Tom in The Big 8 was one of the biggest thrills of my life. The whole showband industry was in a state of shock. One of the legends was gone.'

After the Races ended, it was a subdued Miami that headed back to Dublin before they continued on to a gig in Banbridge, County Down, across the border in Northern Ireland. Less than forty-eight hours later, they would be at the centre of an even greater shockwave, one that would ripple across the entire country.

Chapter 7

The Castle Ballroom, Banbridge, 30 July 1975

Stephen does not recall the gig as being particularly eventful. Even after revisiting The Castle Ballroom, the details of that night's performance do not stand out. 'I do remember that, before the gig, we were mobbed in front of the venue. I had stepped out with Fran to cross the road to buy some sweets. We were halfway back when a gang of boot boys, I suppose you could call them skinheads, surrounded us. For a spilt second, we didn't know what was going on. It was quite scary, but they just wanted autographs. They were asking how we were and they got Fran and me to sign their friend's plastercast, that sort of stuff.'

As they came off stage that night, the Miami were tired

but in good spirits. They ha_____ reception from an audience that_____ course, for the youngsters of Ba_____ opportunity to hear some great_____ to relax, let off some steam an_____ of everyday life in an increasi_____ Ireland. The band was aware o_____ situation, but felt they had not_____ there on a regular basis. Step_____ border scene, but not phased b_____

'Going to the North was_____ These were roads well travelle_____ the band. I had played in th_____ other bands, but it was a regu_____

'The border checkpoints_____ reminder that we were crossi_____ but it was all part of the big a_____ there. It was an exciting plac_____ compared to the Republic.

'Coming into Northern_____ entering a mini Britain. You_____ There were great car-access_____ instru'ments you simply cou_____ same price. Belfast, in parti_____ When we got on stage, it w_____ I think we received a partic_____ for the people there, it offer_____

the three-hour drive back to Dublin. The gear was already loaded securely in the equipment van, which set off ahead of them with road manager Brian Maguire at the wheel. Stephen jumped in beside Tony on the back seat. Des and Fran started a card game as Brian McCoy turned the key and prepared to move off. 'I normally sat up front with Brian,' Stephen says. 'We were both insomniacs and, for me, it was all part of the big adventure and I didn't want to miss one minute of it. But on that night, I got into the back as it was only a short trip home.'

As Brian attempted to turn the van, he found his way blocked by a metal security barrier that was set up across the road outside the venue. These were a common feature in towns and cities across the North at the time, erected as a security measure to keep a control check on passing traffic. 'We had to wait for a man to come with a key to unlock the barrier across the road. Brian Maguire had already left twenty minutes earlier in the van with most of the equipment, but we were delayed.'

It was only a minor delay, and as soon as the barrier was lifted the Miami were finally on their way home. It was a mild, moonlit summer night. The lads were wide awake and soon engrossed in their game of cards.

'Normally, they would be nodding off,' Stephen remembers, 'trying to catch up on some sleep before we got to the next venue. But as it wasn't far, we all gathered round the game and Fran started making jokes as usual.

Tom's death was playing on our minds, but apart from that, we were in good form. Things were going well.'

Up ahead, Brian Maguire, the band's road manager and a native of Northern Ireland, was recovering from an unnerving experience. As he sped along the silent road, he had become aware of a car travelling close behind him. The driver seemed to have been following him at some distance before quickly catching up, sounding his horn and flashing his lights. Brian watched nervously in his rear-view mirror and started to slow down to let the car pass. It overtook him suddenly on a dangerous bend and vanished up ahead. He continued his journey, annoyed at the car driver's behaviour.

Just minutes behind him in the Miami minibus, Fran O'Toole had just marked down everyone's name on the flyleaf of a book to keep scores in the card game when Brian McCoy noticed a red light in the road up ahead.

As the headlights of the minibus appeared from out of the darkness, Thomas Raymond Crozier fingered the heavy pistol in his pocket and looked around at the grim-faced men taking up positions around him.

Crozier was a twenty-five-year-old painter who also served as a Lance-Corporal in the 11th Battalion of the Ulster Defence Regiment (UDR), a locally raised unit of the British army. Tonight, however, he was on duty with his other 'unit' – a gang of terrorists from the Mid-Ulster

Battalion of the Ulster Volunteer Force (UVF). Earlier that evening, he had been instructed to leave his home on Queen Street, in Lurgan, and go to the house of a man called Samuel Fulton Neill, where he picked up a blue Triumph car. Then, he was told to drive to Lurgan Intermediate School to collect two men.

There was nobody around when he arrived at the school, so he parked near the canteen and switched off the engine. He glanced at his watch. He was on time. 'Come on, come on,' he urged them. After only thirty seconds, which to him felt a lot longer, two figures emerged from the shadows. They crossed cautiously to where he was waiting and got into the back seat. 'Drive,' one of them commanded in a thick Northern accent.

Crozier turned the car around once more and headed out onto the road. One of the men was vaguely familiar to him. Some weeks previously, this same man had approached Crozier on the street and asked if he was interested in helping the loyalist cause. Two weeks later, he had met Crozier in a pub in Lurgan and uttered the words, 'You're in', before outlining the rules and regulations of the UVF. His simple remark introduced Crozier to the dangerous world of the paramilitary terrorist.

There was no swearing of oaths at this stage, but the man told him he would be sworn in later. At first, Crozier had merely been told to collect funds for loyalist prisoners in the pubs around the staunchly unionist town. In time, though, the requests had become more sinister. Once he was ordered to lend them his UDR uniform and when he asked why it ws required, the man simply repeated his request.

'I agreed to hand it over, but did not pursue the matter any further,' Crozier would later tell police. 'It would have been unwise to do so. I was not told what he wanted it for nor did I suspect anything. The man was not entitled to it and I explained that I would have to have it back again.'

Now the man leaned forward from the back seat. 'Did ya bring the uniform?'

'Aye, I did, it's there in the back,' Crozier replied.

The man told him to drive in the direction of Banbridge. Crozier claims there was no further conversation. 'I thought it better not to ask where we were going. I knew one of them was in the UVF and I assumed the other one was, too. I was nervous. I didn't know what membership entailed or what they were going to do, but I was sure that we would not be long.'

Crozier was directed to drive through Loughbrickland, a small township located in the rural heartland of County Down, near the border with the Republic. Not far beyond the village, he was told to stop in front of another car which was parked up ahead. Crozier pulled in beside the car, a white Ford Escort, and his passengers got out. As they walked off up the road into the night, one of them turned and told him to wait in the car with the lights off. Then they were gone. He looked around. He was alone.

An hour passed quietly and very slowly. He was starting to doze off when there was a rap of knuckles on the windscreen. The man who had recruited him was standing outside, looking in at him. When he rolled down the window, the man told him to get his uniform on quickly. As he got out and retrieved his uniform from the back seat, the man – who Crozier refused to name in court – issued him with further instructions. 'We're going to stop a vehicle. When we do, you get the names and addresses of the people in it.'

'What I was told and what was going on was far beyond what I had expected,' Crozier would later claim in his confession to police. 'I had no idea what was going on until that moment. My feelings were muddled and I could not think clearly. It was only then that I knew I was going to take part in stopping a vehicle. I didn't ask what vehicle, although I was curious. I knew the men were UVF and I was afraid of finding out what I should not know. I didn't want to get into trouble. I was afraid to ask questions. They would not tell me anything more than I needed to know. Things like punishment shootings were in the back of my mind and I thought that if I did not do what I was told, it could happen to me.'

As he was putting on his uniform, he noticed eight or nine men climbing over a gate in a nearby field. They walked slowly towards him along the road. One of the newcomers asked Crozier if he knew what to do. Then Crozier's former passenger removed something bulky from his pocket and handed it to him. The barrel of the .45 revolver was cold and heavy.

Crozier was given a pen and a notebook and some final orders before the van arrived. It was to look like a regular vehicle checkpoint. In his uniform and with his pistol clearly visible, he was to approach the occupants of the van and get their names and addresses.

'Then I heard two men talking about a bomb and two others went past carrying something. I assumed it was a bomb.'

With that, the headlights of a vehicle pierced the darkness. A man stood out on the road and started waving a red light. When it slowed, Crozier could make out that the vehicle was a light-blue minibus. The driver turned off the headlights, as instructed, and pulled into the side of the road. As he moved forward to get their names and addresses, Crozier admits he noticed two of his comrades were armed with what he could identify as Sterling submachine guns. Another was holding a rifle and all three had levelled their weapons at the parked minibus.

Inside the minibus, Brian McCoy could see that the red light was a torch held by a man who was waving it from side to side. He started to slow the minibus. He turned around and told the rest of the lads that there was a roadblock up ahead and they were being pulled over.

'Again, this was not unusual,' Stephen says. 'We had been stopped before at checkpoints. There would be the usual chat with the soldiers on duty. Sometimes, they would recognise us and even ask for an autograph, so there was no reason for us to suspect that this was going to be any different.'

As the minibus slowed, the figure with the torch motioned for Brian to pull in to the left-hand side of the road. After he stopped, Brian rolled down the window.

'I couldn't hear what was going on, but then somebody opened the side door and we were told to step down out of the van,' Stephen remembers.

As he got out, Stephen became aware of other figures, emerging from the darkness. He could make out one man propped up against a tree, with his rifle pointed towards the minibus. The band mates lined up alongside each other and Crozier stepped forward with a notebook in his hand and started asking for names and addresses. Brian told him they were the Miami; Crozier remembers being somewhat surprised that there wasn't a Dickie Rock among them.

'And then one them started joking with us,' Stephen recalls, 'about us not wanting to be out answering questions. I smiled at that. Fran responded by saying they probably didn't like being out at the side of a ditch at this time of the morning either and they laughed. I still find that hard to understand. Here they were, joking with us, and knowing all the time what they were about to do.'

Suddenly, a car pulled up behind the minibus. To this day, Stephen can recall vividly the appearance of this man at the scene. He immediately caught Stephen's attention and made an indelible impression on him. 'The joking stopped. Everything changed. He had all the bearings of authority, of someone used to being in command. This officer was very efficient in his manner and the others became much more businesslike at his arrival.' He was dressed differently too. Unlike the soldiers in their UDR uniforms, he was in a pair of smart combat trousers with numerous pockets, and a combat smock.

'I admired the professionalism of this man,' Stephen remembers. 'He was good looking and very cool. To me, he looked like 'action man'. I noticed that he was wearing a different coloured beret to the others. His was markedly lighter in colour, while the others were dark. However, it was his English accent that really caught my attention. From my time in London, I had been exposed to a variety of accents and his was a very well-spoken one. He spoke with an educated, curt military voice when he addressed the men standing around us. It was a commanding tone that demanded obedience.'

Now the atmosphere was different. There was no more banter. The musicians were ordered to put their hands on their heads. After a quick consultation with the man who had previously appeared to be in charge, the officer changed Crozier's orders. He instructed this man to tell Crozier to get dates of birth instead of names and addresses. He didn't speak directly to Crozier and at no time did he directly address the Miami band members. But any foreboding that Stephen was beginning to feel was dispelled when Brian, standing next to him, nudged him and said, 'It's okay, Stephen, this is British army', indicating the officer. 'Brian, a Protestant from Northern Ireland, was familiar with security procedure and he probably reasoned that we would be checked and on our way much quicker than if it was simply a UDR check-point. The UDR, although a bona fide part of the British army and its largest regiment, was comprised mainly of part-timers. They had a reputation for sometimes being unpredictable and unprofessional in their behaviour, especially toward those from the Republic.' Des McAlea, a native of Belfast, would also later state that he too considered it a joint British army/UDR operation.

Reassured, Stephen began to feel irritated by the delay. His patience finally ran out when he heard the back of the minibus being opened. 'I got annoyed when I heard them lifting the flap at the back of the minibus. I looked around and I thought, I have had enough of these games. I was leaning over to see what they were doing because my guitar was in there. I had a very unusual guitar, a transparent Dan Armstrong Plexiglas bass, and I was very protective of it. I was damned if I was going to let some awkward soldier manhandle it. It seems naïve but, like Tony, I loved my guitar. But my naïvety probably saved my life.'

Stephen stepped out of line and walked towards the back of the minibus. 'I asked indignantly, "What are you doing?" One of them glanced up and, pointing at my case, asked me if there were any valuables in it. I said there wasn't, that it just contained my equipment.'

Stephen had dropped his hands from his head when he stepped out of line. 'And this soldier, a well-set guy, punched me from behind into the kidneys. It knocked the wind out of me and I gasped. The suddenness of the punch caught me off-guard as well as hurting me.'

Stephen was pushed back into the line, but now he was standing to the right of Brian.

'I hadn't been taking this as seriously as perhaps I should have, but I knew then that something was definitely wrong.'

Chapter 8

It is a cold spring day in March 2006. The leaves and thick foliage of high summer, so obvious in the footage from the aftermath of the bomb blast, have been replaced with bare bark and windswept fields. Stephen and I are standing in silence, looking down through the naked trees into the field where Stephen lay dying beside his friends when the UVF's plot backfired. Stephen's eyes are looking down onto the field as it lies before us today, but he is seeing another scene. I stand to one side, watching as he disappears into his own past.

'We were standing just about here,' Stephen says eventually, his voice quiet as he points at the ground. I have to lean in closer to hear him. I can just make out his words through the noise of the traffic passing yards behind us. 'I had been standing over there, but when the guy punched me back into the line I was at a slightly different angle.

'Suddenly there was a massive bang.'

While the two men rummaged in the back of the van, two others had been placing a bomb under the driver's seat. As they tilted it on its side, 10lb of commercial explosive detonated without warning. The bombers were blown to pieces in a flash. The explosion ripped off their heads, tore off both arms of one of the men and one of the legs of the other. One torso was sent spinning 100 yards away from the road. The blast spread in every direction, ripping the minibus in two. The instant shockwave caught the musicians from behind and propelled them into the air, where they spun in the blinding flash that luridly lit up the surrounding fields for miles around.

The violent roar of the explosion shattered the silence of the countryside. It was followed by the sharp *crack*, *crack*, *crack* of gunfire as the stunned terrorists panicked and squeezed the triggers of their submachine guns and pistols. Bullets flew in all directions. Some were embedded deep into wood and soil; the rest tore through skin, muscle and bone. Dozens of spent cartridges clattered across the road.

We walk over to the side of a ditch that separates the road from the field. Stephen points out exactly where he landed after the explosion had lifted him off his feet. 'I was able to count every one of these,' he says, touching the branches of a tree. 'It was as if I was in slow motion. I could feel every little tiny branch as my body passed through the bushes.'

As he twisted high in the air, he was struck by a dum-dum bullet – a high-explosive bullet modified specifically to ensure maximum damage to whatever it hit. It entered through his right hip and ripped through his body, destroying organs and tearing open arteries, shredding flesh, bone and sinew, before exiting just under his left arm.

We move around to get a better look into the farmer's field, which, now bare of crops, reveals the deep furrows left for planting. Stephen indicates the fifth row in and says this is where he lay, face down in the soil.

'I was in no pain. After I landed, I felt two arms trying to lift me. Fran was on one side of me and Tony was on the other. They had their arms under mine and they were dragging me farther into the field. One of them was crying. They must have been trying to get me away from the carnage on the road, but I collapsed.

'My two brave friends could no longer carry me and as the gunmen jumped down into the field shouting, they dropped me and ran in the opposite direction, away from them, farther into the field. It was there that the gunmen caught up with them. I heard them scream-ing, begging not to be killed. I can still hear them crying out. There was a long, loud burst of gunfire ... and then silence ... '

Stephen trails off and walks slowly towards the corner of the field, where a road sign indicates the direction of Donaghmore, one-and-a-half miles away. I leave him alone for a moment. His account has chilled me. I can't help but wonder about the men responsible for the Miami Showband massacre. From my initial research, I could easily dismiss them as psychopaths who carried out this atrocity without remorse or regret. But they were men who had families, friends, normal lives outside of their 'cause'. How, then, were they able to act with absolutely no mercy for innocent men, who lay defenceless and dying at their feet?

Stephen's next vivid memory of that night is of footsteps approaching him as one of the gunmen, who had just slaughtered his friends, walked towards him, he presumed to finish him off.

As he got closer, Stephen's brain raced with the thoughts of what was about to happen. For a man who had been badly wounded, lying in a field, and who had listened to the last desperate cries of his friends as they were murdered, his memory is remarkably lucid. He can recall exactly what was going through his head. I am curious about this. I remember tales of people who have stared death in the face and who saw bright lights at the end of a tunnel, or how others saw their lives flash before them. But Stephen wasn't experiencing any of those things. He wasn't thinking about dying; he was thinking about survival.

'I heard someone walking towards me. I knew what this meant. I thought, I have two choices. Do I get up on my knees and beg for my life, or do I stay lying here and pretend I'm dead? As I lay there, face down, with the grass against my cheek, I decided, I'll stay here, I won't budge.'

Just as the gunman reached Stephen, he stopped and kicked something, or someone, lying on the ground. It was Brian. The gunman kicked his body again, but there was no response. A split-second passed before Stephen heard him take the final few steps towards him.

'I suddenly felt all the tension drain out of me. All that was going through my head was, I'm probably not going to feel this. It is going to be quick. At that moment, a voice from the road and shouted, "Come on, those bastards are dead. I got them with dum-dums." The footsteps stopped. There was what seemed like an eternal silence. Then he began to walk slowly away from me.'

Stephen still wasn't sure if he had escaped. 'As he walked away, I reasoned that if he does turn around to fire one more shot, his aim may not be that good. His bullet might hit me, but not kill me. I tried to concentrate my mind on not screaming out should another bullet tear into my body.'

But there was no final bullet. There was only the

crackle of flames from the burning remains of the minibus up on the road.

As the silence settled once again over the field, Stephen desperately tried to make sense of what had just happened. He must have been in a shocked state because the first thing that occurred to him was that the Miami would be off the road. He worried that they would not be able to make the gigs scheduled for that weekend. His mind then settled on the memory of meeting a girl with Fran one night after a concert. Fran asked her to retell a story she had told him earlier. Fran and Stephen listened wide-eyed as this girl told them how she had once been shot after getting caught in the crossfire between security forces and terrorists during a street battle in the North.

'She told us that she had just come out of a large public building. She was coming down the steps with her boyfriend when there was a sudden gun battle on the street below. Both of them were hit by stray rounds and her boyfriend was killed. Of course, Fran and I were astonished at this. I suppose we were fascinated to meet someone who had actually been shot and we asked her what it felt like. She said that she remembered lying on the stone steps, but knew that she wasn't dead because she could feel a gentle rain on her face. As I lay in that field, this memory came to my mind. I didn't realise I had been shot, but I knew that I was in a bad way. I longed to feel a gentle reassuring rain on my face, but it never came. It was a beautiful summer's night without a cloud in the sky.

'At one point, I heard a voice calling, "Steve, are you okay?" It was Des McAlea, shouting from where he had landed after the explosion. I think I said I was fine. Then he was gone. I would not see him again for many weeks.'

As his fear grew with the realisation that he was badly injured, Stephen tried to check how much damage he had suffered. 'I had managed to roll onto my back. I slowly brought my hands across my chest and carefully counted my fingers. It was suddenly very important to me as a musician that I had all my fingers. They were all there. I thanked God as I heard my platform shoes click against each other; I still had both my legs. Finally, I raised myself up, almost to a sitting position, to check if my back was broken. I managed to get up on my knees but I found it hard to breathe. I thought that I was still just winded from being punched in the back.'

In reality, Stephen was suffering from massive internal bleeding. One of his lungs had collapsed when the bullet tore through his chest. Of course, he didn't know this at the time. Somehow he managed to get up on his feet. His legs almost gave way, but he steadied himself. As he stood, he realised his stomach was horribly distended.

'I lowered the palm of my hand and I felt this huge bulge. It felt like my stomach was about to explode. I walked in a small circle, fell on my knees, stood up and fell again in a bizarre ritual dance between life and death. Finally, I stumbled over to that tree near the road and I actually swung out of it to release the pressure on my bloated stomach. I grabbed onto a branch and let my legs go. I was hanging on, literally hanging on to my life.'

Chapter 9

Peering out fearfully from a hedge near the field, a terrified Des McAlea decided to make a bid for safety. He was the only one of the five musicians to escape virtually unscathed, suffering no more than some shrapnel cuts to his leg. Like Stephen, he is very lucky to be alive. When the bomb went off, the force of the explosion had blown him through a hedge and out into the field. Momentarily dazed, he raised his head to see what was going on. 'I saw the minibus burning on the road,' he would later recall. 'I stayed down behind the hedge when I heard a lot of shooting, it sounded like automatic fire. I was very scared and stayed as close to the hedge as I could. Then I heard someone running across the field, but I could not tell in which direction they went.'

Thomas Crozier also heard the gunfire as he ran in

blind panic down the road. Crozier had been taking down the names and dates of birth as he had been instructed when the bomb went off. He had seen one man run away ahead of him and instinct prompted him to follow. 'I didn't know what was happening after the explosion,' he would later claim. 'I was at the end of the line-up and those in front shielded me. When I was running, I imagined I heard shots, but they seemed to be just noises.'

When he reached the blue Triumph car, there were already four other men sitting in it. One of them got out and told him to hand over his gun, which was still in his pocket. He gave the pistol to the man, who then urgently told the others to give him their weapons. Crozier got into the car. The driver didn't think he would be able to get past the blazing minibus, so he turned the car around and sped away into the night. Crozier was picked up by police less than a week later.

Des McAlea was waiting to make sure the attackers were all gone before he made his move, but then the hedge he had been hiding in caught fire. Still not sure what exactly had just happened, but fearing for his life, he was forced to make a run for it. 'As I got up to run, I saw two bodies beside me. One of them was Brian McCoy and he appeared to be dead. The other was Stephen Travers and he was still alive, although he could not speak as he was badly shot up.'

Des tried to comfort Stephen for a second and told him he was going to get help. He clambered up onto the road and ran across to the opposite side of the dual-carriageway. There, he noticed a truck that had stopped when the driver saw the carnage. He shouted up to the driver that his friends had been shot and asked for help, but the driver, suspicious of what he had just stumbled across, wouldn't listen and refused to let him into the cab. 'I begged him to take me to the police station and he eventually agreed and let me into the cab. As I was getting in, a car stopped and the lorry driver asked the driver to take me to the police station in Newry.' Once at the station, Des raised the alarm.

Meanwhile, Stephen lay alone in the field, trying to understand what had happened. 'It was difficult to make sense of it all. It's hard to describe what's going through your head when you're trying to survive.'

Suddenly, the silence was shattered again as the noise of an engine roared over the field and the sky was lit up. The sound receded, then returned and stopped overhead. Over the shrill scream of a motor was a massive whoop, whoop, whoop in the air and blasts of wind blew grit into his face. He clenched his eyes shut. Behind his eyelids, a light seared his brain. Then he heard a crackle and the nasal whine of a disembodied voice.

'Roger, six, seven, zero over ...' He strained to make out the words over the noise above him. 'That's a roger

... go again Alpha three six over ... Stand by...' For a second, Stephen thought the ambushers had come back to finish the job. Gradually, he opened his eyes and closed them again as the glare from above blinded him. For an undetermined time he lay there, wishing the noise would go away. The clatter above him moved slowly to another part of the field and the light moved with it. He glanced over the field and could see the light settle on a dark shape lying a few feet away.

'I realised what was going on. A helicopter was shining a searchlight down into the field. I couldn't see it, but I could hear it. As it lit up the field, I could make out objects lying near me, but I refused to recognise them for what they were. In between the noise of the chopper blades, I could make out the chatter of radios up on the road. Fearing the gang had returned, I hesitated before I shouted out for help.'

On the road, vehicles had stopped and flashing lights cast the scene in an eerie glow. Police and army were moving through the debris, calling in for status reports from the helicopter hovering above their heads. From where they were standing, they could see bodies in the field, but they were wary. Having rushed to the aftermath of yet another explosion, they had not yet established what had happened.

They could see the burning remains of a vehicle and one, perhaps two bodies scattered amongst the wreckage.

Beside them, on the other side of the road, a ditch was on fire, the smoke adding to the confusion. The advance units crouched along both sides of the road, keeping a watchful eye over their rifle sights as they awaited further orders.

Officers arriving on the scene had seen all this before. At first, they were cautious as they moved slowly towards the bodies to examine them more closely. A common terrorist tactic was to booby-trap corpses, so they were alert and on guard. Tense and wary, the soldiers and police watched intently and waited. Stephen raised himself to his feet again and, taking a leap of faith, shouted for help. He screamed into the darkness. Finally, a figure moved toward him. A torchlight was shone in his face, temporarily blinding him. 'It's okay, son. It's the police,' a man with a Northern Ireland accent said. Stephen stumbled towards the officer, who caught him just in time as he lost his footing. Slowly and awkwardly, the two men made their way towards a small lattice fence that separated the field from a side road.

'I clearly remember seeing Fran on the ground as we approached the fence,' Stephen told me, 'but all I could focus on was the neatest line of blood trickling down into his palm.'

As the two men reached the fence, an almost comedic scene ensued. 'I still had my platform boots on and when I tried to put one through the diamond-shaped hole in the wire fence to climb over, it wouldn't fit. Every time the officers tried to help me, I'd push them away and try it again. Finally, I conceded and allowed them to lift me over.'

Stephen was placed in the back of an ambulance, but before they closed the doors, he asked the orderly in the back where the others were. 'To comfort me, he said that there was an ambulance for everyone and that the others would be following soon. As we sped off with the sirens blaring, I asked where they were taking me. He said, "Daisy Hill." I'd heard that name before. Daisy Hill … Daisy Hill. Why did it sound so familiar? And then I remembered; I'd heard it in so many western movies. It's the place where they brought dead cowboys for burial. I'd confused the hospital with Boot Hill but, for a moment, I thought, my God, they're going to bury me. The orderly later told me that many times during the journey my hand gripped his calf so tightly that he felt like crying out in pain as he tried to administer to me.'

Stephen's next memory is of being laid on a trolley and the lights of the hospital corridor whizzing over his head as he was rushed to the operating theatre.

'On the operating table, it seemed to me that the doctors were more interested in finding out who I was and what I had been doing in Northern Ireland than attending to me medically. One of them reached over with a scissors and tried to cut my light-blue sweater off, but I stopped him. I said, "I just bought that, take it off, don't cut it," but in a second it was gone. They were pointing at me and firing questions. They were indicating the wounds on my body. A bullet had gone into my right hip and exited under my left arm. There were just these two perfect little holes. They asked me what happened. All I could tell them was that I had fallen through a ditch. They pointed at the holes and I said they must be scratches from falling through the branches. There was very little blood, as all the bleeding was internal, and they seemed puzzled. As they asked me more questions, I realised that I was finding it harder to breathe. They asked me where I was from and I said, "Clondalkin". They thought I'd said "Dundalk" because they then started demanding to know what I was doing up there.

'On reflection, I suppose they were suspicious and wondering what a young man from Dundalk, with its reputation as a Republican hotbed, was doing being brought into hospital directly from the scene of an obvious terrorist outrage. They knew about the other young men being brought in and they were suspicious about who we were. One of them asked me what I was up to. I told them I was playing and he said rather sharply, "Playing at what?" I thought it was strange that he had to ask. After all, I just assumed these people knew who I was. I said I had been playing in a band. One of them, who seemed to be getting impatient, said, "What band? What do you mean?" I said, "The Miami," and he replied, "The Miami Showband?" When I mumbled, "Yes, the Miami," suddenly everything changed. I don't want to suggest that I would have received any lesser treatment had I been someone else, but as soon as they realised that I wasn't a terrorist, that I was an innocent musician, there seemed to be a change in tempo. Suddenly, the race was on to keep me alive.

'They issued orders, more people came into the room, machines were switched on and hummed into life. There were no more questions. It was getting even harder to breathe and I couldn't make myself understood anymore. I pointed at my trouser pocket and somebody found a phone number written on a piece of paper.'

The telephone number was that of a person who lived beside Stephen and his wife in Clondalkin. In the mid-1970s, telephones were a relatively scarce luxury. A common method of communicating was to ask for permission to use a neighbour's number as a contact in the event of an emergency. It was this neighbour who received the call in the early hours of that Thursday morning and who rushed over to Stephen's house to tell Anne that there had been an accident.

Initially, Billy Byrne was annoyed that someone was hammering on his door at such an ungodly hour of the morning, but he was soon jolted into action when the man at the door told him what had happened. Anne dressed quickly while Billy and his wife, Maria, prepared the car for the mad dash to Newry.

Anne was in shock. Just twenty-one years of age, she was being rushed through the night to her young husband's side with no idea of what had happened to him. All she knew was that there had been an accident. She later told Stephen that for the entire three-hour car journey, all she could think of was that no matter how bad it was, as long as he was still alive when she got there, she would be happy. 'She thought I might have broken bones or even lost limbs. All the things that could have happened to me were going through her mind, but she said she didn't mind as long as I was still breathing.'

On arriving at Daisy Hill, they jumped out of the car and rushed to the entrance of the hospital. A security man stood out in front of them, preventing them from going through the doors, and asked Anne who she was. He had a clipboard in his hand and when she told him, he glared at her before trailing through the names with his finger. 'Travers, Travers, Travers,' he mumbled to himself until his finger stopped. Finally he said, 'Oh, yes, … he's dead.' Billy rushed to catch Anne as she slumped down. 'No, it must be a mistake, we were told that he was here, that he was alive,' Billy pleaded with the man. He forced him to check again and he ran his finger down his list once more before looking up and saying, 'Oh yes, sorry, my mistake. He's going into surgery.'

As Anne, Billy and Maria rushed into the hospital, Stephen was drifting in and out of consciousness while the medical team prepared him for surgery. The lights of the operating room above his head started to fade. Then, just as he was slipping under, a man approached from behind and put his hands above Stephen's head.

'I was lying on the trolley, looking up. A tall, grey-haired man was leaning over me saying something in my ear. I turned my head to hear him and I saw a priest's collar. The thought of getting the Last Rites should have frightened me. I would have expected my reaction to be one of utter terror, but I was completely blasé about it. He asked was I sorry for all my sins and I replied, 'Of course I am.'

On the road where the incinerated minibus' charred remains smouldered, dawn broke over a scene of almost unimaginable carnage. One of the only identifiable pieces of the Miami's minibus was the steering column, which stuck up from the mangled remains. A wheel lay to one side, the smell of burning rubber hung in the air, and dog-eared playing cards lay here and there in between ragged bits of metal, pieces of guitar and torn shreds of camouflage clothing. Scattered amongst all of this were body parts. One policeman bent down to pick up an arm he found lying a hundred yards from the wreckage. As he placed it in a plastic bag, he noticed a tattoo on the forearm. He turned it around and, despite the damage, he could clearly make out the letters in bluish ink on the charred limb – UVF.

The policemen were tired, some had been at the scene since they were alerted to an explosion shortly after 2.00am. One of the first to have arrived was Detective Constable Kenneth Hassan of the Royal Ulster Constabulary (RUC). He had been working with CID in Newry when he heard that an explosion had taken place on the dual-carriageway, just seven miles outside the town. Detective Hassan left Bessbrook RUC station to travel the short distance to the scene, but he decided to stop off first at Newry to talk to Des McAlea, who was trying to tell the police what had happened. 'I spoke to this man for a few moments and established that he was a member of The Miami Showband, which had been playing at the Castle Ballroom in Banbridge earlier that night,' Detective Hassan reported. 'His name was John Desmond McAlea and he was in a very shocked state. He didn't make much sense.'

Despite his obvious distress, Des was able to give the policeman some information about what had happened on the motorway just over an hour earlier. 'I asked him a few questions,' Detective Hassan remembered. 'I learned that he had been travelling south from Banbridge in a minibus with four other members of the band. On the dual-carriageway, he said the bus was stopped. The next thing he remembered was an explosion and then shooting.' Detective Hassan listened carefully to everything a shaken Des had to say and, after taking a few more notes, decided to call the home of his immediate superior.

Detective Inspector James Thomas Mitchell listened without saying a word as Hassan relayed the details of what Des had told him. There had been a serious explosion, the young detective explained, adding that he was on his way there now to investigate. Shaking himself from a deep sleep, Mitchell dressed and made his way out into the night. A Detective Inspector with CID in Newry, he was also one of the most senior officers to arrive at the scene in the immediate aftermath of the explosion.

Hassan was already there, with another colleague, Detective Raymond Buchanan. Both policemen had been able to carry out a quick examination of the area and each had studiously taken notes of what they had seen.

'There was quite a lot of debris scattered over both lanes of the carriageway and in the central reservation,' Detective Hassan later reported. 'On close examination, I saw the remains of a smouldering vehicle, axle and wheels, on the roadside, half on the road and half on the hard shoulder. A little further along the road in the direction of Newry, I observed the fully clothed body of a male person lying face down on the road. He was wearing a tanish-brown leather jacket, blue denim jeans and brown boots. I then went into a field which ran parallel to the road but approximately five feet below the level of the road. On climbing the wooden fence, I saw the unclothed remains of a body consisting of a torso and one leg. This was lying stomach down in the field. Below a tree close to the hedge, I saw another body lying face up. This was also a male person and he was dressed in blue denim jeans and a jacket. Farther out into the field, I saw two more bodies both lying face up. They were lying beside each other. The one with his feet towards the hedge was wearing a blue denim shirt and trousers. The other one lying parallel to the road was wearing a brown leather jacket with fur collar, blue denim trousers and a large brown leather belt.'

Hassan pointed out all the bodies to Detective Inspector Mitchell when he arrived. After carrying out his own cursory examination, Mitchell took charge. He summoned the police surgeon Dr Patrick Ward, who arrived soon after 3.00am. Dr Ward was first shown the body of a man who would later be identified to him as Brian McCoy. Despite the fact that it was still dark and a torch supplied to him by a fireman was 'not very good', Dr Ward could clearly see that Brian was dead. 'He was lying on his back in a grass field and he had multiple bullet wounds to his chest, abdomen, right arm and front of the neck,' the doctor noted.

Then he was brought to where another body, that of Tony Geraghty, lay in the field a short distance away. 'On cursory examination, there were bullet wounds in his back, right arm, left chest, right shoulder and skull,' the doctor wrote in his report book.

Again, there was no question of survival.

'Then, at approximately 3.40am, I saw the body of a man later identified to me as that of Francis O'Toole.' Fran had suffered 'multiple head and chest injuries', which the doctor could see immediately had been caused by bullets. After his examination, the doctor conferred with Mitchell and declared that, in all three cases, 'life was extinct'.

Dr Ward also saw what he described as the severely mutilated remains of another two male bodies. These were the two bombers, who had both sustained such massive injuries that the doctor had no difficulty in ascertaining once again that 'life was extinct'.

Meanwhile, Detective Hassan and Buchanan had made another discovery. After showing Mitchell the bodies of the young men in the field, they moved back up onto the road, where they found one of the weapons used by the gunmen. From the top of the embankment, they could see pieces of the minibus lying farther out in the field, blasted away by the force of the explosion. They went farther up along the road to have a look around.

'Back on the road again, I saw a machine gun stuck in

the hedge beside the remains of the vehicle,' Hassan reported. 'I did not touch this gun but then saw another gun, a revolver, lying on the kerbstone that divides the central reservation and the Newry bound carriageway. It appeared to have been damaged by the explosion.'

'The remains of the vehicle were still smouldering at this stage,' Buchanan recalled. 'It appeared to have borne the bulk of the blast and was completely wrecked. On the Newry side of the vehicle, I observed the body of a male person lying face downwards on the centre of the road. He appeared to be dead. There was a lot of debris scattered all over the road. Then, close to the hedge, and convenient to the wreckage, I saw a Sterling submachine gun with magazine attached.' Buchanan took possession of the weapon and waited for the arrival of the forensic teams.

Finally, the order was given to take the dead musicians in from the field. After examining all the bodies, Dr Ward suggested they be removed to the mortuary in Daisy Hill Hospital, where he would carry out a full examination. The ambulances arrived from Daisy Hill soon after and the attendants treaded carefully through the field where the early-morning dew was already starting to settle. Gently, they lifted the bodies from the ground and placed them on stretchers before solemnly carrying the young men to the ambulances. Buchanan was ordered to climb aboard and he accompanied the bodies of Tony, Fran and

Brian on their journey back along the road they had happily travelled only hours before.

The sun was finally starting to come up when a team of forensic experts arrived at the scene. They picked over the numerous items that had been found and carefully documented each discovery. One of the team was James Patrick O'Neill, a constable who was the Scene of Crime Officer (SOCO) attached to Newry. O'Neill had arrived shortly after 4.00am and at a glance he knew he had a lot of evidence to work with. Amongst the carnage, there were vital clues as to what had happened.

His fellow officers had recovered various pieces of clothing and three green berets – one found on the hard shoulder, the other in a hedge and one, the farthest away, more than 400 yards up the road, towards Donaghmore. O'Neill also noted the other items that had been collected. As well as a machine gun with the serial number KR 97933, he also took possession of the pistol Hassan had found. As a police weapons specialist, he had no difficulty identifying it as a 0.38 calibre pistol, with the serial number C5381. He placed it carefully in a forensically sealed bag and labelled the bag. He placed it alongside the other weapons already found by Buchanan and Hassan, each one adding to the increasing bank of evidence. After further consultation with his colleagues, he now engaged in his own forensic study.

'On examination of the scene I found that a bomb had

exploded in a Volkswagen minibus, registration number 5506Z. The vehicle had been cut in half by the explosion. It appeared from examinations that the bomb was in the region of 10–15lbs and had been positioned to the rear of the driver's seat. Fragments of the vehicle and its contents were strewn over a radius of a hundred yards. Fifty feet from the front of the section of the Miami bus and in the Newry direction, I found a pool of blood on the dual carriageway.'

Making his way down into the field, O'Neill noticed that the grass was also saturated in blood. 'The other blood stains in the field were twenty-four feet from the hedge which runs parallel with the dual carriageway.' These stains marked the positions of the bodies of Fran O'Toole and Tony Geraghty. 'The blood stains left by Brian McCoy indicated that he had been shot close to the hedge and inside the field,' O'Neill added. In each pool of blood he discovered piles of spent ammunition – five .45 rounds were found in one bloodied area and twelve 0.9mm bullets were found in another. Strewn all across the area were numerous other bullets, each one spelling out the severity of the assault on the young musicians.

When officers arrived with metal detectors a short time later, they uncovered even more items, including sets of keys, parts of a guitar body, a damaged saxophone and pieces of the minibus. A pair of black-rimmed men's spectacles, with the left frame smashed, was also found. This particular item would later prove a decisive link to one of the killers.

Their examination even recovered parts of the bomb. Gerard Thomas Murray, a forensics expert, noted the blackened rubber plugs and lead wires from what he identified as a short-delay electric detonator. 'The presence of battery casings, and a plate from a clockwork mechanism, indicated that the firing circuit for the device comprised a timer, two HP2 batteries and an un-marked, copper-bodied, short-delay electronic detonator. Commercial high explosive was used as the main charge. The firing circuit described would have allowed a pre-determined time delay to be set and devices employing similar circuits are frequently used by terrorists.'

As no fragment of a metal container was recovered, Murray concluded that the circuit and the explosive charge had been held in some light container, 'such as a bag'.

Scene of Crime Officer O'Neill sealed all the various pieces of evidence in forensic bags and was preparing to have them removed from the scene when a policeman walking farther along the road called out. When his colleagues joined him, they discovered a white car hidden behind a hedge. 'At daylight, a further search of the area was being carried out when a white Ford Escort with the registration number 9528 LZ was found hidden up a lane which runs behind a UDR shooting range located approximately 200 yards on the Banbridge side of the scene of the explosion,' reported Detective Hassan. The car was examined and briefly searched before it was towed away for forensic examination.

Satisfied that he had made a good start in collecting all the clues left behind on the roadway, O'Neill prepared to leave. But as he looked once more over the terrible carnage, he knew his work was far from finished.

*

In the morbid stillness of Daisy Hill Hospital mortuary, a stunned Tony Bogan, a company director of The Miami Showband, nodded grimly to Detective Buchanan, indicating that he had identified the three bodies shown to him as those of his friends and employees. In his statement to police, he wrote: 'At approximately 7.20am on Thursday, July 31, I accompanied Detective Buchanan to the mortuary at Daisy Hill Hospital where I saw the bodies of three male persons. I can identify these as being Brian McCoy, 32, of Raheny, Francis O'Toole, 29, of Bray and Anthony Geraghty, 23, from Crumlin, Dublin. I was a director of The Miami Showband of which they were all members. I last saw the three deceased the previous morning at about 7am when I accompanied them from Galway.'

On a final note he added: 'They had all been in good health and spirits.'

Later that morning, Dr John R. Press, an assistant state pathologist, arrived to carry out a preliminary post mortem on the bodies. He found that three of the deaths had been caused by gunshot wounds. In Tony's case, they were to the head and trunk. Fran had died from shots fired into his head, neck and chest, while Brian was killed by the injuries to his neck and trunk. In all three cases the doctor noted that each man was otherwise in a healthy state and that there were no natural diseases to cause or accelerate death.

Dr Press then removed the ruined, bloody clothing from each body and handed them to Constable O'Neill. He also passed over two copper-jacketed bullets, one removed from the body of Tony and one from the body of Fran. Finally, the bodies were photographed for evidence and reports prepared on each death.

The pathologist also examined the remains of the two bombers, who had also been identified earlier that day. The post-mortem report into the deaths of both men makes for grim reading.

First, the doctor examined the body of the young man who had been identified as twenty-two-year-old Harris Boyle. Boyle had suffered massive multiple injuries. Rigor mortis had already set in and the body had taken on a purplish colour in the hours since death. Most of the top of his head and front had disappeared, leaving only the back half of the scalp. There was no brain. His face had also been blown away, leaving only the fragment of a lacerated tongue and a piece of bearded skin. Dr Press removed part of a battery from what was left of his neck. He noted that most of his hand and the right wrist were missing and that the left arm was mangled. Both legs were torn open, with the left one revealing torn muscles and bone. On what was left of the arms, tattoos bearing the words 'Harris' and 'UVF' were noted.

The other bomber had also been identified. His brother had confirmed that he was thirty-four-year-old William Wesley Somerville. There was also extensive damage to his body. Again, the head had been almost entirely destroyed. Most of it was missing, with just some fragments of scalp remaining. The skin on his torso was almost completely stripped away, exposing the damaged organs within. His entire right arm was missing, as was his left forearm. His legs had been torn away at the knees.

The severity of the injuries to both bodies led Dr Press to record in the post-mortem report that both had been close to, possibly even holding, the bomb when it went off.

'They would have had no chance,' he wrote.

Part III
THE AFTERMATH

Chapter 10

As radios were switched on in kitchens and cars across the country later that morning, few people listening to the news could make any sense of what they were hearing. It seemed the unimaginable had just happened. Bands were special, and the Miami was a household name. In a land that had become increasingly immune to reports of death and destruction from the North, the attack on them plunged people into a new level of disbelief and grief.

Incredibly, considering that it is standard police policy today not to release the names of victims until families have been informed, Helen McCoy learned of her husband's death when she switched on the radio. Neighbours and relatives had called to her house as rumours mounted that something had gone wrong. But it wasn't until the news came on at 8.00am that Helen heard the words herself. 'In the early hours of this morning, three members of the successful pop group, the Miami, were gunned down during an ambush near the border. Among the dead are Brian McCoy ...' Helen would not be able to remember clearly what happened after that. In fact, so severe was her shock that she is still unable to recall anything from the days that followed.

At first, the news was kept from Brian's elderly parents, who were spared the details of how their son had died. There was concern that his father, who had a heart condition, would not survive hearing the truth. Eventually, they were told what every parent fears most – that their child had died.

At the home of guitarist Tony Geraghty, his father Peter, a manager at Irish Biscuits, described his son as 'such a grand lad'. 'How can they shoot someone who was just trying to play music and make people happy?' he begged the reporters gathered at his door. 'Tony was music mad since he was a boy. That's all he was ever interested in. What harm could he do to anyone?' There was no answer to his anguished questions.

In between floods of tears, Tony's fiancée, Linda Hendricks, revealed how she and Tony had been saving to buy a house. They had just bought a car together and were hoping to get married the following year.

Meanwhile, relatives tried to comfort Fran's wife, Valerie. 'She is terribly distressed and is now heavily sedated,' her mother told reporters later that morning. Perhaps as much of a blessing that could be hoped for under the circumstances was the fact that the couple's two children, Rachel, aged four, and Kelly, aged two, were too young to understand what was going on.

It was reported that Ray Millar was safe at home in County Antrim after he decided to drive home from Banbridge after the gig, but according to one radio report, he was 'too shocked to speak'.

Also suffering from the after-effects of the trauma was Des McAlea. He had spent a fitful night in Newry police station, where he had fled to raise the alarm. After questioning by detectives, he was brought to Daisy Hill Hospital, where he was treated for a slight injury to his leg. He was then brought under armed escort to the border and handed over to the police in the Republic, who drove him to his home in Swords, north County Dublin. There, looking exhausted and dishevelled, he rushed into the house for a tearful reunion with his wife, Brenda. A friend described him as 'a very frightened man'.

While Des lay in bed under sedation, Brenda told a reporter outside her door how Des had telephoned her earlier that morning to tell her he was okay. 'Des was hysterical,' she recalled. 'He was shouting down the phone, "They're dead, they're all dead." He told me the boys had been ordered out of the band wagon and then shot.'

One of those trying to make sense of it all that early summer morning was Liam O'Dwyer, Stephen's former band-mate in The Sinners. 'My sister called and said she had heard something on the news about the Miami,' Liam remembers. 'The bulletin was in Irish and she missed most of what was said. All she knew was that something terrible had happened to the lads. I turned on my own radio and heard the tail-end of the report. I still didn't understand why they were on the radio or what was going on. It said that some of them had been killed, but that Stephen was still alive and was in hospital.'

Liam quickly packed a small suitcase and went to a phone box in the town to try and arrange a lift to the North. By chance, he met a man he knew who was on his way to Larne, so he jumped into the seat beside him and got him to drop him off in Newry. When he got out of the car, he sensed the increased tension on the streets of the town.

'I had never been there before, so when I got out of the car, I just asked people on the street where the hospital was. One man took me by the arm and said, "What the hell are you doing here, walking around asking questions like that with your accent?" I didn't know what he was talking about. I explained that I was looking for my friend who was in the band and he said, "Oh, the Miami. Jesus, come with me," and he brought me straight to Daisy Hill Hospital.'

In the corridor, Liam met Anne and the rest of Stephen's family. 'It was a terrible scene, we were all distraught,' he recalls. 'We were just sitting together, praying, when a man approached me and introduced himself as the surgeon. Anne had told him I was an old friend of Stephen's. He took me aside and said, "I've operated on hundreds of bad cases, but this is really bad." Then he said, "Tell me about Steve Travers", so I told him how we had played together as musicians for years. I said he was the sort of guy who, if he gets it into his head to do something, he won't give up. He would see it through to the end. Then this surgeon, Blundell, stuck out his hand and said, "That's all I wanted to hear."'

Under the careful eye of Mr Blundell, Stephen had spent almost four hours on the operating table as the medical team worked to save his life. They had their work cut out for them. The dum-dum bullet, which had entered at his right hip and exploded while still travelling through his body, had exited under his left arm, leaving a barely noticeable exit wound. Internally, there was extensive damage as the bullet had torn through sinew and soft-tissue organs. His lung was punctured and parts of his bowel were perforated.

Stephen would only learn much later how serious his injuries were. About a year after he was released from hospital, he met one of the doctors who had fought to save his life that night.

'I was living in Dublin at the time and one day I answered the door to a very well-spoken man who said he was James O'Neill. The name meant nothing to me, but he stood there and matter-of-factly told me that he had seen my insides. I just thought, What's the story with this guy? He's obviously some sort of fruitcake. He went on to explain that he had been a medical student at Trinity College, but on the night of the incident he had been working as an assistant in Daisy Hill. He then went on to recount all that had happened on the operating table while I stood there listening, with my mouth open. He said he remembered everything in graphic detail, as it was one of his earliest experiences of an emergency medical surgery. Some of the things he described were the attempts to patch up the damage to my large bowel. Every time they would stop the bleeding at one point, a spurt of blood would shoot up from somewhere else. Eventually, he said they had to remove about twelve inches from my large bowel as it was beyond repair. He told me that on two separate occasions everyone else had given up, but this Mr Blundell refused to let me die.'

Outside the operating theatre, Anne stood in the corridor praying for her husband. She was brought into another room and made to sit down and drink a cup of tea. By late morning, the operation was over and Stephen was placed in an intensive-care ward. Anne was allowed in to see him briefly. For a second, Stephen opened his eyes.

'The first person I saw was Anne. I couldn't really make her out, you know your vision is not that great when you first come to, but as my eyes cleared, I saw all these tears rolling down her face. I don't think I had ever seen anything so beautiful in all my life. And the strange thing was, when I looked at her, I absolutely accepted the situation that I was in. I didn't question all the tubes and drips attached to me. I immediately knew that I was in hospital and I was aware of everything that was going on around me. I didn't panic. I remember the first words I managed to say to her. I simply told her that I loved her and she said she loved me. She couldn't say any more, she was crying. She told me later that when I opened my eyes, she knew I was going to live.'

Later, Stephen's family began arriving. His mother, brother and sister, and his in-laws, all crowded around his bed and he can remember clearly the shocked looks on all their faces when he woke up. 'I must have been a bit of a sight. I was lying there, with my long hair and a beard. My mother-in-law said I looked like Jesus on the cross. She is very religious and immediately corrected herself saying I looked like St Joseph instead because it wasn't blasphemous.'

Their initial relief that he had regained consciousness was tempered by the fact that they had been warned he was not yet out of danger. His medical team was still very concerned about his condition and quietly let the family know that there would need to be a dramatic improvement before they gave him a chance of survival. As they watched, Stephen slipped back out of consciousness.

Beyond the hospital's walls, as more details of the horror that had taken place began to emerge, it created what one newspaper described as 'a floodtide of revulsion' across the country. In the North, the four main Church leaders united to issue a statement condemning the murders of the three Miami men. The head of the Catholic Church in Ireland, Cardinal Conway, the Presbyterian Moderator Dr G. Temple-Lundie, the Methodist president Dr Headley W. Plunkett and the Archbishop of Armagh, Dr George Otto Simms, issued a joint declaration urging all their communities to rouse themselves in an effort to break the chain of violence and counter-violence. 'Every murderous deed has its own horror and shame from which all peace-loving people recoil,' they declared. 'We will pray in sympathy for those who have suffered, but not too soon forget the savagery of what has happened.'

Enoch Powell, the British MP for Down South, in whose constituency the attack took place, said the horrific outrage was rendered, 'If possible, more shocking by the fact that it was carried out against people who were peacefully visiting the United Kingdom from another country.'

In Dublin, the British ambassador, Sir Arthur

Galsworthy, was summoned to the Department of Foreign Affairs, where he was told by the Secretary, John Kelly, of the Irish government's concern for the safety of Irish people travelling about their normal business in Northern Ireland. Tánaiste Brendan Corish had requested the meeting with the ambassador to express the government's 'utter condemnation and revulsion' at the brutal murders. In short, the ambassador was told quite frankly that the Irish government felt that not enough was being done to prevent sectarian killings.

In the Dáil, opposition leader Jack Lynch described the murders as a 'bestial deed' and demanded that the Irish and British authorities take steps to ensure that people going about their lawful ways could do so without fear of murderous criminals. The head of the Irish government in 1975 was Taoiseach Liam Cosgrave.

Ironically, the day before the Miami killings he had given a speech to a European security conference in Helsinki on the issue of violence. He was interrupted from talks with other European heads of state, including the Prime Minister of Britain, Harold Wilson, to be informed of developments back home. In his speech, he had told the gathered European leaders that the majority of the people living in Ireland had long held the hope that the two parts of the country might come together in peace at some future time. Now, after expressing his own personal shock at the news of the Miami massacre,

Cosgrave relayed messages of sympathy to the families of the three young musicians.

An early indication of how seriously the leaders of both Ireland and Britain viewed the situation can be gauged by the fact that, for the first time in history, both countries were officially united in condemning a terrorist outrage. After much deliberation, Cosgrave and Wilson agreed to release a joint statement on behalf of their respective governments condemning the Miami killings as 'a criminal and sinister act'. They emphasised how 'deeply shocked' they were by what was 'to be condemned by both communities in Northern Ireland and by the people of both our countries'.

Unionists also distanced themselves from the killings. An official from the Ulster Vanguard – an umbrella group representing members of various unionist political parties – called on the public to help the police to catch the killers.

The Irish music industry, still mourning the death of Tom Dunphy, was reeling from the unthinkable murders of three of the best-loved musicians in the country. Decca Records, the Miami's record company, said all its staff were deeply saddened by the killings. In a statement, a spokesperson confirmed what Fran had told Stephen about his upcoming solo career. 'Decca had planned to launch Fran O'Toole as a solo singer/ songwriter on a new label at the start of September. It is particularly ironic that Fran's first solo record, written by himself, was entitled 'Love Is'. The Miami were Ireland's foremost showband and had devoted their lives to the public in Ireland for many years. They will be sadly missed by their many fans.'

While not going so far as to ban acts from playing in the North, the Irish Federation of Musicians advised bands to make their own decisions in the light of what had taken place. 'The assassinations of the three members of the Miami were carried out by psychopaths who struck at a high-profile profession knowing that the murders would hit the headlines,' General Secretary Paddy Malone told reporters. Representatives of bands and pop groups from across the country agreed to meet in Dublin to discuss the implications for their members. The talks focused on the future of the pop-group circuit, particularly in the North. As an immediate safety measure, it was suggested that all bands change their mode of transport from the gaily painted buses used to promote their acts to more discreet vehicles.

In the North, musicians also met and agreed to make every effort to uphold previous agreements and to continue on as best they could. They asked that owners and promoters of venues provide overnight accommodation, so they could avoid travelling the roads in the small hours. Over 60 per cent of all the touring bands based in the North joined together and issued a plea to their colleagues south of the border to continue to entertain the fans in the North.

However, the damage had already been done. Many acts made their own instant decisions that would affect the entertainment industry in the North for decades. Northern Ireland promoters found themselves with empty venues as managers of southern bands called to cancel gigs. Cecil Thompson, the promoter of the Castle Ballroom, admitted that acts scheduled to appear that weekend refused to confirm whether they would turn up. Even acts from the UK were too frightened to play.

Dickie Rock, the former lead singer of the Miami had been woken at 7.00am that morning by a knock on his bedroom door at the Galway Bay Hotel, to be told that the Miami had been in an accident. After he listened to the news reports, he decided that he would never play in the North again. It was an impulsive and emotional reaction and in the time that followed he would play there again but Rock's knee-jerk response to the horror was imitated across the showbusiness world. It was the end of an era.

All this time, as public feeling swung between grief, disgust and anger, Stephen Travers lay in intensive care, critically ill. Although he had shown some signs of improvement, the doctors were still seriously concerned and his family could only watch on helplessly, praying that he would recover.

'When [they were] off-duty, hospital staff would sit by my bedside and hold my hand,' Stephen remembers. 'Watching a news bulletin, Anne would hear that my condition had deteriorated and she would rush back to where I lay while the nurses attempted to calm her. I was told later that, until Sunday, they didn't expect me to live.'

As Stephen's condition deteriorated, his family was summoned to his bedside. 'They had initially gone back to south Tipperary and Cork, but by the end of that week they were told to come back to the North – though, of course, Anne had remained with me throughout. When they arrived at the hospital, the doctors readied them for the worst. My family doctor had also been put on alert by the hospital authorities.'

Dosed up on painkillers, Stephen slipped in and out of consciousness, sometimes waking up in the dark, wondering where he was.

'I remember on that Sunday they wanted to take me for an x-ray. They wheeled me out, still lying in the bed, but I said I wanted to stand for some stubborn reason. I insisted that I would not have the x-ray lying down and that I would not take no for an answer. They said I was too ill, but I would not listen, so they lifted me up off the bed. I was supported by two orderlies, one on each side. They let me go as they shot the x-ray and then caught me in case I fell. The x-ray finished, they tried to put me back on the bed, but I asked to use the toilet. They backed me up to the bowl and everything came out, my damaged bowel started to work again. The two orderlies stood there gaping, then one of them rushed off to tell the senior nurse, Belle. It was amazing. You would think that all the hospital staff had won the lottery. Belle said the flags were flying. I had not heard that expression before, but I knew it meant that I was going to be fine. I was going to live. My system was kicking into gear.'

Gradually, Stephen's condition stabilised and his body began to repair the terrible wounds it had sustained. He was worried about his friends and continually asked how they were. 'I didn't know that anybody had been killed. I wasn't well enough to hear that. From the moment I opened my eyes, I had been told that some were worse and some were better.' A few days later, the difficult decision was reached when it was felt that it was best to tell Stephen the truth.

'Anne had decided that she would tell me. She came in with a priest, Fr O'Rourke, and she put her hand on mine, finding a spot in between all the needles and tubes. She said, "You know you've been asking about the lads," and I nodded, and she hesitated. I should have been able to work out what I was about to be told, but something in me refused to put two and two together. She tried again. "Well, Steve …" and she clutched my hand tighter and could not say another word. Of course, God, she was only a youngster herself, she was only a child. Fr O'Rourke took over. He just said, "Stephen, three of the lads didn't make it." And, I sort of nodded my head. I thought, Right, okay, and I said, "Brian?" Fr O'Rourke looked straight at me. "No, Stephen, he didn't make it." I said Fran's name and, again, he shook his head. Then I tried to say Tony. But when I opened my mouth, I could not get the word out. I just stared at Fr O'Rourke. I tried to say Tony's name again, but I couldn't. I looked over at Anne and the tears were streaming down her beautiful face. Now, I knew the truth.

'Instantly, I was physically sick. I had tubes in my nose going down into my stomach. They were very uncomfortable. Bile from inside my stomach came up not only through the tubes but also through my mouth. I put my hands up to my face, but it just spurted out of my mouth and my nose, everywhere. I felt it was coming out my eyes and my ears. I felt tugs on my hands. As I recoiled, I must have wrenched at the drips in my arms. That was the first real shock. This was the moment that brought it all crashing down on me. I couldn't talk. I felt dreadful. It was terrible. I was spinning out of reality. I couldn't make sense of it at all. It was like this was all part of some game. You know, when I was younger, I had watched Fran and Brian, already legends, and I had admired them so much. I had joined the Miami only six weeks earlier. Suddenly, I was playing with them, touring with them and enjoying their company. Life was great. Now, I was being told they were dead. It was like we were all acting in some bizarre film. There was an element of surrealism about it, and death was part of this horror movie. How could a pop star be killed? That didn't happen in the movies. To me, Brian, Tony and Fran were superstars. And now they were dead?

'It's hard to explain, even now. After I was told that Fran and Brian were dead, it just felt like another act in a tragic script but still part of the big adventure that we were all on. But when it came to Tony, my mind stumbled. Tony wasn't playing any role. He was like me, a young enthusiastic musician. As the tears rolled down my face, everything I loved about him flashed across my mind. From the beginning, Tony and I had quickly become great pals. Fran said we were peas in a pod and he used to tease us about being "serious musicians". On our days off, we would go back to our house in Carrick-on-Suir and talk about our plans to put our own band together and do our own music. I loved him as a friend and greatly admired him as a musician; he was a great guitarist. Because I could relate more to him as a person, the reality of what had happened began to sink in.'

As Stephen came to terms with the deaths of his friends, the media was reporting that he was showing signs of improvement. Not far from where Stephen lay in Daisy Hill, a man listened to the bulletin, turned off the radio, closed his eyes and said a quiet prayer. His wife had given birth to a baby just days before, but he had been told that the little boy was very ill and had little chance of survival. Like everyone else, he was aware of the Miami atrocity and every day he tuned in to hear if there was any update on the young musician who had been critically injured. As the days went by and Stephen's condition improved, this man decided the young bass player was a fighter and vowed that, if his son also survived, he would name him after Stephen. And he did. A quarter-of-a-century later, Stephen was at a ceremony with the President of Ireland in Áras an Uachtaráin when he was approached by this very same man. He explained how he had sworn that he would call his son after him if they both lived. And how it was a vow he had gladly kept.

Chapter 11

Helen McCoy was woken by the sound of the telephone ringing. She had fallen asleep downstairs after her young son, Keith, had woken her in the middle of the night, but now she was wide-awake and very worried.

'I knew instantly that something was wrong. I glanced at the clock and it was past 7.00am As the Miami had been playing just up the road, I knew Brian should have been home. I picked up the phone and it was Brian's brother-in-law on the other end of the line. He said he had heard something on the news that a band had been ambushed near the border, but when I quizzed him on the details he was vague and sounded distracted. I got the feeling that he wasn't telling me everything he knew. I thought for a second that maybe it was Brian and they had been robbed or held up, but I knew that the money was never carried with the band. I started to get even more anxious. I hung up and immediately dialled Tony Bogan's number, the Miami's co-manager. The phone was lifted after the very first ring and before anyone spoke, I knew immediately that something very bad must have happened. His wife Margaret came on and she blurted it out. She was screaming down the phone that Tony had to go to identify three of the boys. But she didn't know which three were dead. Then she said to me, "Oh God, Helen, maybe Brian isn't one of them."'

Stephen and I are listening very quietly to Helen McCoy's account of the day her life fell apart. We are both sitting in the front room of the comfortable house she once shared with her husband on a suburban street in north Dublin. It was already late in the evening when Stephen and I finally knocked on the door, but we were given a warm welcome and brought inside. Helen offered us a seat and introduced me to her son, Keith, who was five years old when his father died. All around the neat, tidy sitting room are mementoes of Brian. After bringing us some tea, Helen produces a scrapbook packed with photographs of her husband.

We flick through the old black-and-white pictures, marvelling at the sharp suits and quiffed hairstyles. We turn another page and there is a picture of Brian when he first joined the Miami in 1967. In it, he is surrounded by the other lads – Fran, Paul Ashford and a fresh-faced Dickie Rock. They are all astonishingly young.

Brian McCoy had already been recognised as an accomplished musician when, as Helen puts it, the Miami came looking for him. The trumpet player must have found it a difficult move to make as, according to a press clipping in Helen's scrapbook. 'Brian McCoy has turned down offers with some of the bigger named outfits for the simple reason that he is convinced that The Secrets can be big too.'

'And they were,' Helen says. 'They were really starting to make their mark when the Miami came looking for replacements following a split in their original line-up. Looking at the pictures now, I forget the names of some of the other lads in The Secrets because my memory isn't great, but they were all good guys. Brian loved that band and they had a bright future ahead of them. But the Miami, well, the Miami was the biggest band at the time and it was just too great an opportunity to miss.'

She chuckles happily at the pictures of her husband as we turn the pages. Helen is in her sixties now and still speaks with the slightest hint of a northern accent. She heaves a heavy sigh when I ask her how they first got together. 'I met him when I was very, very young,' she says, momentarily looking away from the scrapbook. 'We used to go to the dances on a Saturday night in Armagh. Everybody from the area would go, either to the Parochial

Hall in the town or to the Orange Hall. Brian would have been there too, playing at the socials, as they were called. I was only sixteen and he was six months older than me. We were pals for a long time before we got married because we were so young. Kiddies, that's all we were.'

Helen married Brian eight years after she first met him. He had joined the Miami in August of that year and the couple moved to Dublin to be close to the Miami's base. They were exciting times. 'Once they had even been brought over to the United States and nobody telephoned home at that stage so Brian would write me these long, beautiful letters instead. I remember all their gear was stolen while they were over there, but Brian was delighted because he got a brand new trumpet out of it.'

She laughs. 'There were always people approaching Brian on the street because they were all so well-known, particularly after Dickie came back from the Eurovision Song Contest in 1966. Brian loved being a musician, it was his life. But he was also a family man. He was a very family-oriented guy.'

Stephen tells Helen how he used to sit up front with Brian as he drove the band home after a gig. 'I said to him that he would probably fall straight into bed and be fast asleep in seconds after playing the show and driving through the night. But he said, "Oh no, sure I'll sit for half-an-hour on the children's beds first." He told me he loved to just sit and watch his children sleeping. It was the first time that I ever heard another man say that about his children. I thought my own father was the only man who would do something like that.'

Helen is nodding. She explains that, as a musician, Brian was around the house quite a lot during the day, so he got very attached to his children. He would regularly head off to the seaside with Keith and the dog. Keith remembers being brought to the beach and has many other happy memories of his dad.

His sister Cheryl was only a year and ten months old when their father was murdered, too young to remember him at all. 'She'd love to, but she can't.' Pointing to an old disc, Helen says, 'In fact, she didn't even realise that this record here was her dad's. She was amazed when she realised that her father was singing on it.'

Her voice becomes quieter when we come to one of the last photographs taken of the Miami before they were killed. Helen is vague on the details of all that happened following that phone call to Tony Bogan's wife. Her recollections are a blur of images but she seems to recall that a neighbour, who was distantly related to one of the former members of the Miami, had come in to comfort her as she sat in shock in her dressing gown on the stairs, staring at the phone by her feet.

'I was getting more and more frightened. I remember I was shaking, just sitting there, praying that it wasn't Brian. People from next-door started coming in. They said that they had heard something on the news. Somebody switched on the radio and the headlines came on. The newsreader called out the names of the lads who were killed, including Brian's. Somebody took my arm and said, "Helen, you'll have to get dressed. Brian's dead."

'But you just don't take it in. You're trying to think, who and why or what. What's happening? All the neighbours seemed to be here. The house was packed with people. The girls from next-door came and took Cheryl away, but little Keith here was running around, you know, he was five years of age, he had no idea what was going on. The rest is a haze. Somebody rang my doctor, who was in Cork at the time so they got somebody else from down the road. He came in and handed me two or three little pills and a glass of water. You don't even think about it, you just swallow them and wake up two or three hours later and you don't have a clue what's happened.'

As the house filled with neighbours and friends, little Keith McCoy went out to play with his friends, oblivious to the mounting drama in his home. 'This little kid came out of nowhere,' Keith recalls. 'He ran up to me and said, "Was your dad killed?" I said, "No", but he said, "Yes he was, yes he was. He was shot." And he ran off up the road.'

By lunch-time, Helen's family had arrived and she was taken to her sister's home, where she stayed the night.

'The next few days are indistinguishable. I don't recall the day they buried Brian. I was sedated. Strange as it may seem, that's what doctors did back then when confronted with someone who had just suffered a massive shock. They took the decision out of your hands. I wasn't even at the funeral. It's something I have lived with ever since. That's why I was looking forward to the memorial service in 2006 as it was the first time that I had a chance to attend a service for him. When he died, I didn't know what was going on. I had no control over what was happening to me. Other people had taken over and were doing things for me. People told me what to do and where to go. They meant well, but it still haunts me that I never saw Brian before he was buried.'

Brian's body was brought back to his hometown of Caledon in County Tyrone. Helen says that his cousin, Trevor McCoy, who was also one of his best friends, was doing part-time work with an undertaker and they made the arrangements.

'Trevor had brought Brian's body home the day before the funeral and, that night, I went to see him where he lay in his parents' house. Protestant funerals in the country are huge affairs and I remember this long laneway up to the farm being packed with cars. That's all I could see, there were crowds of people there and I panicked. They brought me upstairs. They were talking about the funeral arrangements. It's funny, just a couple of weeks before it happened, my sister and her husband had been visiting and for some reason we had been talking about funerals. Brian had said that he hated the flowers that people brought and that he didn't want an open coffin or any sad hymns at his funeral. I told my brother-in-law to go ahead with whatever he thought was right because he knew what Brian wanted. At that stage, I didn't care anymore, I just knew I wanted to see my Brian for the last time. I went into where the coffin was and I nervously approached it. I asked to see him and they said that I couldn't because they had been advised not to open the lid. I asked, "Why? What's wrong with him?" because there had been talk about how they found the other lads in an awful state. They told me there was nothing wrong with Brian, that he was all right, but they couldn't open the coffin for me because then his mam and dad would want to see him and that would be too much for them. I could never understand that. It seemed that nobody cared what I wanted.

'Even today, after all this time, it still lives with me, it never goes away. It's always there on my mind, all the time. I have lived with not getting to Brian's funeral for so long that going to the memorial service last year was good for me. It made me face up to things. It brought everything back a bit closer. One of my sisters had thought that it would be the best thing for me. To get upset and grieve properly and she was right. I've subsequently learned that it is important to deal with bereavement in your own way.

'Don't get me wrong. Everything was done for me with the best will in the world. It was a way of protecting me and they were doing what they thought was the right thing. But it can become intrusive. I remember a few days after Brian was buried, a cousin asked me was I going home to live in the North. They were all trying to sort my life out. Keith had just started school and the worst thing would have been for me to take him out of there and put him in another school and have him start all over again. I'm glad that I did not leave my home and uproot all that we had achieved together.'

Helen goes into the kitchen to make some more tea. Stephen is talking to Keith about why he wants to meet the men who killed his father. Keith confesses he got angry when he watched a BBC documentary on the Miami incident which revealed Fran O'Toole had been shot numerous times in the face. 'I heard you interviewed on the documentary, Stephen,' Keith says. 'How you heard one of them saying, "Come on, I got those bastards with dum-dums", and how you had heard the lads beg for their lives. Those guys knew exactly what they were doing and they deliberately set out to do it. That's why I'm worried sometimes that we let them off the hook a little bit by trying to understand their motives or by using phrases like "it was nothing personal".'

'It helps me to believe that because they didn't know us personally, it wasn't personal,' Stephen replies. 'I would not be able to accept it so readily if I thought that somebody who knew me well tried to kill me. I sometimes try to put myself in their shoes. From their perspective, it was a brilliant plan. Look what they could have achieved had they been successful. In their warped minds, the end justified the means. Had it worked, they would have framed an entire country.'

As we have our tea, Stephen talks about how writing about his experiences has forced him to confront certain issues. 'There are compartments in the back of your mind where it's possible to store things, leave them alone and not have to face up to them,' he says. Then he leans over and asks Helen a question so quietly that when I listen back on the dictaphone later, I have to replay it several times to make out what he has said.

'How do you feel now about the individuals who murdered Brian?'

There's a pause before Helen replies.

'If I start to think about it, then I feel angry with them. I have to be honest and say that. There is still some anger there. I try not to think about them but, from time to time, the police have come to my door to tell me that one or two of them had been arrested. This was a long time afterwards. They just wanted to let me know that they had caught these guys and at times like that you're thinking, that's great, I'm so glad. But then when they were released, it really hit me. I just felt that they had done so much damage. They had taken so many lives and destroyed so many families. They were supposed to serve thirty-five years, but one of them got out after just twelve or fifteen years. At the time, it just seemed like it was not enough.'

Stephen points out that at one stage, near the end of the trial, some people had even thought that the judge would have them hanged. 'That's right,' Keith says. 'One of the judges made the comment that had it been a few years earlier, he could have given them the death sentence.'

Stephen turns to Helen. 'You know, it has almost become a cliché to talk about forgiveness. I said in the past that I forgive them, but I sometimes wonder what the word forgiveness really means. Perhaps not carrying it around on my shoulders, like some kind of grudge, enabled me to live a relatively normal life.'

'You got your life back, of sorts, afterwards,' Helen says. 'That's not to say you're not carrying a lot of stuff around in your head, but our lives were cut short. I mean, we lost somebody very close to us, somebody we loved very much, so I couldn't say that I would be able to forgive them so easily. If they arrived at my door and said, "Look, what I did was wrong and I'm sorry", and all that sort of thing, then … I'm a forgiving person, really, I am, but there will always be some anger.'

'What would you say to them, Helen?' Stephen asks.

'I don't know. I'd ask them what brought about the apology. I'd have to find out how it came to that.'

'To see if it was genuine?'

'Yes.'

'And if you thought it was genuine?'

'I would probably say, "Yes, I forgive you", but it still wouldn't stop me thinking, If only … As I said, if they came to me and they said they had something on their mind and they wanted rid of that and apologise to me while they were at it, I would probably accept that. I would never forget what they did and I would still be angry. I would listen to them, but that would be it. I would never have anything more to do with them.'

'I've often thought about what forgiveness means,' Stephen says. 'Does it mean that if I had a gun and the opportunity, I wouldn't shoot those who were responsible? Is that what forgiveness is? I know I wouldn't do that.'

'Well I couldn't do that either,' Helen says. 'If somebody said I could walk up to those who killed Brian and slap them in the face, I would refuse because I'm not a violent person. So to me that's not what forgiveness is …'

'Do you remember the Enniskillen bombing?' Keith says, referring to the horrific 1987 IRA bomb attack that killed eleven people in the County Fermanagh market town during a Remembrance Day service. 'There was a man there who had lost his daughter and one of the first things he did was to make that extraordinary gesture of forgiveness in the immediate aftermath. I could not understand what that meant. Does that mean that it was forgotten? At what stage do you forgive without letting go of what happened?'

'Maybe it just means that they're not going to hold a grudge against that person,' his mum says. 'I suppose if you knew the person who did it, if you both lived in the same town and you knew who killed your loved ones, then it would be a different thing. Because you don't know them, you don't see them in the same way.

'Isn't it harder to forgive a friend than it is an enemy?' Stephen asks.

'I think so,' Helen replies. 'You don't know them, you're angry that they hurt you in that way, but it is a very hard thing to understand. I don't know how to define the difference, to be honest with you.'

I ask both Helen and Stephen if they could envisage sitting down beside these men and talking about anything other than the reasons why they killed their loved ones.

'You could never sit down and talk about the weather or the football,' Stephen declares.

'No,' Helen agrees, 'I couldn't. I would go to a meeting and sit around a table with these guys, but it would have to be for a very specific reason.'

'I have thought long and hard about this,' Stephen adds, 'and I know that I never had any vested interest in seeing these men die in jail. I always saw them as the victims. I considered them victims of stupidity and ignorance. I never saw myself as a victim. Then again, if I had lost someone as close as you did, Helen, I might feel differently. After the incident happened, you have to understand, the one thing that I had to do was get better. Because you need all that positive energy, you need it because if you don't have that, you don't get better. Helen, I had no intention of dying.'

'And you have to get better,' Helen says. 'I understand that. You needed that to get better. You couldn't dwell on the negatives, on the hatred.'

'Whenever I feel angry I never, ever let it linger or develop because I know that if it took root, I might become a different person. It could change me.'

Keith again questions Stephen's description of the Miami murderers as 'victims'. I listen intently as these people who have suffered at the hands of terrorists debate the concept of the victim.

'You know, Stephen, you say they were victims,' Keith says. 'How they were the victims of the society they grew up in. It's like hearing about a random crime and you say, "Oh, well, I blame the parents." Who do you hold responsible? Do you blame their parents? Where does it stop? Sooner or later, the buck has got to stop somewhere.

And if you say publicly, "I forgive them", it doesn't do me any good. It kind of lets them off the hook more easily.'

'Yes, and let's not forget that these people were not stupid either,' Helen adds. 'The people that were involved in all this are calculating and shrewd. They knew what they were doing.'

'I can only forgive on my own behalf,' Stephen tells them. 'I would never presume to do so on behalf of anyone else. I'm not simply saying that their environment or their upbringing is to blame. That would be a pathetic excuse for their evil.'

'But why do you want to talk to them?' Helen asks. 'Do you really think they are going to say sorry?'

'No, I'm not expecting that,' Stephen says. 'The reason we want to talk to them is that when we say, and we will say, these people were engaged in an evil deed, we are not just saying that about faceless, anonymous people. We are talking about real people who grew up in the 1960s, who liked The Beatles, the Stones, The Miami and the other bands of the era. We want to examine how real people can be so blasé about slaughtering the innocent.'

'The fear I would have, if you were going to meet them,' Helen says, 'is that they would know you were coming. I would worry about somebody wanting to finish the job.'

Keith says there would be no logic for them to do that.

'But there is very little logic to what half of them are

doing up there anyway, Keith,' Helen answers, genuine worry on her face.

'No, I would be more worried about where you're meeting them,' Keith says. 'Those guys are always at each other's throats. They have been fighting each other for years and they would love nothing more than a chance to kill each other ... and you could get caught up in the crossfire ...'

'I'm not afraid of that, Keith,' Stephen replies. 'This is an opportunity for them to either make excuses or acknowledge that their violent methods were wrong. However, no amount of spin can ever justify the act.'

Chapter 12

In the aftermath of the ambush, the UVF terrorist organisation released a statement claiming that the band had been carrying bombs for the IRA. In other words, the UVF tried to deflect blame and shame away from itself by blaming the Miami for their own deaths. According to their version of events, instead of the Miami being innocent musicians bringing entertainment to communities on both sides of the border, they were ruthless gunrunners for the IRA. The UVF actually went so far as to describe the shooting of the Miami men as 'justifiable homicide'.

An organisation calling itself the Ulster Central Intelligence Agency (UCIA), which had links with the UVF, claimed that the two dead UVF men – now named as 'Major' Horace, more commonly known as 'Harris',

Boyle from Portadown, County Armagh, and 'Lieutenant' William Wesley Somerville, commonly known as Wesley Somerville, from County Tyrone – had stumbled on the ambush, not participated in it. The group, which also described itself as being connected with 'sympathetic members of the security forces', said that Boyle and Somerville had been leading a UVF border patrol when they came across the ambush. They had gone to investigate the band's minibus and another car parked nearby, and as they did so a bomb had exploded, killing them.

Another, more detailed statement released later to the media by the UVF backed up this claim, adding that its patrol unit had not opened fire until after two of its members had been blown to pieces while searching the Miami van:

'A UVF patrol led by Major Harris Boyle and Lieutenant Wesley Somerville came across a minibus and a car parked near the border about five miles from Newry. Major Boyle was suspicious of the two vehicles and ordered his patrol to apprehend the occupants for questioning. As they were being questioned, Major Boyle and Lieutenant Somerville began to search the minibus. As they entered the vehicle, a bomb was detonated and both men were killed outright. At the precise moment of the explosion, the patrol came under intense automatic fire from the occupants of the other vehicle. The patrol sergeant immediately ordered fire to be returned. Using self-loading rifles and submachine guns, the patrol returned fire, killing three of their attackers and wounding another. The patrol later recovered two armalite rifles and a pistol.'

The UVF spokesman said that the organisation maintained regular border patrols because of the continued activity of the Provisional IRA (PIRA) along the border. Its Mid-Ulster Battalion had been assisting the South Armagh units with border patrols since the Forkhill booby trap, which had killed four British soldiers a month earlier. Finally, it was claimed that three wounded members of the patrol were being treated for gunshot wounds, although they were not receiving this treatment in a hospital.

This bizarre statement put the blame for the tragedy squarely on the shoulders of the Miami members themselves, claiming they had attacked the UVF patrol and hinting that they were IRA members. The reference to the recovery of the armalite rifles – a weapon closely identified with the IRA – was a thinly veiled suggestion that the Miami men were armed gunmen who were operating along the border.

These outrageous claims were greeted by ridicule,

disbelief and anger from everyone attempting to deal with the traumatic aftermath of the Miami killings. Speaking at a charity concert in County Antrim later in the week of the killings, the prominent peace campaigner and outspoken priest, Fr Denis Faul of Dungannon, said the people of the Republic had been revolted by the murders, but that, 'They were even more revolted by the story of lies concocted by the UVF accusing the innocent victims of holding bombs and guns.' He then went on to directly accuse the British security forces of having a hand in the murders. 'Out of the evils comes this good … that these people will now accept that similar stories are put out by the British army after they kill certain people. The British paper wall has been torn asunder by the murder of the bandsmen and the deaths of the UVF men.'

The two dead terrorists were well-known to police. Somerville, a thirty-four-year-old married man from Moygashel Park, Dungannon, had been charged and acquitted the previous year in connection with a loyalist attack in Coalisland. He had been accused of taking part in the kidnapping of two men whose bread van was then packed with explosives and driven into the Catholic Mourne Crescent housing estate. The resulting blast injured twelve people, including a five-year-old boy.

Twenty-two-year-old Boyle was an unemployed single man who lived with his parents at the Killycomaine estate in Portadown. He had no previous convictions but, in

1973, had faced charges of carrying a loaded weapon without lawful authority and under suspicious circumstances. He and two accomplices, including a full-time UDR soldier, were found not guilty of possessing with intent two revolvers and thirteen rounds of ammunition at Teghnavan in Lurgan in 1972. Both men were prominent members of the UVF and held senior titles within the organisation.

As soon as the police identified the two dead men, they set about rounding up people associated with them. Thomas Raymond Crozier would be one of the first to be caught in the net. Meanwhile, the British army carried out a series of follow-up raids and searched houses in loyalist areas of Moygashel. While ammunition and two guns were discovered, no arrests were made. Within a matter of hours, however, the authorities were closing in on the men responsible.

'RUC Question Man About Miami Showband Killings' ran the headline in *The Irish Times* of Friday, 1 August. 'Musicians Stopped by Gang Dressed as British Soldiers – UVF Admits Responsibility' is how the paper revealed, less than forty-eight hours after the atrocity, that police had made an almost immediate breakthrough in the case of what was already being dubbed 'The Miami Showband Massacre'. *Irish Times* crime correspondent Conor O'Clery wrote:

'Three members of The Miami Showband were shot dead after being lined up against a hedge and two UVF men blew themselves to pieces with their own bomb in a UVF ambush that went horribly wrong on the main Belfast–Dublin road during the early hours of yesterday. One man is helping police with their inquiries into the murders.'

The article described how RUC detectives from the newly formed Assassination Squad (A Squad), set up to combat sectarian murders, were working on the theory that the UVF had intended to blow up the van with the five musicians inside. The paper went on to graphically capture the aftermath of the attack:

'The van itself had disintegrated with the force of the blast: leaving only the engine and the back portion recognisable. Around the wreckage were strewn many of the personal belongings of the musicians – a photograph, playing cards, a pair of high heel brown boots, a torn map, a gramophone record, and a book *The Who* by Gerry Harman. The book was marked 'Des, Ray, Fran' where the group members had been keeping the score of a card game.'

On Saturday, 2 August Belfast's *Irish News* revealed that the police were in possession of vital new clues in their hunt for '… the killer gang responsible for the slaying of the three young Miami Showband members near Newry – and twenty-nine Catholics in the Mid-Ulster area – the Murder Triangle. Blunders which the hit squad made at the Miami murder scene – including the premature detonation which killed two of them – are believed to have handed the RUC essential evidence they had been seeking towards ending the activities of the terror gangs.'

Other newspapers covering the story noted how the police did not have to search very hard to find clues to the identity of the killers. The stretch of the motorway near Buskhill had yielded numerous pieces of evidence, including pieces of the detonator, berets, weapons and even one of the getaway cars, which would lead officers directly to those who were involved. In the scramble to get away after the blast, one of the gunmen had left his glasses behind. It would later be revealed in court how he knew the game was up as soon as he read that the police had found them.

By early the following week, it was reported that the RUC was ready to round up the 'terror cliques'. 'Northern Ireland police are poised to pounce on the terror gangs', the *Irish News* declared on Wednesday, 6 August 1975. According to the paper, the RUC was making an all-out effort to solve the Miami Showband murders, while appealing for help from the public. The article noted that the police were certain they had whittled down the number of extremists committing serious crime to 'small but violent groups', and that no effort would be spared to find the men. 'But they cannot be successful without the help of the community,' the Northern Ireland Office added in an appeal for tip-offs. 'Provided that appeals for assistance to the police are heeded, the power of these terror groups can be broken. It's now up to the community to see that this is done.'

By the end of that week, less than seven days after the Miami was ambushed, detectives from A Squad were holding two men in connection with the attack. 'Ulster police were interviewing two men last night in connection with the murder of three pop musicians in an ambush near Newry, County Down,' *The Irish Times* reported. 'Several other people were also being questioned about the attack in which two Ulster Volunteer Force members were killed by their own bomb.' The paper also speculated that the ambush of the Miami as they were returning to Dublin may have been 'an attempt to place a proxy bomb' in the van. 'The group would have been forced to cross the border before it exploded,' the article stated. 'This could have been a means of discrediting the group by claiming they were carrying bombs for the IRA.'

The *Irish Press* of Friday, 8 August revealed that the

two men in custody in Newry police station were being held under tough new laws introduced after the notorious Birmingham pub bombings a year earlier. 'It is understood that six people are now being held in connection with the investigation into the killings. Two of them are being detained under the Prevention of Terrorism Act, the first time the act has been used in Northern Ireland since it was introduced in December 1974. Under the provisions of the act, the secretary of state could apply to have those suspected of involvement in terrorist offences held for more than seventy-two hours.'

As tensions rose across the North in the days following the Miami murders, the police widened their investigations to cover all avenues. One of the possibilities the RUC was exploring were claims that a woman had been approached on the street in the town of Hillsborough, County Down, and told that the Miami shootings had been in revenge for the killing of her Protestant husband in June.

Mr John Presha was one of three prominent Northern Ireland dog-breeders killed in a similar late-night ambush near the border at Newry, as they returned home from a dog show in County Cork. A distressed Lillian Presha said she did not want her husband's name associated with the murders of the Miami men. She pleaded with newspapers that, like everyone in the country, she abhorred the killings and added that her husband had been an innocent man. He was not involved in or associated with politics or paramilitary organisations and she did not want revenge carried out in her name.

It was too late, however; Lillian Presha's pleas for peace fell on deaf ears. A caller to the RTÉ newsroom in Dublin claimed that he represented a new terror group, which would enact revenge for the Miami atrocity. A man identifying himself as Lieutenant Séan Blake said his organisation – the People's Republican Army – had been responsible for the deaths of thirty Protestants since September 1974. They had, he claimed, carried out a series of attacks on police and Protestant paramilitary personnel over the past few months and he warned that there would be fresh retaliations for the murders of the Miami men.

As the RUC disclosed that a 'number of men' were now helping them with their inquiries, they attempted to stem a fresh tide of violence that swelled up over the weekend of the Miami attack, claiming the lives of a seventy-eight-year-old man and a young UDR private. Despite the upheavals in law and order demanding their attention, the RUC was making headway in its investigations into the Miami massacre.

The two men, who had been quizzed for over twenty hours at Newry police station, had both been transferred to another police station, where the interrogation continued. More arrests were likely. The strongest theory the police had was that the ambushers had intended to place explosives in the van and then force the showband members to drive to a pre-selected target in the Republic by holding one of the musicians hostage. Late on Saturday, the RUC revealed that they had extended their investigations to include serious crimes committed in the entire mid-Ulster area over the previous three years. This was an early indication that the police suspected that the gang responsible for the Miami outrage had also been involved in other incidents.

The progress of the investigation was being followed closely in the House of Commons, where MPs pointed out that the area in which the Miami atrocity had been committed was staunchly loyalist. In a sombre address at Westminster on Saturday, 2 August, the Secretary of State to Northern Ireland, Mr Merlyn Rees, confirmed that the RUC was following a definite line of inquiry. He would not state that any particular Protestant group was responsible, but added, 'I understand that an arm with the letters 'UVF' tattooed on it has been found.' Members then listened, in 'stony silence' according to *The Times*, as Mr Rees stood to reveal details of the ambush. 'As a result, three members of the band were shot dead and one was seriously injured. Two other men, believed to have been terrorists, were killed by the explosion. The remaining member of the band was unhurt, but is understandably badly shocked.'

The August Bank Holiday weekend of 1975 was one of the warmest in years. On Sunday, as crowds flocked to enjoy themselves at rivers, beaches and festivities across the country, the temperature gauges hit the mid-80s – the hottest day in Ireland for twenty-seven years. Traffic from the southeast into Dublin was reported to be very heavy as thousands of fans made their way to Croke Park to see Kilkenny take on Wexford in the Leinster Senior Hurling final. It was impossible to find any accommodation in the major resort centres of Tramore in County Waterford, Courtown Harbour or Rosslare in County Wexford, while Dublin's hotels were turning away people from early on Friday afternoon.

On a weekend when the Miami should have been busy entertaining the holiday crowds, Stephen Travers was still critically ill in hospital, while his friends and band-mates were buried amid distressing scenes at three separate funerals.

On Friday night, hundreds of people joined the cortège carrying the remains of Fran O'Toole when it arrived in his hometown of Bray. The sad procession made its way down a mile-long hill to the Church of Lady Queen of Peace on Putland Road. There, the packed church heard a brief service conducted by the Reverend Maurice McManus, who was assisted by the Reverend Dan Breen of Drimnagh, the priest who had married Fran and his childhood sweetheart, Valerie. Among the mourners were television stars and music personalities, including Brendan Balfe, Dickie Rock and Ray Millar, the band's drummer.

The funeral of Brian McCoy, one of two Protestants in the Miami, took place the following day near his parents' home at Caledon, County Tyrone. His removal from his parents' home at Knockaguiney Road was followed by a service at St John's Church. The crowd that filed into the little parish church to pay their respects was evenly representative of Protestants and Catholics. Afterwards, as the funeral passed along the main street of the village, a parade of policemen saluted. Hundreds of wreaths were placed on his grave.

At the same time as Brian was being buried, the UVF was staging a massive show of strength for their young operatives who had been killed in the Miami explosion. Both men were given military-style funerals. Three volleys of shots were fired over the coffin containing the remains of Wesley Somerville when it left his home at Moygashel Park. Men wearing blue forage caps and dark glasses acted as a colour party, and more than fifty men wearing full combat kit lined up and saluted the funeral as it made its way to Killyman Cemetery. The procession stretched for more than a mile, and hundreds of onlookers watched as it passed along the country roads to the cemetery.

From midday that same day, double-decker busloads of UVF men from Belfast and other parts of the province poured into Portadown for the funeral of Harris Boyle. As the cortège left Boyle's home at 20 Festival Road in Killycomaine, masked gunmen fired a volley of shots into the air. An Ulster flag with a black rim covered the coffin and eight girls wearing black glasses and carrying a wreath bearing the initials 'H.B.' walked in front of the cortège. The chief mourners, including Boyle's father and two brothers, William and Samuel, travelled to the church in private cars. The thousands of mourners who lined the route from Killycomaine to Portadown town centre included hundreds of UVF men, many of them in paramilitary dress.

Press photographers who got too close to the mourners had their cameras confiscated by UVF personnel, who removed and exposed film before handing back the cameras. Police directed traffic away from the funeral routes, while soldiers with cameras observed the cortège from a discreet distance. The funeral stopped outside the Ulster Social Club on Bridge Street, where a two-minute silence was observed.

More police and British army personnel formed a strong presence as the funeral passed along the Garvaghy Road, especially at the entrance to Churchill Park, Garvaghy Park and Ballyroan estates – all Catholic enclaves. There were no incidents, however, and the hearse arrived at Drumcree churchyard, where a service was conducted by the Reverend Raymond Hoey, the senior curate assistant of St Mark's Church, who had earlier officiated at Boyle's home.

The Saturday issue of the *Belfast News* carried almost forty death notices for the two dead UVF men, including messages from various loyalist paramilitary groups and from the mid-Ulster branch of the Loyalist Prisoner of War unit, the Mid-Ulster Brigade, UDA Brigade and the Protestant Action Force.

Three days later, on Tuesday, 5 August, the funeral took place of Stephen's musical soul-mate, Tony Geraghty, at Mount Jerome Cemetery in Dublin. Requiem Mass was celebrated by Fr Desmond O'Beirne in St Agnes' Church, Crumlin, not far from where the twenty-three-year-old guitarist had been brought up. The mourners were led by his parents, his brothers, Jim, Dermot and Larry, and his fiancé, Linda Hendricks from Ballyfermot. Also present was the Auxiliary Bishop of Dublin, the most Reverend Dr James Kavanagh, the Minister for Finance, the Parliamentary Secretary to the Taoiseach, John Kelly, and Ben Briscoe TD. As prayers were being read at the graveside by Fr Michael Smith, Des McAlea collapsed and had to be carried away by friends. Ray Millar had also made the painful trip to Dublin to attend Tony's funeral, as did Helen McCoy, accompanied by Fran's brother, Michael. Hymns were sung by Dickie Rock, who was just one of the many showband personalities present.

Before he was finally laid to rest, mourners were told that Tony's family had forgiven his killers. His devastated fiancé Linda said, 'I have no bitterness towards anyone. I want no revenge for Tony. Revenge only prolongs the pain for everyone and I want no one else to suffer what I have been through.'

Chapter 13

The funerals of Brian, Fran and Tony took place while Stephen lay recovering in Daisy Hill Hospital, a place that remains a big part of his life. Although told that his friends were dead, Stephen was still unaware that they had been buried. It would take weeks for him to begin to acknowledge the terrible blow he had been dealt. 'They say Bray came to a standstill for Fran's funeral,' he reflects today. 'I was unaware of what was going on in the outside world. I was still coming to terms with the fact that they were dead, but even that was not sinking in.'

He has a hazy memory of the police coming to interview him in Daisy Hill, and of a succession of friends and visitors arriving at his bedside. 'Gay Brazel visited me at one stage, but he later told me that I didn't appear to know who he was. He said he was looking straight at me, but that I was staring up at the ceiling.'

One memory of his hospital stay that is very vivid in his mind is of being approached by a strong-looking man who came walking, very slowly, toward where he lay.

'I saw a slow, shuffling figure. He came across the ward and, when he got close, he spoke almost inaudibly, as if in great pain. I couldn't understand him. As he leaned closer, I could see that he was crying. Tears were rolling down his face. He put his hand out, but I couldn't take it. Mine were lying motionless on the bed, connected to drips and tubes. He took my hand in his and with tears falling down his face, he spoke quietly to me. "I am so sorry for what my people did to you and your young friends." And that was it; he couldn't say another word. He was too upset. I felt so sorry for the terrible grief of this stranger. He wanted to apologise on behalf of his people, even though there was no need. I squeezed his hand as best I could and, for a brief moment, we silently cried together.'

Physically, Stephen was finally showing signs of recovery. When he was considered well enough to leave intensive care, he insisted on being transferred to a ward with other patients. He wanted to be among people, but when he was finally brought to a small ward, the other beds in the room were empty. There was a large window at the end of the room through which he was kept under observation. 'The weather was very warm, but they wouldn't give me any liquids to drink. It was almost unbearable. I would beg for water, but my system was still unable to accept anything. I was being fed intravenously and had gone from over ten stone to less than six-and-a half. There was a dramatic change in my appearance. After a few days in hospital, I looked quite gaunt. But I was young and strong and, from the moment I lay in that field, my mind was fixed on getting better.'

Stephen firmly attributes his eventual recovery to the life-saving skills of the surgeon, James Blundell, a man he remembers as an imposing figure who commanded great respect from his staff. 'During one of his visits to my bedside, I took the opportunity to quiz him on my condition. I asked him why I couldn't breathe properly. I was under the impression that the soldier had caused some injury when he punched me back into line. Mr Blundell explained that my lung had collapsed. With great patience, he went through the operational procedure with me and admitted that, at first, they didn't know what was wrong with me when I was brought in.'

As part of the research for this book, Stephen wanted to meet James Blundell again. He managed to track him down to the outskirts of Bessbrook, County Down, where he lives today. On a wild, stormy night, we pulled into the driveway of his imposing house; we knew we had the right place because Blundell's name is emblazoned on a bronze plate outside. Stephen rang the bell and through the glass at the side of the door we saw a figure approach.

An elderly man opens the door and, for the first time in thirty-one years, Stephen shakes the hand of the surgeon who saved his life. Blundell is eighty-two, but is still a big man. He has a hearty handshake and lively, inquisitive eyes. He welcomes us into his home and brings us through to the kitchen, which reminds me of a large country farmhouse. We are invited to sit at the huge table and offered a drink. I join him in a glass of whiskey. Medical journals are splayed out across the table. Blundell removes these before he sits down beside us.

It is a curious meeting. Blundell launches into conversation as if we've all known each other for a very long time. Stephen and I relax and enjoy the chat. Retired for many years now, he is from a time when medical practice was a lot different from today and he regales us with tales of how it was not unusual for doctors to smoke. 'In fact, there was one head surgeon who used to go on about the evils of cigarettes long before we knew anything about the associated problems and we looked on him as some sort of nutcase. I never smoked in front in him in case I received a long lecture, but I smoked behind his back for years. I only quit about ten or twelve years ago.'

James Blundell was senior surgeon in Daisy Hill Hospital the night Stephen was admitted. I ask him if he remembers that day. 'Oh, aye, of course I do,' he replies with a grin. 'He was such a bloody mess, I can tell you that. An anaesthetist by the name of Tony Tracey and I worked very hard to keep him alive. I remember well how Tracey had to compress his aorta to keep his blood pressure up until we got more blood into him.'

I ask Blundell if he was aware of what had happened earlier that morning, considering there must have been a lot of confusion with all the bodies being brought to Daisy Hill.

'Not really. By the time I arrived, the other nurses and doctors could tell me that he was a member of The Miami Showband. I knew that he had been shot, but I didn't know much apart from that. To be honest, at that stage, we were really just concentrating on keeping him alive. We got him up on the table, Tracey had a drip fixed up and we got to work. I'm sure we must have worked on you for over three hours.'

Stephen asks about the anaesthetist, Tony Tracey, and his role in the operation. He wonders if it was normal for him to be asked to squeeze someone's heart like that. 'No, not at all,' replies Blundell. 'An anaesthetist normally monitors the patient while he is unconscious and lets the surgeon get on with the job. But I had to get Tracey involved because I could see your pressure was dropping dangerously fast and I knew you were losing a lot of blood.'

Blundell said he had treated a great number of shooting victims around that time, so I asked if he had ever come across a case similar to Stephen's, where the victim had been shot with a dum-dum bullet.

'I don't remember treating anybody who had been shot with that kind of bullet in particular. But some gunshot wounds could be most peculiar. I remember I treated one girl and I couldn't understand why she was still alive when she was brought into us. She had been shot in the square of her back and had an exit wound through her stomach directly opposite. Initially, it appeared that the bullet had gone right through her. But we discovered that the bullet had actually hit her pelvis and deflected around her body, avoiding all the vital organs. She survived – but we did think Stephen here had had his chips. He was in a really bad way. Only for Tracey, who kept his aorta compressed until we finally got his pressure up, Stephen would not have made it. He was a real mess.'

Blundell looks admiringly at his famous success story and adds, 'Aye, you're a very lucky man.'

Stephen was still conscious when he was first brought into the operating theatre and says he can remember machines being switched on as he lay on the table. 'Oh yes,' Blundell says, 'we were probably taking x-rays to see if there were any foreign bodies like bullets still in your body.' Stephen asks if the police would have been allowed into the operating theatre to ask questions. 'No,' Blundell replies firmly. 'Not unless it was important from a medical point of view. The only time we admitted police was during post mortems.'

Stephen also described waking up after surgery. The overwhelming sensation was one of unbearable heat. He can still recall the torture of being allowed only a drop of water on his tongue.

As the weeks passed, he recovered gradually. He remembers how he knew he was getting better when he became angry at a perceived slight by an Indian doctor who came to check on him. 'I asked him if I would be okay. I expected him to say, "You'll be fine", you know, "You're doing great", that sort of thing. But this man was from a different culture and he answered, "Well, we've done all we can for you. The rest is up to you." Now this is not what I wanted to hear. As a child, when I cut my knee my parents said, "Of course it will get better." I wanted sycophantic reassurance. When I didn't get it, I got upset. It was the first time someone was brutally honest. I said, "Listen here, if I have to stick my chest out as far as that ceiling I'll show you what a survivor is." Instead of being offended, he patted me on the arm and quietly said, "Young man, you're on your way."' Blundell laughs at the recollection.

Although he was improving physically, Stephen became increasingly anxious about staying in hospital in Northern Ireland and questioned the safety of his surroundings.

'On the one hand, this was all another part of the

adventure. I was still stuck in this surreal movie. You're trying to escape from the bad guys and you're not really afraid because it's a movie after all. It's not real. It was all part of a crazy journey that I had embarked upon with the Miami. Then, in my more lucid moments, I'd think, hold on, I'm a witness to all this, and the idea became planted in my mind that I might be a target. I didn't feel comfortable in the hospital anymore. I was worried that somebody might come in and finish me off. I wanted to get out of Northern Ireland and demanded that they transfer me to another hospital in the Republic.'

Blundell remembers Stephen's state of mind at the time. 'Within thirty seconds of meeting him, he brought it up and no matter what I said, it made no difference. He was convinced that these devils would try to come in and finish the job. It was obvious that no matter what we said it was not going to have any effect, so the best thing to do was get him out. It was a major problem and I could see there was no point in me sitting down and trying to reassure him. He was in a state of high anxiety.' As Stephen became more agitated, the surgeon decided to transfer him to another hospital, even though he was still very ill. That was the last time, until this night, that Stephen had seen Mr Blundell.

Later, after we had said our goodbyes and are back in the car, I say to Stephen that it must have been an unusual experience to meet the man who saved his life. 'Well, even more important to me is the fact that, had I died on the operating table, my daughter, who I absolutely adore, would not be alive today. There is a ripple effect when something like this happens that stretches far into the unknown. Not only do I owe him my life, but I owe him my daughter's as well. James' modesty can't obscure his incalculable value to my family.'

On the way home, we talk about Stephen's eventful trip back across the border in the ambulance.

'I don't think they told me until the morning of my departure that I was going to be moved. Everything was arranged. As I was being put in the ambulance, Ray Millar suddenly arrived. He jumped in the back to talk to me, but I remember his awkwardness. It was the first of many such reunions when friends simply didn't know what to say. I know now his life had been turned inside out. He truly loved the lads and had a very difficult time getting his head around it. Years later, Ray would name his baby son after Fran. Being treated differently by my friends was something I found difficult to get used to. It would always make me recall one of my favourite Eagles' songs, 'New Kid in Town'. There is a line, "Even your old friends treat you like you're someone new." It signalled that my life would never be the same again.'

Once the ambulance pulled out of the hospital grounds, Stephen's spirits started to rise. The drive to the border was just another adventure.

'Police cars drove in front and behind, their lights flashing all the way to the border. The convoy was brought to an unscheduled halt when I insisted on having an ice cream. There was some concern about it in the ambulance. They wanted to get me safely over the border, but now all my anxiety to leave Northern Ireland was overwhelmed by this maddening desire to taste ice cream. I made such a fuss that the motorcade was forced to come to a halt outside a petrol station along the way. The orderly came back with an ice-pop. I was only allowed to barely touch it with the tip of my tongue before he took it away, but it was so good, so good to taste something from normal life again.'

At the border, the convoy was taken over by An Garda Síochána. 'A garda stuck his head in, smiled at me and said, "Stephen, we won't take too long. We won't be stopping for any red lights."'

In little over an hour, the ambulance arrived at Elm Park Private Nursing Home in St Vincent's Hospital in south Dublin. Stephen recalls a marked difference in attitude between the two hospitals.

'When we got to Elm Park, they brought me up to my room. I was still on a trolley, but a nun insisted on waiting for the arrival of the Miami's director, Tony Bogan, to complete all the forms for my admission and to sort out the health insurance before I could be lifted into the bed. I thought it very insensitive compared to the treatment in

Northern Ireland, which had been second-to-none and absolutely free of charge. Here, one of the first considerations were the health insurance and the means to get paid. They should have known that money was not going to be an issue.

'The people there were great, they couldn't have been nicer. I have always had an obsession about cleanliness and I wanted a bath every day, even though it wasn't very practical. A very kind male nurse would help me. He was extremely patient. He would slowly manoeuvre me into the bath, add some water, but not too much that I'd slide down and drown. I'd just sit there for what seemed like hours, literally contemplating my navel, staring at this raw rip down my body. The medical team in Daisy Hill had no option but to cut me open to find out what was wrong. The operation left a great jagged tear all the way down my stomach. I would look down at my body and marvel at it.'

Following his release from Elm Park, Stephen stayed in Clondalkin for a few weeks. Anne, together with his friends Billy and Maria Byrne, kept a watchful eye on him as he shuffled slowly and awkwardly around the house and garden. 'I felt immensely proud the first time I managed the stairs unaided. It took almost half-an-hour and it felt like Everest, but I climbed them.' Finally, the doctors gave him permission to travel home to Carrick-on-Suir, which still remains his favourite place on earth. 'I was overwhelmed with goodwill,' he remembers. 'The Carrick people closed ranks to protect my privacy. Strangers were told that I was staying with relatives up the country. Journalists from all over the world had come there seeking interviews, but my friends diverted them. They circled the wagons and gave me the space I so badly needed.'

Nonetheless, Stephen was struggling with the attention he was now receiving. 'I had difficulty being the subject of local fascination for something that I hardly understood myself,' he reflects. During the quieter periods, recuperating at home with Anne, he was very much aware that he had married someone very special. 'She never, ever molly-coddled me. If she thought there was something I could do for myself, she encouraged me to do it. Anne realised that I had to regain my independence. When the novelty wore off and everyone got back to their own lives, we had to manage ours. At the end of the day, there was just the two of us. She put on a brave face most of the time. Many years later, she confessed that she would stay awake at night listening to my breathing, terrified that I would die.'

The young couple was lucky to have some very special people around when they needed them. 'We will be eternally grateful for their kindness,' Stephen says. 'Our mortgage was around £30 a month and Anne's young brother Bertie and her sister Marie offered to get jobs to help us pay it, even though they were still in school. Of course, that was out of the question, but it was a beautiful gesture. They are still two of the kindest people I know.' The Miami's management team continued paying Stephen's wages of around £55 a week. They also paid the hospital bills and loaned him money to buy a new bass guitar.

One day, one of Stephen's oldest friends, Liam Doherty, came to the house. He offered to take Stephen for a walk. Gingerly, they dressed him and led him to the front door. Slowly, the two old friends walked along the riverbank to look at the swans. 'We stayed chatting for a while and it was good to get out into the fresh air,' Stephen remembers. 'I think it was the first time I had been properly outdoors since the incident, but when we returned Anne became very concerned. I was as white as a ghost. That little walk had drained me. She thought I had overdone it and was going to die.'

His dogged determination to get better suffered a few inevitable setbacks. One incident in particular reminded him vividly of the trauma he had endured.

'Another good friend of mine and one of the greatest rock drummers I have ever heard, Alan Murphy, by then a garda, had cycled twenty-six miles from Kilkenny to see me. I was thrilled to talk to him and when the visit was over, I insisted on driving him back. Everyone thought I was crazy, but it was important to me. I was testing myself. It was another milestone, the first time I had driven a car since the incident. I had to do it. My brother Michael agreed to come with me as a back-up driver. They put the bike in the boot of the car and prepared to set off on the half-hour trip to Kilkenny. I had a leather jacket on and it felt like it was all that was holding my stomach together. We spent quite some time adjusting the seat and seatbelt before I was comfortable enough to set off.

'Finally, we got going and reached Kilkenny without incident. Then a strange thing happened that reminded me sharply how dangerous memories were still just under the surface. On the way back, we turned a corner near Nine Mile House and there was a police checkpoint just up ahead.

'It was a routine garda check for tax and insurance. There were three or four cars ahead of us waiting to go through and as I pulled up behind them I began to panic.

'I stared hard. I could not get it out of my head that this was an army checkpoint. Suddenly, I was back on the road to Newry. Perspiration was pouring off my cold forehead. I considered putting my foot on the accelerator and bursting through the checkpoint to get away. My brother must have noticed that something was wrong. He leaned over and said, "It's okay, it's only the guards." I took a deep breath and rolled down the window. The garda leaned in and said, "Stephen, how are you? Are you feeling better?" He obviously just wanted to wish me well, but I could hardly answer him. I just smiled and mumbled a few words, rolled the window up and got the hell out there. "It was only a checkpoint, it was only a checkpoint," I told myself. Yes, it was only a checkpoint, but it was also much more than that. For me, it was another step on the road to recovery, another bridge crossed.'

Chapter 14

From the earliest days of Stephen's recovery, there had been speculation about whether or not the survivors of the Miami massacre would ever play again. Stephen even remembers being asked if there was a future for the band when he was still in hospital. 'It wasn't that long after the incident before the subject had been broached by members of the Miami management team. They had spoken to me while I was in hospital in Dublin, and I was asked how I would feel about it. I made it clear very quickly that I wanted to get back up on the horse as soon as possible. It was something I definitely wanted to do.'

The Miami management had agreed to give just two newspaper interviews – one with the *Evening Herald* and the other with *Spotlight* magazine. Both featured the difficult question of whether Stephen thought the Miami should reform. 'It is easy to understand why there was such an interest in our story. The country was embroiled in a terrible conflict and needed a symbol of survival. But the idea of playing together again began to get a bit scary. I knew it would be a challenge for me, an important obstacle to get over.'

He remembered how the first time he picked up a guitar again, it brought him back to that night.

'Shortly after leaving hospital and while still in Clondalkin, Billy brought home a bass guitar that the Garda Band had offered to lend me. He laid it on the bed and said, "How about giving this a go?" I knew this was a test. The last time I had a guitar in my hands was on the night of the incident. I was lying there, propped up on pillows looking at this guitar. By a strange coincidence, it was a Dan Armstrong bass made by the same company as the one I had lost that night. I picked it up and it felt right. As I sat there, gingerly easing the thick strings onto the fretboard, I realised that I was at the very beginning of a second chance. Music was therapy and I knew that it would be my salvation.

'My plans of forming a rock band with Tony or joining Fran on his solo attempt to take on the world had disappeared in a flash of light and thunder, but here was tangible proof that I still had a musical voice. I was determined to use it.'

After weeks of being ensconced in the protection of

his beloved Carrick-on-Suir, Stephen left for a meeting at the Miami headquarters in Parnell Square, Dublin. As he walked slowly up the stairs to the Topline Promotions office, he met Des McAlea coming down towards him. After the shooting had died down, Stephen had heard Des' voice calling him, asking if he was okay. Des had fled the scene to get help and they had not seen one another until now. Stephen found it an odd experience, talking to the only other survivor of the massacre. 'We were never close friends. Of course, Des was very welcoming when I joined, but he was totally focused on his career and had very little time for anything other than the job at hand.'

I asked Stephen if the fact that they were both survivors had any bearing on their feelings towards each other now.

'If you are referring to the bond that survivors with a shared traumatic experience sometimes claim to have, then, no, that is not the case with us. We are both members of a very exclusive club, but we don't have that bond. We come from very different backgrounds and maybe because of that we each had our own way of dealing with the experience. We didn't really speak about that night. We stopped on the stairs that day and it took all of five seconds to exchange pleasantries. It was strange and not at all what I had expected. Afterwards, I would even wonder if this man resented me because his friends had died and I had survived. Perhaps I had a touch of survivor's guilt.'

After discussions about getting the Miami back on the road, Des took a leading role in the creation of the new line-up.

'Des had wanted to select the musicians but the management insisted that I be there, too, to gauge the musical quality of the applicants and to make sure that I would be happy working with certain people. I remember sitting on a stool in the same room in the George Hotel where I had had my own audition those few months before. We had dozens and dozens of people applying for the job. They would come in and play and I would listen and jam along with them. After the hundredth time playing 'Johnny B. Goode', I was sick of it. Some of those same guys who were coming in told me afterwards that I appeared to them to be totally emotionless.

'The management would stare at me to see what my reaction was, but I just sat there and made no comment whatsoever. Des would discuss the applicants with the management as I packed up my bass and went home. They would ask for my opinion on a particular musician, but I don't think I ever had one. I found that I couldn't care less because if a guitar player was here, he was only here to take Tony's place and I really couldn't get my head around that. While I was enthusiastic about getting the Miami back on the road, I realised that the mechanics of putting it all back together was going to be harder than I could have imagined. We had spoken about finding replacements, but we had to correct ourselves as we realised that nobody could replace the lads.

'We agreed on one thing though – we would put a band together that couldn't really be judged against the original. We wanted a keyboard player, but we didn't want him to sing because we felt he would be compared to Fran. We eventually settled on a keyboard player whose vocals would be limited to harmony. We needed another vocalist, but instead of engaging a trumpet player who, like Brian, could sing, we got a sax player with excellent vocals. The guitar player we finally selected was not a rock guitarist like Tony, but one who came from a country-music background.'

When the newly reformed Miami was finally unveiled to the world, it consisted of the three original members – Ray Millar on drums, Des McAlea centre stage as front man and Stephen, to Des' right, on bass – and three new recruits – Des O'Flaherty on guitar and vocals, Norman Clifford on sax and vocals and Noel Ryan on keyboards.

Stephen was happy to see Noel in the ranks because he was a man with whom he found he had some things in common.

'He was from Waterford, only sixteen miles from Carrick. I always admired him as a keyboard player. He had been with The Big 8 in Las Vegas. Ironically, Noel was in the car with Tom Dunphy when Tom was killed just two days before my friends died. We always had a good laugh. We didn't take ourselves too seriously as pop stars. Noel had a great image. He looked like a young Elvis and the girls simply adored him. Norman Clifford was a journeyman and he knew that this was a great way to raise his profile. You could not deny the man's ability though and he would go on to make a name for himself, also with The Big 8.

'Dessie O'Flaherty was a gentleman, literally, to his fingertips. He was a fine guitarist and a fabulous singer, but I think he was sometimes like a fish out of water as his real passion was for country and folk music. I always thought he was brought in as the token country artist – country music was still a religion in Ireland. Although we were a pop group, Dessie would cover songs such as The Bellamy Brothers' 'Let Your Love Flow' or the many hits at the time by Glen Campbell.'

Stephen's initial apprehensions about going back on the road were assuaged when he realised how well the new band gelled.

'They were all fabulous musicians and covering the hits of the day, together with Miami originals, was not going to be difficult for them. The image of the band was tremendous. We had been choreographed and dressed impeccably and everyone moved and looked like stars. Des was very excited. He was fronting one of the best bands ever to take to the boards in Ireland. There was no better man for that job than Des. Nobody could match the charisma and talent of Fran O'Toole but, in fairness to Des, he never pretended to claim otherwise. Cynics thought that the new band would get the sympathy vote; that people would come to see us the first time around out of curiosity. But the truth is that the band was so good that it would have been successful even without the notoriety that preceded us.'

However, despite the meticulous preparation and hype surrounding the biggest relaunch in the history of Irish music, something just didn't feel right to Stephen.

'Very often I got the impression that some people didn't know whether to shake our hands or genuflect. I started to realise that we had become national icons, but for the life of me I couldn't tell what we were icons of. We were certainly brand new. There had never been anybody in the history of this country in our position before. Our band had been shot, bombed and half of us murdered. Can you imagine it? It wasn't like we had been in a car crash like The Real McCoy where the members had been badly injured. This was something so completely different that nobody, least of all me, knew how to handle it. It was as strange for us as it was for the onlooker. The whole country was still coming to terms with what had happened and I remember thinking that, somewhere along the way, we had fallen into the Twilight Zone.

Shopkeepers or petrol-station attendants looked at me like I was an apparition. People knew what to say to Brendan Bowyer or Red Hurley, but they didn't really know how to approach me. They would say, "How are you Stephen? Are you feeling better?" That's not really the rock 'n' roll dream. It was more like a rock 'n' roll nightmare. Even my old schoolteachers treated me differently. I started to feel that this was not what I had bargained for.'

Things were happening very fast for Stephen as the new Miami burst back onto the scene. He had joined the band as a bass player with guys who were already very famous. If nature had taken its proper course, he would have steadily achieved similar status, but now, all too quickly, he was the star. The bright spotlight swung around onto Stephen and that was the start of two crucial things in his life – the reconstruction of him as a performer, and the dismantling of him as a musician.

'As a teenager, all I ever wanted was to play bass like Paul McCartney or James Jamerson. I always saw fame as a necessary evil, but acceptable if it were in appreciation of my work. Now I was famous, but not because of my musical ability. That was the nagging doubt that would steadily creep up on me, the one that still haunts me to this day. It's the fear that people might see me as something that I'm not or, worse still, something that I don't want to be.'

By November 1975, after going through the motions of doing endless photograph shoots, interviews and rehearsals, the new Miami was finally ready for their first public performance. They decided to play outside Dublin to tighten up their new line-up and set at a far remove from the intense media interest in the capital. *Nationwide*, a top BBC TV programme, won the right to film the relaunch at The Seapoint Leisure Centre in Salthill, in Galway, one of the largest ballrooms in the west of Ireland.

'We arrived the day before and the BBC filmed around Galway. We did all the usual TV stuff, doing interviews and talking about our return. Because they were set up to film the live performance, the crew had placed equipment in the dressing rooms back in the venue. We felt we needed some space of our own to change and prepare mentally for the gig. I asked the owner, Noel Finan, if there was someplace we could get a little more privacy. He said we could use downstairs.

'Underneath the ballroom, there was a huge restaurant built to cater for the holiday crowds. It was as large as the ballroom upstairs, taking up the complete ground floor, but when we got there to change, we realised there was no room there either. It was packed with media from all over the world. There were TV cameras, men with clipboards shouting instructions into their headsets and engineers moving lighting equipment and cameras around. When we walked down the stairs, press men pushed each other out of the way to get a photograph. There is actually a picture of me, taken before we went on stage that night. I have my white suit on and I'm pulling on my boots. I've glanced towards the photographer and my face just says it all. My expression is a look of, Please, just give me a chance, I'm trying to get my boots on, how interesting can that be?

'Everything about that night was surreal. In the old days, before a gig we would have had tea and perhaps a sandwich, but earlier that day we had dinner with the mayor of Galway. I didn't know whether I was more like Elvis or Lazarus.

The place was rammed to the rafters and there were hundreds outside still trying to get in. We had a garda and venue-security escort to get us through the crowd. As we approached the stage, Jack Flahive, Secretary of the Irish Federation of Musicians, had begun the introductions, calling out each of our names. A huge roar went up, which caught me completely by surprise. It caused me to stumble backwards. I had expected to get up on stage, say a quick hello and launch into some number like we always had, but the screaming and cheering of the crowd was overwhelming. For the first few minutes, we were unsure of ourselves. We anxiously watched each other's hands to synchronise our playing as we could not hear the music. I tried to lip-read Des' vocals. I was quite surprised – the people couldn't care less whether we played in or out of tune. Everyone was simply thrilled to see us back.'

I asked Stephen if it was perhaps an outpouring of emotion from a country that was expressing its relief.

'Absolutely, and in the beginning it was great to be up there on stage, although it was obviously with some mixed feelings. Then you get the sieve out and you let the sand pass through. You begin to believe all the stuff you want to believe and let the doubts fade. Perhaps it was therapy for the audience. I know it was certainly therapeutic for us.'

Next, they played a smaller gig in Wexford, to iron out any remaining teething problems and to make sure the lads were comfortable together before the big show in Dublin. For Stephen, their first performance in the capital's TV Club on Harcourt Street is another experience he will never forget.

'It was a Tuesday night and the management had told us to get to the venue early. As I approached Harcourt Street, a garda stopped me. He said, "Sorry, young man that road is closed, you will have to take another route." I said I had to go down that road and he asked me where I was going. I told him I was going to the TV Club and he said, "Well that's the problem, you won't be able to get there tonight." I could see that there were crash-barriers all the way down the street and I asked him if there had been a bomb scare. "No," he said, "the Miami are playing here tonight." I couldn't believe they had to shut down the street for us. I said to the policeman, "Well that's okay, I'm the bass player, I have to get up there." He looked at me and said, "Oh, yeah, and I'm the drummer. Now, get out of here, off you go." He wasn't having any of it. I had to find a telephone box and put a call through to Seán Sharkey, the manager of the venue. I was told that it wouldn't be possible to talk to him because he had a big night on. I told the person on the other end that there probably wouldn't be any show at all unless they got him on the line immediately. Eventually, he came on and I told him where I was. I was only a couple of streets away and they sent out a car to bring me in. It was like some sort of CIA operation.

'I had played the TV Club many times before, but we never received a reception like we did that night. There were champagne corks popping and dozens of celebrities lining up to shake our hands. It was an emotional evening. As we stood behind the curtain waiting for Larry Gogan, the legendary Irish DJ, to finish his introduction, the crowd was chanting its modified version of the old Al Johnson song, 'Mammy'. Once again, the audience all sang in unison, "Miami, Miami, I'd walk a million miles for one of your smiles, Miami", the great venue shook. The excitement was tangible. The capacity crowd had huge banners with our names on them and they were waving their customised Miami scarves from side to side.

Massive crash-barriers had been erected in front of the stage to prevent the audience from climbing up. The atmosphere was brilliant. There's a scene in one of my favourite movies *The Last Waltz*, where former band leader Ronnie Hawkins says to Robbie Robertson, "We're in the big time now, boy." Every time I see that movie, it reminds me of our return to the TV Club.'

The band walked off the stage drained by what had been a very emotional experience for all involved. For Stephen, the cheers ringing in his ears were tinged with great sadness. 'We had succeeded in resurrecting the Miami name, but at times during the show I would glance over at one of the new lads and see Fran, or Tony or Brian in their place. I couldn't get them out of my head. It unnerved me, but I got on with the job at hand and tried not to think about it.'

He had just experienced the genuine warmth and love of fans who had known the Miami well and who would have regarded them as friends.

'We weren't distant pop stars. You can go to U2 concerts now, but you can't sit at the side of the stage and chat to them afterwards. Security considerations today even prevent the fans from asking for autographs. This was not the case in 1975 with the Miami; we were on first-name terms with many of our fans. They would shout up to us, "Hi, Fran", "How's it going, Steve?" and we would say, "Hi Marie or Barry …" Fans would sit with us and

Fran was always delighted to talk to them. The band was always happy to sign the souvenir cards and made a point of personalising autographs. The band photocard was a very valuable connection. Even shy girls, who would never have dreamed of approaching a musician, had an excuse as they summoned up the courage to get their cards autographed. This broke the ice and made it easier for them to talk to their favourite performers.

'That depth of feeling still exists more than thirty years later. Irish showbands and beat groups played a huge part in the lives of young Irish people then and, very often, loom large among their happiest memories. In 2005, on the thirtieth anniversary of the incident, Des, Ray and I, together with the cream of Irish showbiz talent, played at a commemorative concert at Dublin's Vicar Street. Three decades on, and the capacity audience was openly and unashamedly emotional. There was genuine affection there and it was obvious that, even today, The Miami Showband continues to enjoy the love and respect of the entire country.

'The Troubles in the North had seriously contaminated the lives of all who lived there, but the Miami massacre brought home to the entire island that nobody could be complacent. We had become almost immune to the news that a solider had been killed in Belfast, or somebody had been shot in the Creggan or on the Falls or Shankill; it was a million miles away. It wasn't the North so much as the North Pole. Very few in the Republic had known anyone directly affected by the Troubles, but now people from Kerry to Donegal had friends who were murdered.'

The depth of feeling for the Miami was illustrated to Stephen shortly after his recovery. He remembers walking into the band's office and casually asking the staff if he could read some of the 'get well' cards. He expected a handful, but what he was shown astounded him. 'I thought there would have been some on the mantelpiece or pinned to the wall. But there were sacks and sacks of mail and most of it was unopened. Letters had arrived from all over the world. I was shown a careful selection. The goodwill expressed towards us was phenomenal.'

By the mid-1970s, the halcyon days of the showbands were long gone, but the Miami had metamorphosed into a modern pop group. The terrible tragedy that befell them catapulted the group into a league not experienced by any band for many years. They discovered that the miraculous rebirth of the Miami had injected the entire Irish music scene with fresh popularity and enthusiasm. 'The bands still on the circuit at the time of the incident were either the remains of the big showbands or those going through a transition period,' Stephen explains. 'The Miami had successfully reinvented itself and was a prime example to other bands that it could be done.'

The reformed Miami played to packed houses over the

next few months before Stephen's new-found fame began to overwhelm him. Slowly, the nagging doubts he had started to feel about the merit of playing in the Miami began to surface.

'It never went sour for me; I don't think I would use that phrase, but I wasn't happy. I've thought many times about this. You know what they say about lottery winners, that money won't make them happy? Well, until you win, you don't know that for sure, do you? It was the same for me. At first, my new-found celebrity status was like winning the lottery and, initially, it made me very happy. You see people on reality television programmes today who will do anything to become famous. I had become famous for this thing and some people reckoned that maybe it had been worth it. A friend of mine even said that some people have all the luck. After all, on the surface, I was fine. I was playing and I was successful. Eventually, though, the celebrity buzz wears off.'

The turning point was to come during a gig in Blackrock, near Dundalk, where, ironically, Stephen had played his first gig with the Miami. It was another sold-out show with a massive crowd, but throughout the performance Stephen was distracted by one man, who stood directly in front of him, watching him closely.

'This guy was just staring at me; he never bothered with the rest of the band. He just stood there, dressed in a long coat, his hands in his pockets. He started to freak me out a bit. All I could think about was that we were very close to the border. Was this guy going to pull a gun out and blow me away? I walked off the stage in the middle of the show and went back to the dressing room. The rest of the lads were left standing there, wondering what was going on. The road manager rushed in after me and asked if I was all right. I was standing at the mirror, holding my head in my hands. The colour had drained from my face. I didn't feel well. He asked me what was wrong. I said, "Look, there's a guy out there just staring at me. He's not listening to the music and he's not interested in the rest of the lads." I pointed out that we were close to the border and he said, "All right, I'll go and check him out." The roadie, together with the security guards, called this guy aside. I'm sure this man got a bit of a fright himself because it turned out that he was just there to see us play. He admitted that he was fascinated with me, but there was no gun and he was no threat.

'I went back and played on, but the experience affected me profoundly. It was the only time in my life that I have ever walked off a stage. That man had made me confront the truth that for some people, it was the Miami massacre that fascinated them, not the band. There would always be this element of voyeurism and it unsettled me.

'When I got home that night, I told Anne that this was not what I imagined it would be. People were screaming and shouting my name and celebrities were patting me on the back. I was getting no satisfaction at all out of it and I told her that I didn't want to do it anymore. She didn't said yes or no or we'll miss the money or anything like that. She just nodded and that was that. I went to the Miami office the following day and told the management about my decision. They were stunned. I think they would have gone to the ends of the earth to get me to stay. They asked me if it was a question of money. I just sat there shaking my head, but I could not get it through to them that I wanted out. It went from gentle persuasion to emotional blackmail. They showed me a map and pointed out every city, small town and village in Ireland, saying, "Do you see this place here? You're a hero to all these people. How can you let them down? How can you just quit like this after all the support they've shown you?" But my mind was made up and I handed in my notice.

'Things came to a head very soon afterwards. It was getting close to Christmas and we were playing at the Fairways Hotel in Dundalk. Tony Bogan and Joe Tyrell, the two former members of the Miami who had become directors of the company, took turns to drive the personnel van. On this particular night, Joe Tyrell was on duty. It seems he had all his family's Christmas presents stolen from the back of his car that day and, consequently, was in bad humour. It obviously didn't help that he was also faced with my leaving the band.

'We had a fraught confrontation in the hallway of the hotel which made my decision all the more definite. Shortly after Christmas, I agreed to stay until the summer holidays. I felt silly after the confrontation with Joe, but I was angry at how I was being treated. They had tried the good-cop/bad-cop routine to get me to stay, but nothing was going to change my mind.

'They finally accepted the fact that I was leaving, but asked me for one final commitment. They said they would appreciate it if I didn't tell anyone about my decision. They wanted it kept secret so it didn't impact on dates for the year ahead. I had no problem with that. I just wanted to get out of the limelight and get my head together.

'The following day I was driving back to Carrick-on-Suir, feeling great and seeing a light at the end of the tunnel. I switched on the radio and there it was on the news, that Stephen Travers was leaving the Miami. I could have frozen in my seat. This was supposed to be a big secret. I couldn't understand how the news got out. Later, I learned through Julie Boyd, a showbiz gossip columnist who was known for her ability to make or break a band with just one review, that *Spotlight* magazine had passed on the news to Radio Luxembourg.

'This proved particularly awkward for me as I hadn't told the band. The first they heard of it was on the news bulletins. When I came back, not only would the management not talk to me but Des and the rest of them were also very cool towards me. The experience just convinced me that the sooner I got out of it, the better. I didn't care about trying to explain at this stage. I felt that they would eventually understand and, after a while, come to terms with my decision. As it turned out, it did affect the band. Noel, in particular, couldn't make the adjustment and he left shortly after I did. He says he saw it as the first chink in the armour of the invincible Miami superband. They would eventually settle on the excellent musician, Peter Eades, to take my place on bass.

'When summer came, the management asked me for another favour. They suggested that I take a week off so they could try out the new guy. They wanted to test the water, to see how the crowd reacted. Effectively, they were trying to sneak him in the back door while nobody was looking.

'I fulfilled my obligations to the Miami and walked off stage for the last time a week later. I had no regrets. I could not wait to get out. I hated the celebrity. I felt like I was famous for all the wrong reasons. I hated being pointed out in the street, singled out in a crowd with people asking for my autograph. I just didn't want to be a part of that anymore.

'I remember the shame I felt at having become this caricature. I went for a meal with Billy Byrne and his father-in-law in the Green Isle Hotel one day. We had just

Miami vocalist Fran O'Toole (centre standing) with The Bay City Rollers, the year before he was murdered, 1974.

Happier times – one of the last pictures ever taken of the band, June 1975 (left to right) Brian McCoy, Fran O'Toole, Des Lee, Stephen Travers, Tony Geraghty and Ray Millar (seated).

Above left: My father, Patrick Travers, pictured in his Irish army uniform before the outbreak of the Second World War. Above right: My mother, Mary (Torpey) Travers, pictured in Paris shortly before the German occupation.

A photo of me from my school days at Green School, Carrick-on-Suir, 1959.

Me, ever the musician, already embracing the 'look', aged nineteen, 1970.

Wesley Somerville and Horace 'Harris' Boyle, two of the men involved in the ambush. Both were killed as the bomb they were placing onto the Miami minibus exploded prematurely.

Photographs taken just a few hours after the murders. An estimated 10lb of commercial explosives devastated the minibus.

The new Miami (back row, left to right) Dessie Flaherty, Stephen Travers, Norman Clifford and Noel Ryan (centre) Des Lee (seated in front) Ray Millar.

The first gig after the ambush – we played to an emotional sell-out crowd at The Seapoint Leisure Centre, Salthill, Galway, late 1975.

In a quiet moment of peace in the aftermath of the murders, myself and Anne relax at home in Carrick-on-Suir, County Tipperary, 1976.

Our happiness was completed with the birth of our daughter Sean in 1992.

Life after the Miami. Above left: The *Nightlife* magazine picture is of The Movies, my second adventure with Liam O'Dwyer in Carrick-on-Suir (left to right) Michael (Sheriff) O'Hanlon, Pat Ryan, Liam O'Dwyer and Stephen Travers, 1978. Above right: The Crack (left to right) Martin McElroy, Tommy Lundy, Ronan O'Callaghan and Stephen Travers, 1981. Above: The Great Hunger (left to right) Stephen Travers, Maurice McElroy and Jim Bradford, 1984.

In 2007, during the writing of this book, I returned to the scene of the murders. Above left: the spot where I lay seriously wounded. The bodies of Tony, Fran and Brian were found only feet away. Above right: meeting former RUC officer James O'Neill, acting Scene of Crime Officer for Newry and one of the first officers on the scene after the ambush, 2007.

The scene of the Miami massacre today. A bus shelter now stands on the exact spot where our bus was parked in the early hours of 31 July 1975.

In 2007, I met with James Blundell, the surgeon who saved my life.

Myself with Johnny Fean, the world's foremost Celtic rock guitarist. We are music soul-mates and regularly tour together today, 2006.

Meeting President Mary McAleese and Dr Martin McAleese at Áras an Uachtaráin, 22 May 2002. President McAleese paid tribute to our 'outstanding contribution to Irish entertainment'.

sat down to enjoy a quiet Sunday lunch, but before long the chef and kitchen staff were all standing around the doorway, craning their necks to have a look. We thought there was an emergency and we looked around to see what the problem was. Eventually, the mâitre d' came over and asked if I would mind signing autographs for them. Although they probably just saw it as a bit of fun, I was embarrassed that somebody from my own hometown would have to endure this.

'But now I was free. I didn't have a plan for the future, but I wasn't worried. My life had always been a bit like that. It was simply a case of worrying about it later.'

Stephen couldn't have known that events in the North were about to intrude on his life once again. The consequences of 31 July meant he would have to relive what had happened all over again.

Part IV
THE SCALES
OF JUSTICE

Chapter 15

By January 1976, the police had arrested the second man who would eventually stand trial for the murders of the Miami men. James Roderick McDowell, a twenty-nine-year-old optician from Princeton Drive in Lurgan, was tracked down when the police found his broken spectacles at the scene of the ambush. He joined his co-accused, the twenty-five-year-old painter, Thomas Raymond Crozier, on the stand when the case was brought before Belfast City Commission in October of that year. Both faced charges of murder. Crozier had already admitted being at the roadblock, but denied any involvement in the killings.

In the intervening months, Stephen had been enjoying his new-found freedom, revelling in the fact that, for the first time in a long time, he had the space he needed to think and to come to terms with the events of the previous summer. He reflects now that perhaps he had rushed into the decision to rejoin the Miami and get back on the road. It's understandable that the desire for some form of normaity probably made a lot of sense at the time, giving him an alternative from focusing on what had happened. Once he had stepped out of the glare of the limelight, however, he was able to start coming to terms with the past year of his life. He spent the first few weeks after he left the new Miami pottering about at home with Anne, relaxing in the beauty of Carrick in the summer and taking long walks by the riverbank, where he often went to find peace and silence.

One day in mid-1976, he returned from one of his walks to find two gardaí waiting for him in his kitchen. It was a sign that life was about to lurch in a new direction once again.

The officers told him that arrests had been made in the North and that two men would soon go on trial for the murders of Fran, Brian and Tony. They asked Stephen if he would attend an interview with the detectives investigating the case.

Initially, Stephen felt only too happy to help, but admits that he didn't really know what he was getting into. It is obvious that the memories of how he was forced to confront his pain still unsettle him deeply. Bizarrely, he found himself at the receiving end of 'police procedure'.

'We were aware that there had been arrests made very early on, but then we didn't hear anything else for quite some time. My first reaction when I was told that people had been arrested was one of relief. I was glad that somebody had been caught, although I wasn't terribly surprised because, again in my naïvety, I took it for granted that the good guys always got the bad guys. I didn't have any doubt that somebody would be held responsible and that justice would be done. Of course, today, I'm a bit older and wiser and, unfortunately, a little cynical.'

Stephen had preferred not to follow the case too closely, confident that justice would triumph, however long it took. 'I was more engrossed in putting my own world back together. Somehow, I had managed to get on with it. It was all part of my strategy for reconstructing my life. I was taking things one day at a time and not dwelling on what had happened. If I had allowed myself to carry the tragedy around in my head all day, every day, I would have gone mad.'

As he spoke with the gardaí, however, he began to realise just how much his carefully worked out coping mechanism would be tested. 'I agreed to meet with the RUC officers to tell them what I had seen that night. It was not out of a desire for revenge or for any reason other than to do the right thing. I was told that I would have to meet them in Dublin Castle. Apparently, there was no other place where they felt safe enough to conduct their inquiries.'

Stephen travelled to Dublin with Des McAlea, who had also agreed to make a statement. When they arrived, they were met at the gates of Dublin Castle and led deep into its confines. 'Des and I were brought into a room by a senior garda officer and introduced to two well-dressed detectives, who were seated at a long, polished table. Initially, they were very welcoming and friendly, they made us feel at ease, and I was not at all nervous as I sat down with them. I was curious to hear what they had to say about the arrested suspects. The interview started off nice and slowly. They asked us how we were getting on and how we were feeling. There was quite a nice atmosphere of bonhomie in the room, as if we were all in this together.'

According to Stephen, at this point everything was going very well.

'While one of the detectives scribbled away in a notebook, his partner leaned over and said, "Right, lads, you may be able to help us further. Perhaps you may have remembered something else about the night since you last spoke to our colleagues."

'He then took out a folder and removed a sheaf of black-and-white photographs. He handed one to me and I looked at it. I can still see it clearly in my mind. It was a picture of a field with a fence down one side taken in broad daylight. He asked me to pass it on to Des, who studied it for a moment. The detective then asked if we recognised it. I shook my head. The detective took it from me and said, "That's the field, lads. That's where it happened." But it was taken from a particular angle that I didn't remember and, anyway, the last time I was there it was lit only by a starry sky. Then he handed me another photograph that he said was of the same field, but taken from another angle. I just said, "I'll take your word for it," and smiled. He didn't smile back. The other officer was alternating between taking notes and studying our expressions. His partner handed me a third black-and-white picture. It had a white background with what looked like a black rectangular bar in the middle. I turned it this way and that, but I couldn't for the life of me make any sense of it.

'I glanced up, thinking he had handed me the wrong picture, and noticed the officer on my left had put his pencil down. Both were now staring at me intensely. I asked what it was and one of them said, quite casually, "Oh, that's what you get for playing around with bombs." That's exactly what he said. I said, "Oh! Is that a bomb?" And he replied, "No, it's not. That's the guy who hit you in the back." I looked at it again and said, "I'm afraid you've given me the wrong picture, this is not a person." I tried to hand it back to him, but he pushed my hand away and said, "No, that's okay, Stephen, you take a good look at it. Go on, show it to Des." The atmosphere in the room had suddenly changed. I looked more closely at the photograph. Surely this couldn't be a person? But it was. It was a burned torso without legs, arms, or head; no limbs whatsoever. It didn't resemble a person in any way; it was more like a melted bar of chocolate. I asked what he meant when he said it was the person who hit me and he said, "Oh, it's him all right. We took him off the road with a shovel."

'I stared at him and he dispassionately met my eyes. I realised that this was some sort of test. He was looking for a reaction, to see if we had ever seen anything like this before. I got angry. What the hell were they treating us like this for? I looked around at the gardaí in the room, but they sat off to one side, just observing. Their demeanour hadn't changed. The picture had dropped out of my hand and landed on the desk, where Des picked it up. Now he was looking at it with an expression of shock and horror. Seemingly, this was common behaviour for policemen when dealing with terrorist crimes. I was told afterwards that they employed similar scare tactics when they interrogated the men they had arrested.

'The next subject on the agenda was one I hoped wouldn't be brought up, although I knew it was inevitable. The detective told us that it would be very difficult to get a conviction unless we gave evidence in person. Des and I had hoped that the case would be cut and dry and that our signed statements would be enough to excuse us from a court appearance. "Look," I told him, "forget it. There's no way we are going back to Northern Ireland. My God, you have the people who did this. What more can we do?" But he just shook his head. "They'll probably walk free if you're not there."

'I told him we were both terrified at the thought of having to go anywhere near the North. We were both adamant that we were not going to do it; Des, born and reared in Belfast, was white with fright. The officer shook his head again. With a trace of anger in his voice he said, "Fine, but know this – not only are you letting your friends down, you're also helping these guys get away with murder." I glared at him and summoned up the courage to reply, "Well, if our friends were here, they would prefer for us to stay alive." He didn't say anything and I thought, That's it, they're not getting anywhere with us. Just then, he came back with something that pushed my button. "Ah, I know," he said quietly, "this is just because you've been threatened."

'I asked him what he was talking about. He said it again, less interested this time, "Oh, it's just because they've threatened you. Didn't you know? These guys have a price on your head; you're on their list, you're a marked man, Stephen. They know you won't go up there to give evidence against them because you are too scared." I asked him if they really had said that and he replied,

"Oh yes, and they're relying on this very reaction from you both."

'"Who the hell do they think they are?" I said. "Give me the dates, I'll be there."

'I don't know if it was true, if the threat was genuine, but that's what swung it. I have the very Irish characteristic of reacting with my heart rather than my head. It may well have been true; it made sense that if they could get to us before we gave evidence against them, then I'm sure they would have tried. In retrospect, I realise that we were taking a huge risk. We were not just dealing with a bunch of renegade terrorists. We posed a threat to a lot of people. We were up against something a lot more sinister than we could ever have imagined. We were about to implicate many more important and dangerous people than just the two foot-soldiers in custody.'

As soon as Des and Stephen agreed to give evidence in person, the mood in the room changed once again.

'They promised they would make it as easy and safe as possible. They explained that there would be a preliminary hearing to first establish if there was a case to be heard. They offered to hold the preliminaries in Newry as opposed to Belfast, as Newry was closer to the border. We nodded, resigned to the fact that we had agreed to step into the lion's den.

'I drove my car out of the castle, but instead of heading south, I drove up and down O'Connell Street in a daze. I turned around on Parnell Square and drove back down the length of the street to the other end. When I got there, I turned again and drove back up the other side. I knew Dublin very well, but I could not make any sense of where I was. I was in shock at what I had agreed to do and the more I thought about it, the more terrified I became. I knew I was going to have to see it through. There was no way back. I tried to convince myself that, all along, I was probably looking for a good enough excuse to do my duty. Now, I had one.'

The preliminary inquiry to hear the case against James Roderick McDowell and Thomas Raymond Crozier was scheduled to take place in the Magistrate's Court at Newry a few months later. Before dawn on the day of the hearings, Stephen woke and gently kissed Anne before he slipped out of the bedroom. He was leaving the house early in order to meet Des and Tony Bogan at the Crofton Airport Hotel on the Dublin–Belfast road, a place that held a particular significance.

'That hotel was one of our calls – one of the places where the band members would meet the bandwagon when they were travelling north. We had a call at compass points all around the city. If we were heading south, we would meet at up at the Green Isle Hotel. For the west, we would meet in Chapelizod. As I got dressed that morning in the half-light, it occurred to me that the last time I was at the Crofton Airport Hotel was to travel to the Castle Ballroom in Banbridge. I tensed at the thought. As I left the house, I began to feel increasingly uneasy. Usually a good sleeper, I had hardly slept the night before. Anne was dreadfully worried about me; she was terrified of me going back up North and fretted that I wouldn't come back. I assured her that I would be fine, but of course I was nervous.

'It was very early, only about four in the morning, when I got onto the main Clonmel–Kilkenny road at Glenbower. Suddenly, I felt a surge of nausea. I pulled the car into a little layby, opened the door and leaned out. I heaved once or twice, but I wasn't sick. Then, without warning, a huge wave of emotion welled up deep inside me and I started sobbing my heart out. It caught me completely by surprise. I just sat there, both arms on the steering wheel, crying like a lost soul. I remembered an old school friend had once asked me if I had cried with pain when I was shot. It was a strange question. I hadn't, but now I suddenly remembered that when the shooting started, I had cried out for my mother. It was a primal scream, a desperate call for help. The sudden memory of it stunned me. I thought about all of this as I sat sobbing in the car. I have a wonderful ability to store things in the back of my mind. I can lock them away and forget about them. But the memories hadn't gone away, they were back, haunting me.

'I stayed like that for a few minutes. All the frustration

and renewed terror poured down my face in a stream of tears. Up until then, there had been an element of bravado. I had put on a brave face and convinced myself that I had to do this for the lads. I was on a mission of righteousness, but for those few minutes in the car, my guard slipped and I was in danger of losing control. All I could do was slump over the steering wheel and wait for the strength that only God can grant in a dark moment. Eventually, I got it together long enough to get out of the car and take a few deep breaths.

'It was completely unexpected. It hit me like a ton of bricks. "What the hell am I doing here?" I asked myself, "I'm way out of my league. How can I take on the world like this? I'm just an ordinary person." I was terrified of the unknown, but underneath it all, there was a sense building up that this was the right thing to do, that it was important, not just for us as survivors, but also for the lads. I had known all along that, one day, I would have to face up to things – that the moment would come which, as Lady Macbeth said, would be "a spur to prick the sides of my intent" – but I had pushed it as far away as I could. I got back in the car and took a deep breath. I felt calmer and soon was as right as rain. I continued my journey in peace, having got over my moment of doubt. By the time I met the others, I must have appeared very composed and relaxed. Des, in comparison, was so nervous that he was shaking.'

After meeting Tony Bogan and Des McAlea, the three drove to Dundalk police station, where they were switched to an unmarked garda car for the short drive to the border. 'The Irish detectives were well armed. There was a huge revolver jammed between the driver and passenger seats. I was fascinated by the sight of it, wondering why he needed it as they were only taking us a few miles up the road.'

As they raced across the border into no-man's-land – the area between the two border posts – two speeding sports cars came from the opposite direction. The swap occurred in seconds. Des and Tony were unceremoniously ushered into one car and Stephen was quickly placed in the other.

'It occurred to me later that they were taking precautions in case we were attacked. If the terrorists actually managed to knock out one car, they would still have at least one witness alive. Well and truly in adventure mode, I expected to hear someone say, "Hello, my name is Bond, James Bond." It was very obvious that we were still in danger from people who posed a significant threat, but there are times when even the most serious circumstances can take on a light-hearted atmosphere.'

The RUC detectives sped them on their way to Newry, where later that morning Des and Stephen would have their first glimpse of some of the men who had tried to murder them. The policemen who accompanied them to the court said that the two suspects would be arriving by armoured car from Belfast. Soon, from below came the sound of a door opening and steps on the stairs up into the court from the holding cells.

'It was then that I saw the two of them for the first time since the murders. At a glance, they looked like hard men. They were broad-shouldered, like bouncers. But as I watched them, I could see they weren't as big and tough as they first appeared. In fact, they looked scared; not confident at all. They looked over at Des a few times, but they didn't look at me at all. The amazing thing was that they didn't scare me. In fact, I felt sorry for them. They no longer had any authority. Their guns had been taken away and they were nothing without them. Something very strange occurred when I was giving my evidence at the preliminary hearings, something that has stayed with me ever since. On describing the uniform, cap and cap badge of the officer in charge of the murders, I was told by both the defence and prosecution that I was mistaken, that part of my evidence was being discarded. Later, I wondered if this was the first sign that a cap, or ceiling, was being put on the investigation.'

The detectives investigating the murders said they had enough evidence to go to full trial. After hearing all the statements, the judge set the trial dates to be heard at Belfast City Commission in October 1976. Until then, Stephen and Des were free to go.

Chapter 16

As he was led into the packed courtroom, James Roderick McDowell knew he was facing a long stretch in prison, the only question in his mind was – how long? He had already admitted his part in the killings of Fran O'Toole, Brian McCoy and Tony Geraghty. Now, on 9 October 1976, the first day of his trial, there was only one way he could plead – 'Guilty.' The scientific evidence against him was so overwhelming that it rendered his only other option irrelevant. In the words of one newspaperman covering the trial, the evidence was 'devastating'.

When he had fled in panic from The Miami Showband ambush, McDowell had left behind a vital clue – his spectacles. They had lain on the road, smashed to pieces among all the other debris from the terrible slaughter, until the forensic police teams had discovered them, and bagged and labelled them. A detective who had worked on the case later revealed the significance of the find, saying the broken glasses had proved crucial in tracking down those responsible for the triple murder. The reason for this was that James McDowell was one in 10,000 – a man who needed a very special type of lens.

The police undertook the painstaking task of placing the glasses on the face of the killer. They went through over 100,000 optical files held by opticians in Newry, Portadown, Lurgan and Dungannon. It took time, but in the end it proved worth the effort. They established that only seven people in the infamous 'Murder Triangle' used lenses like those found at the scene. After that, it was a simple matter of elimination. The remaining pieces of the puzzle fell into place very quickly. McDowell was an optical worker by trade, but when detectives went to interview him, he was off work, sick with 'flu. When they did finally catch up with him, they knew they had their man.

Standing next to McDowell in court was his co-accused, the pale-faced twenty-five-year-old from Queen Street in Lurgan, Thomas Raymond Crozier. Unlike McDowell, Crozier denied the charges against him, but he must have been seriously worried as the trial began.

Opening the case for the prosecution at Belfast City Commission, Mr Liam McCallum for the Crown stated that both of the accused were said to have been non-commissioned officers of the Ulster Defence Regiment and were wearing their uniforms at the time of the murders. The clipped language in the trial accounts captures the serious mood of the court hearings. 'It is a sad and shocking thing to relate that at least two of the men who stopped the showband's van – Crozier and McDowell – were wearing the uniforms of the UDR,' Crown counsel stated. He declared that the purpose of the two accused was to murder all the members of the showband, who were travelling in the minibus. He acknowledged, however, that no person had come before the court who could explain exactly what the main purpose was in placing a 10lb bomb in the Miami van.

Crown counsel suggested one reasonable conclusion. '... the bomb was, in effect, an anti-personnel device intended to kill or maim everyone in the vehicle. The objective was to get the showband members back on board the van with the bomb, which would have exploded a short time later. One would have been left with a very serious explosion. If the men had got away and the minibus travelled on a short distance before the bomb went off, there would have been great difficulty on anyone's part in establishing what had happened. But the plan did not come to fruition. The bomb exploded, killing two men who died by their own act. Then, other men opened fire on the members who were lined up facing away from the minibus. It was then that Fran O'Toole, Tony Geraghty and Brian McCoy were killed.'

Fran O'Toole had been 'literally riddled with bullets' as he lay on the ground. Mr McCallum stated that eighteen of the twenty-one bullets fired had struck him, and any one of those would have killed him. Evidence would show that Tony was likely shot from behind, about eight or nine times, while he was standing. It was shown that Brian McCoy was hit by three bullets fired at him from his right side and one from the left.

The court was then told the details of what had happened during that night and also that Crozier had admitted being at the scene of the crime and being a member of the UVF. 'It is not a large leap,' counsel said, 'to conclude that this was a UVF operation. The crown would suggest that, having regard to the fact that he was a lance corporal in the UDR, that he was not someone expected to be naïve about the character or the intentions of these men. It is quite inconceivable that any man in the company of these men could not have anticipated that the evening was very likely to result in the deaths of some unfortunate persons. The crown would say that the common objective was murder.'

Counsel for the crown then went on to outline details of the weapons found at the scene. One sub-machine gun that had not been fired and one that evidently had been fired were recovered, as well as two revolvers – one that had not been fired and one that had. It was believed from ballistic reports that there was at least one other weapon, and possibly two, used in the killings.

Des McAlea and Stephen then gave their accounts of what had happened that night. McAlea confirmed that the band had been playing at the Castle Ballroom barely an hour before they were halted at what they thought was a security-forces checkpoint, and that they were asked to get out of the minibus so they could be searched. They were lined up at the side of the vehicle, facing a ditch. At that point, he noticed a number of men emerging from the dark. His impression was that this was a joint British army and UDR exercise because all the men were wearing military uniforms; some wore green berets, others wore black ones. McAlea said that one man who seemed to have some authority was McDowell. He said that he had left the line-up to move his saxophone in the minibus and that when he got back he forgot to put his hands on the back of his head. 'One of the lads got very aggressive and this man I took to be McDowell,' McAlea told the court. Asked by McDowell's defence counsel how he could be so certain that it was McDowell, McAlea replied that he had 'a photograph of him in my mind'.

The next time he saw McDowell was in court.

McAlea described to the court how the band members were first asked for their names, addresses, ages and dates of birth, before one of the soldiers said that names and dates of birth would do. While this was going on, McAlea said he noticed two other men at the back and to the side of the minibus. Without warning, there was an explosion.

'It all happened so quickly. I was lifted off the ground and into the ditch. After that, there was a burst of automatic fire and at that stage I realised we were in trouble, so I stayed as close as I could to the ditch. I remember calling out the lads' names and there was a second burst of fire. I was unconscious for a while. The wagon was on fire and so was the ditch. The fire was getting closer to me so I had no alternative but to make a move. I rolled out onto the grass and saw Brian McCoy. He appeared to be dead. Stephen Travers was injured, he was only able to say a few words. I realised I had to get out as quickly as I could. I made a run for the main road, in the Banbridge direction. I stopped a lorry, but the driver was loathe to bring me to Newry. A man and his wife who drove up in a car took me to Newry, where I reported the matter.'

He testified that he had seen at least one machine gun and a rifle in the hands of the group who had stopped them. There were about six or seven men in the group in all. In response to further questioning, McAlea said that at no time were members of the band aggressive, adding that they had always been friendly with the security forces.

When cross-examined by counsel, McAlea said it was normal procedure when stopped to produce some form of identification. On most occasions, they showed photographs of the band and this seemed to be good enough because they could be identified easily. He added that when they were stopped that morning, they saw nothing extraordinary about it, but that they were always tense in view of what was happening in Northern Ireland at the time.

Then it was Stephen's turn. He stood, gave his name and declared that he was now living in County Tipperary, but at the time of the incident had been living in Dublin. He recalled lining up with the band on the road and at one stage naïvely walking back to the vehicle to check that his guitar was not being manhandled. He had asked the soldiers, who appeared to be foraging through the cases, to be careful with his guitar. They had asked if there were valuables in his small case, but he had replied that it only contained some electronic sound processors. He was then pushed, or rather punched, back into line, but now to Brian's McCoy's right. Then, the taking of names began.

'I remember quite vividly what happened next because it struck me that I never heard Mr O'Toole referred to as "Francis". He was always referred to as "Fran". Just then there was a loud bang. My first instinct was to run. I saw Mr McAlea going into the ditch. Everything became very bright. The impression I got was of things moving very, very slowly, as if in slow motion. Then I fell into the ditch and I think the others were falling on top of me. I heard a burst of machine-gun fire and a short time after a voice said, "Come on, these bastards are dead. I got them with the dum-dums." Then there was another explosion, which, in retrospect, seemed to be in the petrol tank. I heard two or three more bursts of machine-gun fire. I then heard Mr McAlea asking me if I was okay.

'When I heard talk of the dum-dum, I thought they were blanks as I didn't feel any pain. This convinced me that I was not hurt, but, in fact, a bullet had entered my right hip and came out under my left arm.'

He was then asked if he could point out the men who had stopped the bus that night. When Des had been asked if he recognised the people in the dock, he was just about to point them out when there was a bit of commotion at the back of the courthouse. The two wives or girlfriends of McDowell and Crozier had arrived in court and were making a scene, waving their hands at the accused, chewing gum, talking loudly and acting like it was a circus. 'I don't know whether it was a coincidence or whether it was timed, but it certainly seemed to rattle Des, although he still pointed them out,' Stephen says today. 'However, I didn't recognise them at all. I very much wanted to be able to throw in my tuppenceworth and say, "Yes, that is them", but I didn't. I had been briefed and strongly advised that if I recognised them, then I was to say so in a loud, clear voice. However, if I didn't, then I was to say so. When it was my turn, I had to say I didn't recognise them.'

Over the next few days of the trial, attention shifted to Crozier, who was still maintaining his not-guilty stance. He had been arrested on 7 August – just one week after the killings – and questioned in the CID room at Newry RUC barracks about his movements on the night of 30 July. One session lasted over four hours.

At first, he told the police that he had been at home all night, denying that he had anything to do with any murders. One detective revealed in court that Crozier had also initially denied being a member of the UVF in the Portadown–Lurgan area. When this was put to him, he said he was in no way involved in illegal organisations, but confirmed that he was a member of the UDR. Crozier also admitted that he had known Harris Boyle and Wesley Somerville, the two bombers who were killed in the explosion, but he denied that he had been with them in the early hours of 31 July. Despite his protests of innocence, police noted that Crozier was a worried man. His demeanour in the interrogation room, one detective said later, was quiet and he appeared to be deep in thought. He slumped in the chair with his head down and mumbled replies to their questions only after they had been put to him several times.

Crozier finally cracked when the policemen changed tactics and asked questions from a new angle. He became emotional and upset when they asked about his job, wife and family. The police sensed they had found his weak spot and they pounced. They were convinced that Crozier was hiding something in relation to the Miami murders and this probability was put to him. He shook his head. Then they asked what he had done with a car he had collected from the home of Samuel Fulton Neill on the night of 30 July.

'"He started crying," the detective said, 'and replied, "I wasn't there." When asked again if he was at the scene of the murders, he dropped his head and made no comment.'

Another member of A Squad gave evidence that he felt sure that Crozier would have told the truth but for fear of the UVF. The detective claimed that Crozier had told him he was afraid to tell the truth because he was frightened for his wife and family. When asked of whom he was afraid, Crozier had answered quietly, 'The UVF.' When asked if he was a member of that organisation, Crozier had said that he thought he was because a month earlier a man had approached him to join and that same man had told him a fortnight later, 'You're in.' He denied that he had attended any meetings or sworn an oath.

Another detective claimed in court that when he asked Crozier why he had become involved in the Miami incident, he replied that it was for the same reason he had joined the UVF. Asked if he had done so voluntarily, the accused indicated that he was under pressure. 'I was afraid. Things like punishment shootings were always in the back of my mind. The men did not tell me any more than I needed to know. I took it that I was not to ask. I was prepared to do whatever I was told to. I was prepared to do it rather than face a punishment shooting.'

In court, Crozier said he had been a member of the UDR at the time he joined the UVF in a pub in July 1975, repeating that he had been approached by a man he knew who had asked him to join the UVF. He said he was not at liberty to say who the man was. When asked if there was any inconsistency in belonging to the UDR and the UVF simultaneously, Crozier told his counsel that they were both legal organisations at that time. The judge pointed out that the UVF had been proscribed for the second time in October 1975. Pressed as to why he could not give names, Crozier replied, 'If I gave names of men who were members of the UVF, my life would be in danger. I knew the man previously by sight, but not to talk to. The man said I would be sworn in at a later date before he then outlined the rules and regulations of the UVF.' Crozier told the court that it was only on the night of the killings that he realised that the UVF was a body that would resort to violence.

When prosecuting counsel detailed the forensic evidence

relating to the guns used at and recovered from the scene, Crozier insisted that six shots fired from a .45-type revolver had not been fired from the gun he admitted, in direct evidence, to having in his possession at the scene. 'That was not the weapon I had,' he told the court. 'My weapon was definitely not fired.'

Questioned further by counsel, Crozier said he had no intention of using the gun given to him and felt the others were only displaying their weapons for the purposes of the checkpoint. When he was given instructions about stopping the van, he did not ask any questions because he knew the men were UVF and it was safer not to ask any questions. Crozier maintained that he was not told about the members of the Miami at any time during the operation, insisting that he found out there was to be a roadblock only a short time before the band's van arrived. 'I knew something illegal was going on, but I had formed no conclusions. I knew it was an illegal roadblock, but did not know what its purpose was.'

The judge asked him, 'Did you not ask, "What sort of carry-on is this?"'

'No,' Crozier replied. 'I got no indication of what was going to happen. They made it clear they were not going to tell me. When I started asking questions one man said to me, "The other men know what they have to do. And you know what you have to do."'

A detective from A Squad, which was still engaged in

an ongoing investigation into the murders, said that, for security reasons, the UVF frequently did not tell participants in their operations what was to happen or who was to be involved until the last possible moment.

Under cross-examination, Crozier agreed with prosecution counsel that, as far as he was aware, the members of the showband were completely innocent and law-abiding people. He had never heard anything to suggest otherwise and accepted that they were just musicians returning home after a gig. Crozier acknowledged that some UVF men had murdered the three musicians and that the ambush looked like a plot to murder every member of the Miami group. Crozier further agreed that two UVF men had been killed at the scene and that another man had pleaded guilty to the three murders. He also agreed that there were four or five UVF men still unaccounted for and that they had used their weapons ruthlessly that night.

In his summing up, prosecution counsel said that from the evidence given by twenty-five-year-old Thomas Raymond Crozier in his statement to police after the murders and from his evidence in the witness box, he could be found guilty of aiding and abetting in the crime.

Crown consul would not say that Crozier had actually fired the bullets that killed the showband members, but that he did 'aid and abet the common design' of the men who did.

'He was taking part in the common design, dressed in the uniform of the UDR and armed with a revolver which he did not trouble to ascertain was loaded or not. He was guilty of wilful blindness because no one who made the slightest enquiry into what was happening could have failed to realise what was in view. In relation to that, one must remember that he was a mature person of twenty-four and had the experience of serving for some three years in the UDR and had just newly joined the UVF. The crown maintains that this naïvety, in the circumstances, is quite incredible. If one looks a little further and considers the facts of the accused's statement to the police, and his own evidence in the witness box that he had been given a warning on his arrival at the scene and at a later point he heard talk about a bomb, he could not have failed to have been aware that some outrage was to be committed. In short, the crown would say that the accused is guilty on the strength of his own defence.'

The details that emerged during the trial revealed the brutality meted out to the Miami men and prompted the judge in his summation to state that the two accused were lucky to escape with their own lives as the death penalty had just been abolished. Referring to the 'devastating' nature of Crozier's statement to the police while he was in custody, Lord Justice Jones said that no one reading it would come to the conclusion that the accused was right. 'In my clear view, Crozier was a man who would lie, whether on oath or not, it matters nothing if it suited him to do so.'

The judge then said he found Crozier guilty of the murders in that he had acted throughout with the objective of killing the occupants of the vehicle, who happened to be members of The Miami Showband. He held that Crozier may or may not have known who they were, but that he did know the object of the exercise and who was present. He had worn a military uniform, had taken the names and addresses of the group outside the minibus and had carried a revolver. There had been several persons involved and while Crozier admitted having a .45 revolver in his possession, in law he also was in possession of the other weapons, which included a Sterling submachine gun. The judge said that he held Crozier equally to blame in relation to the possession of the 10lb bomb that had exploded at the scene.

Crozier's clergyman had given evidence that the accused had been sacrificial in his duty to his parents and had been known for his kindness to his mother. However, Lord Justice Jones said the extreme gravity of the offences made the previous clear records of both men of little force. In sentencing Crozier and McDowell, Lord Justice Jones said they had been found guilty of a number of offences of the utmost gravity.

'You went with others to kill a number of persons who were passing along this road. The result was a massacre.

People who acted as you did on that night must be made an example of. Such atrocities must be stopped. Some years ago the term of imprisonment for murder was life, but in cases like this it should be seen to be really effective. As I am empowered to do, I declare that thirty-five years, a period which I recommend to the minister as a minimum period, which, in my view, should elapse before the minister should order your release, to be, in this case, considered your life sentence.'

Chapter 17

The thirty-five-year sentences imposed on McDowell and Crozier were the longest ever handed out for murder by a court in Northern Ireland. The convicted killers were also sentenced to shorter terms on charges of having guns and a bomb in their possession with intent to endanger life.

After the verdict was read, jubilant detectives spoke to reporters outside the courthouse. Buoyed by their victory in court, the policemen still investigating the case said they could now account for eight of the nine men who they believed made up the gang that set out to murder the Miami. Two of the attackers had died at the scene when the bomb detonated prematurely; two had just been jailed; one man who they had questioned and released had been shot dead outside a Lurgan pub shortly afterwards; and three others known to have taken part in the triple murder had been charged with serious offences unconnected with the Miami murders, but which would put them away for a number of years. According to one newspaperman who spoke to the members of A Squad outside the court, only one man was known by police to have escaped the massive murder hunt.

'I learned that, within a matter of days of the murders, the police had netted seven survivors of the murder gang. But they were able to associate only two of them with the actual killings – not because of a lack of evidence but because of fear. And the one man who, it is alleged, could name them, said he would be putting his life and the lives of his wife and little baby in danger if he identified them. He is Thomas Raymond Crozier of Queen Street, Lurgan, and a former lance corporal in the UDR.

'When the blast occurred, several of the group and the gunmen were blown off their feet. Then, the shooting began. Was it panic or design that left Tony Geraghty, Fran O'Toole and Brian McCoy dead? Whatever the answer, Crozier, a twenty-five-year-old painter, and McDowell, a twenty-eight-year-old optical worker, were yesterday on their way to Crumlin Road Prison to start a seventy-year sentence between them.'

There would be further arrests, and five years after McDowell and Crozier began their sentences in Crumlin Road, a third man stood trial and was subsequently jailed for his part in the killings. Police vowed that the file on the triple murder would remain open until the entire gang was brought to justice. Presumably, it remains open to this day as some of those suspected of being involved in the Miami massacre remain free men; others have died in the intervening years.

For his part, Stephen agrees with the generally held view that only the foot-soldiers were brought to trial while the ringleaders got away.

'Essentially they were scapegoats. They took the fall and refused to name the others at the scene. The death squad of 31 July had close ties with the British security forces. The fact that the officer who arrived on the scene had an English accent and immediately took charge of the operation was ignored. It was never satisfactorily explained why all of them were armed with standard-issue British weapons and uniforms. When it was brought up in court, both myself and Des were told that we were wrong in our descriptions of the English officer. This, to me, proves that they either refused to believe the possibility of collusion or, as I have always firmly believed, there was a cover-up.'

Stephen is not the first, and probably won't be the last, to believe there was some level of collusion between the paramilitary organisations and the authorities in Northern Ireland.

Only one month after the deaths of Harris Boyle and Wesley Somerville in the explosion, the official UVF magazine *Combat* carried a full page of notices of sympathy to the relatives of the dead men. Two of these were submitted by members of the UDR. One read:

> 'The Loyalist members of A Company 9 UDR County Antrim wish to convey their deepest heart-felt sympathies to the families and friends of Harris Boyle and Wesley Somerville.' Each notice was accompanied by a depiction of the regimental crest, appearing as if it were an official mark of respect for the dead terrorists.

When quizzed about the death notices, the UVF openly boasted to newspapers that they not only had members in the army but that those very same members were passing on intelligence to the organisation:

> 'We do not stop our members from becoming involved in the security forces. Some of them are attached to the RUC, UDR and several full-time regiments. They are not only active members of the UVF, but they are also feeding us vital information on security and Republicans.'

The UVF spokesman then said that many operations carried out against 'Republicans' by UVF units and associate groups had been ordered as a direct result of intelligence information gathered from inside the police and security forces.

Top British government officials and security chiefs played down the claims. Colonel Peter Hicks of the UDR said that anyone who knew anything about UVF infiltration, or infiltration by any other group, should contact the military or RUC immediately. He pointed out that in the past the UDR had quickly weeded out people who were discovered to be actively involved in political parties or paramilitary organisations. 'We have a very careful screening process to make sure there is no infiltration by paramilitary organisations,' he said, adding that any member of the UDR who was charged with a terrorist offence would be dismissed immediately. The army employed a special team for the purpose of checking the backgrounds of UDR applicants before they were admitted to the regiment. They even had access to RUC records and could seek the views of senior policemen when considering an application. In the immediate aftermath of the trial, senior officers vowed that they would find out how Crozier and McDowell had slipped through the UDR screening process.

In August 1975, the same month that the death notices appeared in *Combat*, members of the SDLP – the principal political party of the nationalist Catholic community in Northern Ireland – claimed that a loyalist death squad was operating from within the ranks of the

UDR. This allegation followed the murders of two GAA supporters, Sean Farmer and Colm McCartney, who were both shot in the back of the head after being stopped at a checkpoint near Altnamacken in County Armagh on 24 August 1975. The two men were returning from the All-Ireland football semi-final between Derry and Dublin in Croke Park when they were stopped at a roadblock manned by what appeared to be UDR soldiers. Tragically for the two innocent sports fans, it was another UVF ambush and they were both abducted, shot dead and their bodies left at the side of the road. A documented RUC patrol had passed through the checkpoint less than an hour before the two men were killed, and while the members of the patrol were suspicious, their concerns were ignored when they radioed back to base.

The bombings and the killings would stretch on into the next two decades. Some of the most infamous incidents would form the basis for a series of tribunals of inquiry that would begin to unravel the true extent of collusion that many, including Stephen Travers, maintained had existed all along.

*

The trials left their mark on Stephen. He found it traumatic to face up to the memories of 31 July 1975. He had once again been forced to run the gauntlet by attending the hearings in Belfast, his own anxieties exacerbated by the very real fears that he could be taken out at any time. The police had been so concerned for the safety of their key witnesses that they had flown them by helicopter from Bessbrook army base to Belfast to avoid assassination attempts on the road.

After giving their evidence, Stephen and Des McAlea had expected to be flown back out to Bessbrook, from where they would be escorted to the border. Stephen describes the arrangements.

'The police told us that they would get us to Belfast, we would give our evidence and we would be away after a couple of hours. They assured us that they wouldn't detain us any longer than necessary. We were once again taken separately by fast cars to Bessbrook, and then brought from an underground area to a landing pad. I saw this chopper coming down with soldiers sitting in the doorways on either side with their legs dangling over the sides. I thought, Oh my God almighty, we have to get into this thing. The noise of it coming down didn't help the fact that I also suffer from a fear of heights. We clambered into it and they pulled the doors across and gave us some headsets so we were able to talk to the pilots and each other.

'When we landed, we were ushered across to the courthouse and led to our places on the stand, where we gave our evidence.

'When we were leaving, they informed us that we

would have to stay an extra night in the city because the wind was too strong to fly us back out. We suspected that they just wanted to keep us around in case we were needed back in court. We were petrified. We told them we had to get out of the North because we feared for our lives, but they assured us that we would be okay. After our evidence was heard, we spent the remainder of the day upstairs in a restaurant called The Buttery and it was after dark before they decided where they were going to take us. Des, Tony Bogan and I were driven to a small hotel outside the city. We had convinced ourselves that we were going to be targeted, so we barricaded ourselves in that night. I'm sure there were police on duty outside, but it made no difference to us. We were definitely nervous. We put a heavy chair against the door handle for security. It was terrifying.'

On their way back to the border after the trial, the convoy of police cars passed the spot where the ambush had taken place and the detectives with Stephen pointed out the field. It was the first time he had seen it since the night of the massacre. He asked them to stop, but they declined, citing their rendezvous deadline with the Irish police as an excuse. He caught a glimpse of the lattice fence, then it was gone.

After the trial, Stephen thought often about the two convicted killers who were beginning their lengthy sentences. He derived no satisfaction from the fact that justice, at least in the eyes of the law, had been seen to be done.

'I had fulfilled what I felt was my duty to the lads, but it did nothing for me personally to see them punished. As they were led away, all I could think of was how people living parallel lives could meet so tragically. I wondered what they were interested in. Did they like music? Would they remember hearing 'Hey Jude' or seeing 'Rock Around the Clock' for the first time, just like I did? I thought it possible that they, like so many Northerners, might have walked along the same beach on holiday at our local seaside town Tramore, in County Waterford.

'These men were not aliens. They had families. We may have had so much in common. Where did we diverge? Where did we start to drift apart? I've never felt like they did, so frightened by what was perceived to be a threat to my way of life that I could carry out murder.'

The lack of clarity about the events surrounding the night of the attack would leave many other unanswered questions in Stephen Travers' mind for the next thirty years.

It is still unclear what the UVF had hoped to achieve by planting a 10lb bomb in the back of a bus full of innocent musicians. As we would learn, sometimes the answer to that question depends on who you talk to. Stephen maintains that, had they succeeded, if everything had gone to plan, they would have destroyed the good name of the Miami forever and, by extension, cast a doubt on every person living in the Republic.

'It is impossible to find a finer example of unselfishness and bravery than that shown by the young men who sacrificed their lives in the act of bringing happiness, joy and respite from the Troubles to their people. When no one else seemed to care, showbands were very often the only light at the end of an otherwise dreary week for thousands of young people with little else to look forward to. Facing obvious danger, the Miami, armed only with their talent and a burning desire to bring together communities of all political and religious persuasions, paid the ultimate price.'

If the terrorists could frame the most innocent and trusted members of society, then the entire country would be regarded with suspicion. It was a two-pronged attack as success in their evil venture would also have driven a wedge between the two communities in the North.

'They wanted to plant the bomb in the van, wish us luck and send us on our way. Later, perhaps in Newry, or even back in Dublin, the bomb would have exploded and killed every one of us. Nobody would have known about the roadblock. We would surely have been written into the history books as terrorists. From their point of view, it was a brilliant plan and not a bad night's work had it succeeded. However, it begs the question – was this their first or last attempt to employ such a strategy? Because if not, then how many other innocent people have been buried while the lives of their friends and families were condemned under such false circumstances?'

As it was, it turned out to be a night's work that ended in chaos and disorder; a disaster for the loyalist paramilitary gang that carried it out. Perhaps their biggest mistake was to leave survivors – an oversight that was to prove their undoing.

Stephen returned to Carrick after the trial ended in late 1976 and attempted to pick up the pieces and get on with his life. He found himself once again retreating into the only thing that could offer him solace – playing music. He even joined his old friend Liam O'Dwyer, from The Sinners, in a new band they called The Movies. He was going back, he reflects, to be the person he was before he stepped out of the minibus that night. But no matter how hard he tried, the demons still haunted him.

'I thought I could pick up where I had left off and pretend all this had never happened. It was the start of thirty years of denial. I almost subconsciously tried to reconstruct everything in the manner of the way it was before July 1975. We got the band together with pretty much the same format as The Sinners and we played the same places. But it was too late. People couldn't help but see me as a tragic figure. It could never be the same again.'

Regardless of anything he tried to accomplish in later

years, the Miami massacre followed Stephen around, a silent spectre forever hanging over his shoulder. He felt he could not move on or ever hope for success based purely on his musical ability. As a teenager and up until the tragedy, Stephen Travers had been widely regarded as a musician of huge talent. Now, he was stigmatised by the mark of tragedy.

'I couldn't just throw away the years of experience and become something else, but if you consistently fail to make sense of your life, you begin to see yourself as a failure. It was a confusing time, and still is to this day. Even if I was told chapter and verse exactly what happened and who ordered, planned and carried it out, it would still be difficult to make sense of the event. Only now, through writing this book, have I begun to confront some of the things I had put out of my mind for all those years.'

He never allowed himself to think about the slaughter. If he had to speak about it, he divorced himself from the person to whom it had happened. He never really acknowledged that it was himself he was talking about. The alternative, he knew deep down, was too terrible to contemplate.

'There are some things that are still too difficult to remember. The small, personal stuff like sitting up, talking to Brian on the way home from the gigs, Fran's jokes. It's the memories of times like that that are the hardest to dwell on. Whenever I think about the lads, I put them back on the stage where they were safe and happy. I don't think I accepted that they were killed. If the truth be told, I still find it hard to accept that the whole incident happened, and that it happened to me.'

Stephen left The Movies during the summer of 1978, after three years in the band, because he had come to realise that this attempt to retrieve his former life hadn't worked.

'I wasn't happy because I couldn't get back to this vision of normality that I longed for. I reasoned that perhaps normality would be found back on the national circuit. Des McAlea quit the Miami in 1978 and asked me to join him and Ray Millar in a new venture, which we called Starband. I needed a kick-start to get back on track as a musician and when it didn't work with The Movies, I tried it with Starband. It was a high-profile outfit; we had a female singer called Dee McMahon. By pure coincidence, I found out that her boyfriend was a brother of Bugsy O'Reilly, with whom I had shared a flat back in 1969 in London. We were managed by Louis Walsh, who had managed Chips. He was a real go-getter even then. I always liked Louis. Behind the tough public image, he is one of the good guys and we remain friends to this day.'

Stephen sold his house and moved to Portmarnock, just outside Dublin, because he felt his future lay in the capital. Starband enjoyed relative success, but Stephen became distracted again fairly quickly and went his own way to form a Ska band with Aonghus McAnally. But before the band had even got off the ground, Aonghus left unexpectedly to take an acting job on Irish television. Crackers, as the band was known, became The Crack. They released a critically acclaimed single called 'When the Time Comes' from their album *Dawn of The Crack*, but the fact that the live music industry was in serious decline denied the band the opportunity to remain solvent.

'There had been an effort by established musicians to revive the showband scene in Ireland,' Stephen recalls. 'Ballroom owners and band promoters got together under the chairmanship of Enda O'Riordain, former manager of The Cowboys. Enda was well regarded as an organiser and tried to revive the fortunes of a dead industry, but I could see that there was no future in it.'

Ballrooms had played no small part in their own demise, in fact, by refusing to move with the times and reinvent themselves as modern entertainment centres. On the whole, the owners wouldn't reinvest in their businesses. Most ballroom managers refused to promote original bands, even though they had some of the best musical talent in the world at their disposal. Having said that, it is only fair to point out that ballrooms were essentially 'dance' venues rather than concert halls.

Original bands didn't want to restrict their work to dance music, and so the ballroom era was bound to come to an end. Many of the bands were writing and performing their own material, but they were, to a great extent, ignored. Soon the ballrooms were competing with hotels, which offered comfortable facilities and licensed bars. Hotels employed DJs at a fraction of the cost of live bands and one by one, the ballrooms started to close.

'The future of any band depended on success outside of Ireland. It became the yardstick by which bands were measured. Ireland seemed to lack the confidence to recognise real talent. There were exceptions, but even they had to foster the illusion that they were about to crack the international market.

'By the early 1980s, it was simply not possible to earn a living as a musician in Ireland. Things were catching up on us. I had put everything I had, all my earnings, into The Crack and I was still paying people wages long after it came to an end. It was then that we – Anne and I – decided to go to London.'

Before he left, Stephen contacted an old friend and musician, Joe Carroll, who was based there. He offered Joe his services on the live circuit.

'He laughed when I first asked for a job and said he couldn't afford me. I asked what he was paying and he said £10 to £15 a night. I told him, "Well, it's £10 to £15 more than I'm making at the moment."

'When he realised I was serious, he agreed to take me on. I promised to stay for six months, until I got my feet on the ground. We then embarked on a crucifying circuit of playing in half-empty pubs six nights a week. We played every wedding and gig we could get and, within two months, Smokey Joe Carroll had become a star in west London, and he never looked back.'

Stephen found comfort in the anonymity of London. People who approached him after gigs didn't know who he was and he could enjoy their compliments without the Miami being brought up. Once again, he was being appreciated solely as a musician.

'It was a culture shock for Anne, uprooting and transplanting to multicultural London. Initially, she was very dubious about settling down there, but after six months we bought a house in leafy Hillingdon in west London and, for the first time in quite a while, it felt like I was getting back to something resembling a normal life.'

Chapter 18

John James Somerville was born near Coalisland on New Year's Eve 1944. He had three brothers and two sisters and his family were members of the Presbyterian Church. On leaving school at the age of sixteen, he began work as a factory clerk in Moygashel, but left after about eighteen months to join the Royal Navy, in which he served for nine years. By the time he left the navy, in 1971, he was married with a son and a daughter. He found it hard to get work in the economic slump of the early 1970s and was unemployed for six months. It was during this time, he says, that he became aware of 'the IRA's increasing activities across the province'.

To Somerville, it seemed that things were getting out of hand. At one stage, he claimed, shots were fired through his mother's window. He was of the opinion that there were two laws in the province – one for Protestants and one for Catholics. To him, the civil rights marchers and the IRA were one and the same, therefore he objected to their right to protest in public. Somerville hated the IRA and claimed that nobody, not even the army or the police, seemed able, or even willing, to stop them, which meant in turn that he had little or no respect for the RUC, even though one of his brothers was a policeman.

It was not difficult to get involved with those who had taken the law into their own hands. For an unemployed young man in Moygashel, joining a paramilitary group was easy. Somerville would later say that to be in the company of these people was as natural as breathing, eating or drinking. Even his brother, Wesley, was a member of one of the gangs. He would also assert that it wasn't only 'his type' that was involved. He would claim that 'the respectable and the wealthy, who drove around in big cars' were also engaged in such activities.

Ironically, Somerville maintained that, in his opinion, law and order had broken down and he would later try to justify his barbaric actions as an attempt to restore what he perceived to be an acceptable way of life.

One of the first criminal acts he admitted to was the hijacking of a CIÉ bus in February 1973, near the border at Aughnacloy. In an incident remarkably similar to the Miami ambush two years later, the driver of the bus was stopped at a checkpoint manned by a soldier in uniform and waving a red torch. Armed with a revolver, Somerville, along with a number of other men, boarded the bus and forced the driver to go down a narrow, secluded lane. The passengers were ordered off and robbed while the bus was set on fire. The frightened driver was told to inform his company that, in future, the passengers and drivers of buses travelling over the border would be shot.

In April 1973, Somerville was involved in a plot to bomb a house owned by the Devlin family who, it was claimed, had refused to serve members of the security forces in their shop. The 2lb gelignite bomb exploded on the windowsill, damaging property but causing no injuries.

Somerville's next terrorist attempt would prove more successful. It was a quiet night in Fall's public house in Aughnamullan, near Coalisland, on 20 November 1974 when Somerville walked in with another armed man. They opened fire on the few regulars inside, hitting publican Patrick Aidan Falls and fifty-five-year-old Alphonsus Quinn. Falls bled to death on the floor of his bar, but Quinn survived, even though he had been shot in the neck.

Eight months later, at approximately 11.00pm on the night of 30 July 1975, Somerville was driven from Portadown to the Newry Road. There, along with his brother Wesley, he was handed a 0.9mm pistol and ordered to take up position on the road near Buskhill and wait for the arrival of the Miami Showband. In a statement to police on 23 September 1980, he claimed, 'I was told what I had to do was cover the rest of the men. I was wearing my ordinary clothes at the time. I left the group of men and walked some forty to fifty yards away and took up a position in the hedge at the side of the Newry–Banbridge road. I stayed there for something like five minutes. Then the Miami Showband van came along, which was stopped and pulled into the same side of the road that I was on. I couldn't see what was happening, only that the lights of the van were dipped, but I couldn't be sure of this.

'The van remained at the side of the road for a short time and I stayed in the hedge, keeping cover. Suddenly, there was an explosion and a blinding flash came from the direction of the van. I got out of the hedge and ran towards the van. It had been blown all over the road and spilt petrol was burning along the road. I made my way to the point were the van had been stopped, but I couldn't get near it with the heat. There was nothing that could be done and someone shouted to get out of it. I went along the road towards Banbridge and, on doing so, I heard gunfire coming from a field to my right. It was serious, brother, desperate. I got into a car and was driven away. It may be the understatement of the year, but may I say at this time a heart-rending experience for all concerned. I trust that God would heal the wounds in due time. As far as I'm concerned, I'm sorry. I would like to make it clear that the gun which I had wasn't fired during the incident.'

Somerville would later discover that his brother had been killed that night. The only thing he would say to police about his brother's death was that he had never seen his body, but believed he had died in the explosion. Later, he would organise the headstone for Wesley.

When first questioned about the various terrorist offences in which he had been involved, Somerville denied all knowledge of them. He acknowledged that his brother had been killed in the Miami explosion, but refused to admit that he himself had been there. He told the police that he had confessed his sins to God, but would never confide in man.

He was quizzed over a number of days in September 1980. At first, he denied any wrongdoing, but then confessed his involvement in the Miami ambush late in the evening of the 23rd, after he had spoken to a 'Christian' officer. 'I'll admit nothing,' he said repeatedly. 'I will only admit anything that I have done wrong to God.'

Somerville was joined in his cell by a police officer, who declared himself a fellow Christian. The officer told Somerville he believed him to be a committed Christian and proceeded to talk with him about their shared faith. Somerville finally broke his wall of silence and started to speak about the peace he had found since accepting Jesus Christ into his life. The officer recorded their exchanges as follows.

'We continued to speak of Jesus Christ and things in connection with the Bible and the positions in which we both now found ourselves as Christians. I spoke to Somerville about God's conditions for the believer in Christ, and also related to him the promises of God. I explained that, as an investigating police officer, it was my duty to serve God in the society where I lived and worked. I said that I had a responsibility to society and that, as a policeman, I had to pursue my duties impartially in the furtherance and the prevention of crime.

'Somerville, in return, explained that he appreciated what I had said and accepted what I had to do. He then said that he wished to make a statement to me on the basis that he felt I was a sincere Christian. He said that he now wanted to explain his part in the Miami Showband murders.'

Somerville agreed to tell the detective what he knew, on condition that he would not divulge the names of the others involved. In his statement, Somerville reflected on his past. He confessed, 'During the years since leaving the navy, I have done things that an animal wouldn't do and that is the brutal truth. It's like smoking or drinking, the first butt or drink maybe tasted bad, but you eventually become brainwashed and addicted to it. Even your mind can come to the place where you enjoyed it. It's like the devil saying, "Sure, it's sweet." It got to me a couple of times that my conscience didn't bother me. It just got to the stage where I felt justified doing the things I had done.'

He then described how his mind had become warped through his actions, but that since the day of his conversion, he had on many occasions felt guilty about some of his past actions. 'Memory would always bring these things back to my mind,' he admitted. 'As I look on things since becoming a Christian, I now know that I was a prisoner of Satan.'

He went on to speak about the changes God had made to his life and the problems he still faced every day, complaining that the same people who had condemned him when he was involved in violence also condemned him when he became a Christian. As to his present situation, he said, 'My conscience is clear. And even if hanging was still here, I would not be afraid. [This is] what God did for me in Christ, he had taken away fear of men and fear of death and prison.' Somerville paused, then added, 'The world would be full of Christians if it wasn't for the fears of man.'

Since his conversion, Somerville said, he realised how wrong he had been. He now knew what was right for him. He said God was the most important influence in his life and made him feel content. He added that he didn't want to blame anyone else for the things he had done and felt that he was fully responsible for his own actions, and prepared to suffer the consequences. When asked if he was upset, he said that he wasn't, that the thought wasn't 'causing me any problems'. One of the detectives asked how he felt about the future. Somerville replied that he knew he was going to prison for twenty years, but he wasn't bothered. When he was asked how he thought jail would affect him, he replied, 'I won't know until I get there. I'll just have to wait and see.'

Later that same evening of 23 September, he was questioned about other incidents, but would only say that he could not remember anything else. 'It is hard to think back. You would find it hard to think back to what you had done six or seven years ago.' He was pressed further about other matters that had occurred between the years 1974 and 1976, but denied any knowledge of them. 'They have nothing to do with me. The last thing I was in was the Miami job.' When asked again how he felt about his brother being killed he replied, 'I really don't want to discuss that.'

One of the detectives wrote: 'I asked him if he had handled guns or explosives on occasions other than the times he had admitted to and he replied, "I can't remember but it would be stupid for me not to tell you after telling you about the Miami and the other things."'

The officers pressed him on other incidents, but he stated that he couldn't remember. Sitting in what appeared to be a pensive silence, he finally said, 'I never knew who brought the explosives or who made it up. It was usually left somewhere.'

Despite further attempts to get him to talk about other incidents, Somerville would say no more.

On 26 September 1980 – almost three years to the day since he claimed Jesus Christ had entered his life – John James Somerville was arrested and formally charged with the murder of Patrick Aidan Falls in Fall's pub. After being cautioned, he replied, 'Nothing to say.' Directly afterwards, he was arrested and formally charged with the murders of Fran O'Toole, Tony Geraghty and Brian McCoy. After each charge, he gave the same reply, 'Nothing to say.'

When his case came to trial in November 1981, Somerville pleaded not guilty to the murders of the Miami men. He pleaded guilty to the murder of Patrick Falls.

He did not give evidence during his four-day trial, but on 9 November 1981, having being found guilty of the murders of all four men, he made an unsworn statement from the dock. 'I pleaded guilty to the things I am guilty of. I had no intention of murdering these three men. So far as I can see, if I had accepted an offer by CID to become a police informer, it would have a totally different bearing on this case. People are totally wrong when they say I killed members of The Miami Showband. I accept full responsibility for the things I have pleaded guilty to.'

As he stood to hear the verdict against him, Somerville reflected on all the bad he had done in his life and, not for the first time, asked God to forgive him. Passing sentence, Lord Justice Gibson referred to the role Somerville had played in the Miami massacre.

'If anyone had tried to escape, his duty was to protect the members of the gang and the secrecy of the exercise. The purpose of the gang was to kill … I am generally opposed to recommended sentences, except in psychiatric cases or when the accused has committed a long series of atrocious crimes.'

The judge then told the court that the Miami incident had aroused 'tremendous public interest and revulsion'. In keeping with the thirty-five-year minimum sentence imposed on the other men convicted of the killings, the judge said he must observe a degree of uniformity. He sentenced Somerville to life for each murder, with a recommendation that he serve not less than thirty-five years in prison. Somerville was also convicted of a series of lesser charges relating to the possession and use of guns and explosives. The jail terms for these offences were to run concurrently with those for murder.

As he was led out of the dock, Somerville turned to the court, raised his arm and gave a 'V' sign for victory. Then he shouted, 'No surrender', before he disappeared from view.

One year later, Somerville appealed his conviction and life sentence to the Supreme Court. In February 1982, his appeal was dismissed by Lord Justice Jones and Justice MacDermott and he was returned to jail. With that, the last of the Miami trials was over.

Part V
RECONCILIATION

Chapter 19

In London, Stephen Travers was working hard to survive in the city he remembered fondly from his youth, though he had little or no time to enjoy the sights and sounds of the capital. This time round he had responsibilities – a new home to pay for and a young wife who depended on him.

Their new life in England had taken some getting used to, but at least – unlike 1980s Ireland – there was no shortage of work. Stephen readily accepted every gig and function he was offered. It didn't matter if it was a dance, a christening, a wedding or a wake, he gladly turned up night after night in every corner of London with his bass guitar, ready to play any style of music that was required. He found that his showband apprenticeship stood him in good stead for the life of a jobbing musician.

On one occasion he arrived at a club, only to be told that the advertisement was incorrect and the band playing that night needed a drummer, not a bass guitarist. Stephen was reluctant to walk away. Instead, he casually mentioned that he could quite easily hold down a rhythm and, for the first time in his life, he sat behind a drum kit. 'My hands were so tired afterwards that I found it difficult to count my money. But I pulled it off and the gig went so well the band even offered me a permanent job as their drummer. I declined. I was more ambitious than that. I needed to build a good life for Anne and me.'

Despite the daily challenges of making a living, Anne and Stephen were happy in their house in the pleasant London suburb of Hillingdon. As the months passed, life started to move further away from the past.

'I was playing fifteen engagements a week. I did a lunchtime jazz session at a French restaurant in Pinner every day and seven nights a week at various clubs and pubs throughout Greater London. On Sundays, I had a late date in Clapham. If there were twenty days in the week, I would have worked them. My profile as a musician in London began to grow and I experienced a relaxation and peace that I hadn't known for a long time. My confidence returned and I began to look forwards instead of backwards. I wasn't Stephen Travers anymore, I was Steve Travers. A subtle difference I know, but nevertheless it was a step away from the person I used to be. Gradually,

I disassociated myself from Stephen altogether. I didn't think about him at all.'

Stephen had never suffered any of the effects that psychologists expect for a person who has been through his experience. He didn't have nightmares, he didn't wake up with the sheets soaking in sweat and it was possible to go through a day without thinking about the incident or the lads.

'Of course, I could never forget them. Now and then I'd find myself smiling at the memory of one of Fran's jokes. Maybe I'd be on stage in some small east London club and I'd remember walking out with the Miami to the screams of the crowd and it would all come back. Not how it all ended, just the good times. The chats with Brian as we journeyed back from some prestigious venue, the fun, the jamming with Tony in my home in Carrick-on-Suir. But I'd just smile and play, happy to move on with my new life with Anne and comfortable in the knowledge that it was finally slipping further and further behind me.'

Stephen paid little attention to events in the North and was not even aware that there had been a third trial for one of the Miami murderers. After his own experiences in the trials of McDowell and Crozier, he was content to let justice take its course while he concentrated on getting on with his life. By the mid-1980s, however, the Troubles broke into his life once more as the conflict spilled over into Britain. In 1982, the IRA exploded two bombs at a British army ceremonial parade in London's Hyde Park and Regent's Park, killing eleven soldiers and wounding fifty soldiers and civilians. On 17 December 1983 a bomb exploded outside Harrod's during the busy pre-Christmas shopping period, killing six people and injuring nearly ninety.

A year later, the IRA almost succeeded in assassinating the British Prime Minister, Margaret Thatcher, and her cabinet when they bombed the Grand Hotel in Brighton. On 7 February 1991, members of the British cabinet came under mortar attack during a session at 10 Downing Street. A few days later, on 18 February, a bomb at Victoria Station killed one person and injured thirty-eight. Given the rise in tension on the streets, Stephen decided to present himself to the local police.

'I was concerned that, in the event of an incident, the security forces there might add one and one and get three. The fact that my name might show up in connection with a previous terrorist incident worried me. I called into Uxbridge police station to make my presence in the area known. To be honest, the desk sergeant looked at me as if he didn't really know what I was talking about. And, of course, I never heard from them again.'

In 1987, Stephen turned his hand to a new business. Together with three others, he founded *The Irish World* newspaper.

'It was an opportune time for such a venture as half the

population of Ireland seemed to be living in the UK. There was a strong sense of community among the Irish immigrants and our weekly was very well received. The excellent *Irish Post Newspaper* was long established in Britain, but because of the huge Irish diaspora there was ample room for a second Irish paper. We worked, to say the least, on a low budget. In the absence of a professional editor, I was elected to do the job. Up to then, the only experience I had in media was as a child helping my dad bundle Catholic newspapers for the Legion of Mary. However, I rarely refuse a challenge and in my innocence and naïvety, I took up the position with great enthusiasm. At first, I struggled to come to terms with the printers' and typesetters' methods and jargon, but my confidence had returned to such an extent that *The Irish World* got off the ground and, in 2007, celebrated its twentieth anniversary. I was very proud when Damien Gaffney, the outstanding *Irish World* editor, was the first to break the news of the IRA ceasefire. Sadly, Damien died from an asthma attack some years later. He was a great loss to the profession.'

Once *The Irish World* was up and running successfully, Stephen set his sights on further opportunities in the media. As soon as he had proved himself a competent newspaperman, he applied for a broadcasting licence after Douglas Hurd, the then British Home Secretary, had indicated that he would grant extra local radio licences.

'We hoped to be successful in applying for an Irish community radio licence, but as the bombs began exploding in British cities, our hopes for a positive outcome to our plans faded. It appeared that the British authorities were reluctant to hand over exclusive airtime to any Irish entrepreneur during those uneasy times. I am happy to say, however, that neither Anne nor I ever encountered racism or anti-Irish bias of any kind during our time in London. I love that city and its people and I'm very happy to return there on a regular basis for both business and pleasure.'

The disappointment at not getting a broadcasting licence, coupled with a natural restlessness, eventually persuaded Stephen to leave the newspaper business.

'I am happiest with a challenge, but not very comfortable with the day-to-day running of normal business. I decided to leave my media mogul pretensions behind and find something I was more at ease with. From my time at the newspaper, I knew that I was a natural organiser and co-ordinator. Somehow, I had continued playing music during my publishing era and four hours' sleep a night seemed to be sufficient. A chance request by a club owner to help him "get some good bands" started me on my career as a music agent. At first, I saw it as a compromise between a steady job and music, but soon I realised I enjoyed the work and continue to do so. I love the interaction with musicians of all genres and feel especially proud of my part in keeping music live during a period when discos threatened the livelihoods of real musicians.'

Stephen also continued performing during this time, and it was while playing the occasional gig in London that he formed a musical partnership that is still going strong. Guitarist Johnny Fean had also emigrated to London in the mid-1980s, following the break-up of his legendary band, Horslips. Johnny had felt that his group too was a hard act to follow and he struggled to survive in the bleak economic climate in Ireland, before jumping ship and washing up on the busy live-music circuit in London.

'Johnny and I had been introduced to each other by the Irish blues legend Rory Gallagher at an awards concert in 1975. I had always admired Johnny's playing, but apart from the occasional nod, we didn't come into contact again until St Patrick's Day 1991, at a concert at Wembley. This particular encounter lasted all of ten minutes. His schedule, like mine, was hectic and we only had time for a quick chat. Although it would take another five years, it was written in the sand that we would work together and when we did eventually form a band, we humorously called it The Psycho Pats. We teamed up with the much-sought-after keyboard player Dave Lennox, whose CV included tours with Cream's Ginger Baker among a host of other top artists. Drummer and percussionist Danny 'Bongos' Smith gave us the beat and together we stormed many of the music venues of London and across the southeast of England.

'When the band eventually ran its course, Johnny and I continued playing as a duo and made the best of the situation. The liquor licensing laws in the UK at that time were such that most live-music venues used duos rather than full bands in order to avoid the necessity of paying for an expensive entertainment licence. Occasionally, people recognised us from our previous backgrounds. They would come up to us at the gigs and say in amazement, "Aren't you Johnny Fean and Stephen Travers … what are you doing here?" Of course, it was a lesson in humility as we had both played to capacity crowds in Ireland for years, we had both headlined at such great venues as The Royal Albert Hall, yet here we were, playing to a hundred people in a pub in London. But we knew the world didn't owe us anything. We were grateful to be playing and earning a good living. We both had a past to be proud of and a burning desire to develop further as musicians, but this time away from the glare of the spotlight. There was no pressure to conform to a strict set list or travel long distances to gigs. People came to hear us, not to look at us. Generally speaking, the vast majority of our audience had no idea about our history. They simply knew us as two guys who were pushing the boundaries of Celtic rock and blues and they loved it. Sometimes, when we took it too far and indulged ourselves, a venue owner would remind us to keep it commercial. We usually agreed to return to more mainstream stuff and keep them happy, but we still slipped in the odd interesting chord or timing for our own amusement. The discipline we had both learned on the road in Ireland was invaluable to us as musicians.'

Johnny and his wife, Maggie, decided to return to Ireland around the time as Stephen and Anne arrived at the same conclusion. Stephen and Johnny continued to work together and today tour throughout Ireland and the UK with various drummers, including Mick Rowley and Blendi Krasniqi, whenever the opportunity and their busy schedules allow. So far they have declined to tour farther afield, despite numerous lucrative offers. It is a musical partnership born of mutual respect that enables two highly acclaimed artists to indulge in their shared passion. For audiences who like to witness two unique musicians playing their hearts out, their intimate gigs across Ireland have become something of a special treat.

Stephen and Anne had been considering moving back to Ireland since January 1992, after Stephen had experienced the greatest day of his life when their daughter, Sean, was born.

'From then on, Anne and I were determined to move back to Ireland to provide Sean with an Irish education. We started to look at our options. I was eager to live in the countryside, but Anne loved city life. We found a compromise in the one place that seemed to offer the best of both worlds – Cork. Anne's sisters live there and I fondly remembered playing city-centre venues, such as The Stardust, The Arcadia and The Majorca in Crosshaven, with the Miami. Cork people are renowned for their good nature and, in 1975, I clearly recall being told that the churches were packed to capacity praying for the Miami and for my recovery. The city by the Lee was the perfect choice. But I must admit that I still wave the blue-and-gold of Tipperary during the hurling clashes between the two great counties, while my wife and daughter tease me with the red-and-white of Cork.'

Stephen returned home in 1998 – the same year that a peace, of sorts, was finally reached with the Good Friday Agreement. Despite some outrageous terrorist atrocities, in particular the Omagh bombing in August of that year, the agreement paved the way for the long process of reconciliation and dialogue, and also an honest examination of past events.

In December 1999, the Hamilton Inquiry was set up under Mr Justice Liam Hamilton to undertake a thorough examination of the 1974 Dublin and Monaghan bombings. In 2000, Justice Henry Barron took over as presiding judge, and the tribunal's work continued. Soon after, Stephen was given the opportunity to officially set down his account of the night of 31 July 1975 when he was asked to appear before Justice Barron.

'When I was first contacted about appearing before the inquiry, I felt relieved that, at last, my own government was about to look for the truth. When I think about it now, it is incredible that no Irish official ever interviewed me or asked me any questions about the incident. Although three prominent Irish citizens had been murdered, not one member of our police force ever took a statement from me. I am absolutely convinced that, until then, no Irish government cared as long as the murders of its young men were neatly packaged and placed on some high shelf to be conveniently filed away and gather dust. To use a well-worn but perfectly apt cliché, "they didn't want to know". That, in itself, poses a serious question – why didn't they want to know?'

It's a question that remains unanswered to this day.

Judge Barron and his assistant questioned Stephen about the incident and seemed genuinely interested when he described a British army officer who had arrived to take charge of the operation on the night. 'I relived the events of that night again and, though I found it difficult, I was more disappointed to discover that the experience had not gone away after all those years. The horrors all too easily paraded themselves in the forefront of my mind, as if they had only happened the day before.'

It was during this period that Stephen met Margaret Urwin, secretary of Justice for the Forgotten, a campaign group that was founded in 1996, initially to assist the bereaved family members and survivors of the Dublin and Monaghan bombings of 1974 and the Dublin bombings of 1972 and 1973, but which also looks into other incidents. It was through Justice for the Forgotten that Stephen would learn many disturbing facts about the events he had found himself caught up in more than twenty years before.

He soon became aware that the Miami massacre was far from an isolated case. It was, in fact, only one in a series of crimes perpetrated by a particular gang that operated on both sides of the border over a period of years during the mid-1970s. While the Miami killings were particularly shocking because the pop group was a household name and the attack therefore received a huge amount of publicity, for the men who had carried it out it was not very different from the dozens of other, less well-known murders they had notched up. Members of this gang are suspected of taking part in the Dublin and Monaghan bombings of 1974, the Dundalk bombings of December 1975 and the gun-and-bomb attack at Donnelly's Bar in County Armagh in December 1975 among many other atrocities.

It has been well documented in the years since the Miami incident that the people who carried out the killings were members of the Glenanne Gang, which included members of the RUC, the UDR and loyalist paramilitaries. It is now widely accepted that throughout their campaign of terror, the gang was assisted by members of the British security services. McDowell and Crozier were both soldiers serving with the UDR, the largest regiment of the British army in Northern Ireland, as was John James Somerville. As soon as they were caught and charged with the murders, all three men were dismissed from the UDR. This meant they could be described as ex-UDR, which enabled the authorities to distance them and their crimes from the security forces. The UDR used the 'bad apples' argument to describe the actions of these men, claiming they were the exception rather than the rule.

However, according to revelations in the *Irish News* newspaper in May 2006, which were based on research by the Pat Finucane Centre and Justice for the Forgotten, the UDR was seriously infiltrated by paramilitaries, proving what many had suspected for a long time. The newspaper had uncovered official Whitehall files in which it was estimated that 5–15 per cent of UDR soldiers were linked to loyalist terror groups. Among these groups was the Glenanne Gang, which were said to have operated out of James Mitchell's farmhouse at Glenanne, near Markethill in County Armagh. James Mitchell, who is now in his eighties, had once been a member of the RUC Reserve. Allegedly, it was from this farmhouse that he provided a base for the making of explosives and the storing of guns.

The most notorious individual associated with the Glenanne Gang was Robin Jackson, often referred to as 'The Jackal'. Jackson hailed from Donaghmore, a town just one-and-a-half miles from where the Miami musicians were murdered. He died of cancer in 1998, but is suspected of having been involved in over one hundred murders during his lifetime.

Over the intervening years, there have been many suggestions that the mysterious officer whom Stephen saw arriving on the night was Captain Robert Nairac, an undercover agent for the SAS in Britain's dirty war against the IRA. He has been described as everything from 'an aloof dreamer' who had his head in the clouds to a man with a cold heart and ruthless determination. In his book, *The SAS in Ireland*, Fr Raymond Murray claimed that Nairac was an associate of Harris Boyle. Both men have been accused of taking part in the murder of IRA man John Francis Green in County Monaghan in 1975. Significantly, one of the weapons used in the murder of Green, a Luger pistol, was also used in the Miami murders.

In 1987, the man who would become the Lord Mayor of London, Ken Livingstone, caused an outcry in the British House of Commons during his maiden speech when he claimed that Nairac was quite likely to have been one of the names behind the Miami Showband massacre. Livingstone based this claim on the word of Fred

Holroyd, a former intelligence officer, who knew Nairac. Holroyd, first arrived in Northern Ireland in 1974 and claimed had been forced to resign from the army two years later. Since then, he has made persistent, well-documented claims that, during his time, there the British army was engaged in murder, kidnapping and assisting loyalist paramilitaries in Northern Ireland.

The British officer's name hit the headlines again in 1999 when a woman who claimed to have been Nairac's lover said he had confessed to her his involvement in the murder of the Miami. It may never be proven either way whether it was Nairac who arrived as the Miami men were being questioned. Certainly, an admission can never come from the soldier himself. He was just twenty-nine years of age when his cover was blown and he disappeared at the hands of the IRA in May 1977. His fate remains unknown, but one of the more popular, if gruesome, stories told is that his body was disposed of by being minced into pig feed.

In late December 1975 and early 1976, members of the Glenanne Gang, which, according to the Pat Finucane Centre, included members of the security services, went on the rampage, murdering eleven people over the course of a few weeks. On 19 December 1975, a section of the gang bombed Donnelly's bar in Silverbridge, County Armagh, killing three people, while another section carried out the bombing of Kay's Tavern in Dundalk earlier the same evening, killing two local men. Just a few weeks later, on 4 January 1976, two other units killed three members of the O'Dowd family and three members of the Reavey family on the same night.

In June 1976, the Glenanne Gang attacked the Rock Bar in Keady, south Armagh. This attack was carried out entirely by serving members of the RUC, who were subsequently arrested and brought to court. During the trial of the policemen charged with the attack, the fact that there were no known loyalist paramilitaries involved was used to dispel suspicion of police and terrorist collusion. It was held up as an example of how a few officers, having been traumatised by the loss of their comrades to the IRA, could lose control. However, one of those eventually convicted, William McCaughey, would later reveal the true extent of security-forces collusion with terrorists.

McCaughey was also convicted of the shooting of a Catholic shopkeeper, William Strathearn, in April 1977, which in turn led to the jailing of another RUC man, John Weir. McCaughey and Weir served over ten years for their involvement in the killing. In prison, Weir claimed that the two others who had been with him that night were Robin Jackson and another well-known loyalist, R.J. Kerr. It was stated during the trial that Jackson and Kerr were not being charged 'for operational reasons'. Despite such overwhelming evidence, there has never been official acknowledgment by the British authorities of collusion between the security forces and terrorist gangs. The British government has always blamed collusion on individuals, who, it claimed, were acting alone.

There was also evidence that some of the Miami murderers had been caught engaging in terrorist-related activities in the weeks before the Miami massacre, but, inexplicably, had not been charged. In June 1975, Jackson and Thomas Crozier were caught in possession of weapons in a field. There is documentary evidence that suggests John James Somerville and Wesley Somerville had also escaped serious charges a year before the Miami massacre. On 5 March 1974, the Somerville brothers and another man, Trevor Barnard, all from Dungannon, were caught red-handed putting a bomb in a bread van in Coalisland. Barnard was the only one to receive a prison sentence.

The involvement of these members of the Glenanne Gang in the Miami Massacre came to light through letters written by Colin Wallace, an Armagh native who was based in British army headquarters in Lisburn, to one of his superiors; the letters subsequently came into the possession of Justice for the Forgotten. In one letter Wallace refers to the 'Protestant Task Force', one of many cover names used by the Glenanne Gang.

'I have been told recently that most of the loyalist sectarian killings that took place in Armagh and Tyrone this year [1975], including the Irish showband murders two months ago, were carried out by the Protestant Task Force. There are also rumours that the group is linked to the Special Duties Team at Lisburn. The whole business is really chilling.'

The Special Duties Team to which Wallace referred was a British army unit attached to army headquarters in Lisburn. The team issued instructions to 'Four Field Survey Troop', which was Robert Nairac's unit, based at Castledillon in County Armagh. There was a later attempt to discredit Wallace, who was convicted of manslaughter, although this conviction was quashed.

It is widely believed – although never proven – that those arrested, charged and jailed for their parts in the murder of Fran O'Toole, Brian McCoy and Tony Geraghty were on the periphery, while those who were really central to the crime were never brought to justice.

In spite of all this, at the very least Stephen was afforded the opportunity to set down officially his account of the night of 31 July when he was invited to appear before the Joint Oireachtas Committee on Justice, Equality, Defence and Women's Rights, which was examining the Barron Report into the bombing of Kay's Tavern, Dundalk, and other atrocities, including the Miami Showband murders.

As the years passed, however, Stephen found himself, somewhat reluctantly, becoming fascinated by questions regarding the significance of the Miami murders in relation to the wider story of the Troubles. 'It was like uncovering parts of a detective story. And as each revelation came to the surface, I found myself becoming more and more intrigued by what had happened to us and, in particular, the others who were there that night. I wondered who they were, what they were like and if they ever thought about their actions and regretted them.'

It was during one of these meetings at the offices of Justice for the Forgotten that Margaret Urwin suggested arranging a memorial service to commemorate the thirtieth anniversary of the murders.

'At first, I was dubious as the families and survivors had not been in contact for many years. Fran's wife Valerie had remarried and moved to Canada with their two daughters, Kelly and Rachel. Fran's parents and brother, Michael, had passed away. Tony's fiancée, Linda Hendricks, was now married with her own family. Brian's wife, Helen, lived with her son Keith in Dublin, but I had spoken to her only briefly on the telephone at the time of the twenty-fifth anniversary, five years previously. Though I had never confronted it, I think now that perhaps I was suffering from 'survivor's guilt' and dealt with it by avoiding contact with the families and friends of Tony, Fran and Brian.

'Margaret offered to make exploratory enquiries. To my amazement, she called me to say that Helen and Keith McCoy, Joan O'Toole (Fran's sister-in-law) and her sons and Tony's brothers and nephew had all agreed to meet to discuss the service. It was an emotional meeting, during which we all agreed to hold an inter-denominational service at the Pro Cathedral in Dublin on Saturday, 30 July, the day before the thirtieth anniversary. As the meeting was coming to an end, in a moment of what I can only describe as over-enthusiasm, I suggested a concert to celebrate the lives of the lads that might even raise some funds for a permanent memorial. The suggestion was greeted with raised eyebrows. Brian's son Keith was the first to break the silence. "It sounds fantastic," he said, "but do you think anyone would come?"

'His question went through my heart like a knife. What had I done? What if Keith was right? Perhaps the Miami was just a faded memory in modern Ireland. Failure in such a venture could embarrass the families and, even worse, damage the cherished memories, impressions and dreams of their children. But weighted against that was the very strong feeling that I couldn't let Keith think for one second that his dad had been forgotten. I reassured him that people from all over the country would love the opportunity to celebrate their heroes. "After all", I said, "this is what I do for a living; organise music events. It will be a huge success." We agreed to explore the idea further but, despite my reassurances, I couldn't shake my own apprehension.'

Although the inter-denominational service for the

Miami was held on a Saturday during a bank holiday weekend, Dublin's Pro Cathedral was packed to capacity. People who couldn't get inside the building stood out on the street and joined in the prayers from there. Those fortunate enough to be inside said it was one of the most emotional and moving services they had ever witnessed.

The mass was conducted by Fr Brian D'Arcy and Reverend Robert Dean, an Anglican rector. Dana, a former MEP and one-time Eurovision winner, sang several hymns, including 'Abide With Me', 'How Great Thou Art' and 'Make Me a Channel of Your Peace'. There was also a musical tribute from former Miami Showband singer, Dickie Rock. Stephen is still touched by the memories of that day.

'I could hardly believe it as the tears began rolling down my face. I felt embarrassed that anyone might notice. Anne or Sean hadn't seen me cry since the death of my mother in 2001. I kept my gaze towards the high altar. It brought home to me very forcibly the final truth that Tony, Fran and Brian were dead. Why else would we be at a church service, praying for them? I was made acutely aware of the terrible consequences of death as my wife and daughter, on either side of me, gently took my hands. Where were Tony's children? The beautiful angels that were never born. I gripped my family's hands now with a renewed feeling of love and terror. What if …?'

After all the emotion of the service, Stephen was

determined that The Miami Showband 30th Anniversary Memorial Concert, as it was now called, would have to be the biggest and best of its kind ever staged.

'I knew that, to achieve this, I would have to get the biggest stars from that era on board. How could I even contact the most important names from the Irish showband and beat-group scene of 1975? I had lived abroad for so long; would they even remember me? I knew I needed a strong team. My first call was to the former Miami bass player, Paul Ashford. Paul had joined the Miami with Fran and Brian and was devastated when they were killed. Paul had long since left the band, but remained prominent in the Irish music scene. I knew that he had kept in touch with all the musicians in and around Dublin.

'Paul was excited about the project and immediately suggested getting Mike Hanrahan, Chairman of the Irish Music Rights Organisation, involved as the concert producer. I only knew Mike as the vocalist and guitarist with the celebrated band Stockton's Wing. I had booked them for a Wembley concert in 1991. But, as I would discover, Paul's confidence in Mike was well founded. My friend John Murphy, an accountant in Macroom, County Cork, was a mine of information. John had contact details for every major star from the showband and beat-group years. Together, we started making tentative phone calls. There was great interest and genuine goodwill.

Although some artists immediately offered their services, we found that many wanted to know who else was going to perform. We were making headway, but it could all have collapsed like a house of cards.

'This was unknown territory. Some of the artists themselves doubted their own popularity and drawing power. They had their own misgivings; it was a long time since they had topped the charts. Most were now in cabaret or management, while others had retired. I didn't yet feel confident that this would be a success. I knew I needed 'the King', the one man who could change everything. If I got Brendan Bowyer on the bill, I knew everything else would fall into place. But Brendan lived in Las Vegas and I had not seen him for many years. I called him, despite my doubts, even as the phone was ringing. I got through to his answering service and left a quick message. I didn't hear anything for about four days when, while out walking, my mobile phone rang. I didn't recognise the number, but I could see that it was American. "Is that you, Stephen?" the unmistakable voice asked from the other side of the world. "This is Brendan. I was away for a few days, but I just got back home to Las Vegas and listened to your message." I waited with bated breath. "I'm thrilled about the concert, it's well overdue. I'm calling to say that if I have to swim the Atlantic Ocean, I'll be there for the lads."

'From that phone call, I knew we had a concert.

Everyone breathed a sigh of relief when I told them. The momentum had begun.

'Word spread like wildfire. Suddenly, the concert was the bill to be on. We had the famous Vicar Street venue in Dublin and the best performers of their day were gathering for a unique one-off event. But through it all Keith McCoy's words still rang in my ears, "It sounds fantastic, but do you think anyone would come?" There could be no place for complacency; we had to shout it from the rooftops. Mike, Paul, John and I formed a committee and Margaret Urwin kindly took on the role of secretary. Between us, we bombarded the media with details of the concert. It was far easier than we had imagined; everyone was delighted to help. The newspapers, TV and radio, north and south of the border, all got behind the project to such an extent that I was asked on many occasions what PR company we were using. The interest was incredible. We were completely inundated with requests for interviews.

'During this time, there were a number of fortunate coincidences which Carl Jung might have called synchronicity. Others, anticipating the thirtieth anniversary, had commissioned, or were in the process of producing, TV documentaries, radio programmes or were writing articles on the Miami incident and began to get in contact. One such project was already well under way by a Belfast film company called DoubleBand Films. I agreed to take part in their documentary, which was entitled *The Day the Music Died*. It was an excellent production, which had a huge impact on viewers when it was aired during the week of the anniversary.

'Up until 2005, very few journalists had contact details for me. I had remained very private, but now I found myself in the full glare of the media spotlight once again. Every morning, I told myself that it was worth going through and I steeled myself for the same question that would be asked four or five times each day, "Can you tell us what happened on that fateful night?" I had to relive the incident every time. It was harrowing, but what amazed me most of all was the huge interest shown by the young reporters and interviewers who appeared horrified that such an event had ever happened.

'It dawned on me that most of the thirty-somethings, the very people who were poised to take charge of the country, knew little or nothing about the Miami Showband massacre. I wondered how they could avoid a similar outrage in the future if such a painful and hard-won lesson of their recent past had been so readily forgotten, conveniently airbrushed out of history in the intervening years. I did my best to tell our story with dignity and sensitivity for the families and friends of the lads. To this day, I remain very much indebted to all sections of the media, not just for their help with the concert but, more importantly, for keeping the memory of Tony, Fran and Brian alive. The publicity for the concert was so intense that the Vicar Street event became a memorial in itself.

'Up until the day of the concert, we continued with the manic round of interviews and photo-calls. The Miami Showband's former road manager, Brian Maguire, had just parked his people carrier outside Vicar Street that evening when my mobile rang. It was a reporter from the *Belfast Telegraph*. He asked me to comment on another memorial ceremony that was being held in Northern Ireland to commemorate the UVF men who murdered Tony, Fran and Brian. He told me that large crowds were attending the unveiling of a permanent memorial in Portadown to those who had died in the act of planting the bomb in the Miami van. I told him that I was pleased that the men were being remembered, but hoped that the act itself was not being honoured. Ironically, I felt deeply offended when he told me that fifteen marching bands were taking part in the event. I wondered how these musicians could use their God-given talents to celebrate the slaughter of the best of their own kind.

'I tried to put that call out of my mind and walked into the Vicar Street auditorium. Inside, the prestigious venue was like an Aladdin's cave of celebrities. I felt like I had opened my *Spotlight* magazine annual and it had somehow come to life. Between the mayhem of sound checks and the barking of producer Mike Hanrahan, I witnessed tearful reunions of icons of the 1960s and 1970s. I was overwhelmed and deeply humbled. Bren Berry of Aiken Promotions told me that the concert had been completely sold out. He added that we could have packed the venue many times over. I was particularly delighted and emotional to see Keith McCoy busy in his role as production assistant to Mike. Des Lee was already doing his sound check, despite the fact that his wife Brenda was dying. That wonderful lady had insisted on Des taking part, even though she only had a few weeks to live.

'The night was an unparalleled success. During the concert, I slipped away unnoticed and quietly went up onto the balcony, behind the audience, to watch the opening acts. There, I witnessed a sight which has been etched in my memory ever since. Everyone, the entire crowd, was on their feet applauding. Just two rows in front of me I saw the representatives of three generations with their arms linked and thoroughly enjoying them- selves – my teenage daughter Sean, my wife Anne and Philomena Lynott, the mother Phil Lynott. Philomena was representing her famous son's lifelong friendship with Fran O'Toole. I watched them for a moment. A tear rolled down my cheek before I turned and walked away.'

The sudden burst of publicity around the anniversary of the Miami massacre generated a new level of interest in the band and the fate that befell them. The thirty- somethings to whom Stephen had referred, who had seen the documentary or read about the incident in the newspapers, included myself. I sensed there was more to this particular story that needed to be told. I had heard about the band and was vaguely aware that they had been involved in a notorious accident. When I asked people of my own age what they knew about the Miami, many had similar recollections. Older people knew more, but the details were fading. The flurry of headlines about the concert and the memorial mass brought it all back again for many, but soon enough the moment, as it always does, would pass and it would recede again into the mist.

'I watched the excellent documentary that was screened and was immediately fascinated by the story of the Miami. The film depicted the early days of the band and featured interviews with, among others, Stephen Travers. Any sense of foreboding in the story was brilliantly cast aside as the film-makers recalled the excitement and fun of the showband years. This was not just about death, it was very much about the excitement of life. The viewer was lulled into a false sense of security; suddenly there was a scene of a bomb exploding in a city street. There was an ominous change in the mood of the piece. I was struck by Stephen's calm account of what had happened to him and found myself marvelling that he was still on the planet at all after all he had been through. I decided I wanted to talk to him. I got in touch with the editor on the show, Jonathan Golden, who kindly passed on my message to Stephen. He phoned one night and we spoke briefly before arranging to meet in Cork.

When we did finally meet, one of the most fascinating aspects for me was the fact that Stephen had forgiven the men who had carried out the attack. Now I was even more convinced that here was a man who had a story to tell. We talked at length about how best we could achieve that, but it was only later that he would reveal the central desire that motivated him – to meet the men who had murdered his friends.

It would lead to one of the strangest encounters in both our lives.

Chapter 20

It was a glorious sunny Saturday in 1975 and Chris Hudson was sauntering along Dublin's trendy Grafton Street. The young postman was enjoying his time off, strolling on the city's most fashionable thoroughfare, admiring the girls and occasionally stopping to listen to one of the many buskers. Over the bobbing masses of heads, he caught sight of a familiar face.

'I knew it was Fran O'Toole straight away. I called out to him and he grinned and waved his hand. I was really happy to bump into him again – it had been ages since we'd hung out. We exchanged the usual greetings and we talked about the Miami. He told me they had just taken on a brilliant new bass player and it was really working out. He appeared excited about his new album. He was in great form and I was delighted for him. Fran was destined to be a big star and it was brilliant to witness it all coming together for him. He loved touring and live gigs and mentioned that they were due to play the North again soon.

I remember saying to him, "Oh, Fran, is that okay? You should be careful up there", and he replied, "No, no, not at all – the ballrooms are neutral ground. Nobody would bother us there." That was the last time I spoke to him. Two weeks later, he was dead.'

Like so many Irish people in their twenties and thirties during the mid-1970s, Chris Hudson will always remember where he was when he heard the news that the Miami had been attacked. As we sit together drinking tea, he tells Stephen and me about that day.

'I was out on one of my rounds near Blackrock, so I didn't hear a news bulletin until late afternoon. But I was passing by a shop where a mutual friend worked. She came out and asked me if I had heard about the band. At first, I thought she was talking about Tom Dunphy's car crash, which was on everyone's lips. But she said, "No, I'm talking about the Miami, didn't you hear? They were killed." I stared at her, trying to work out what she was talking about. "Killed in a car crash?" I asked, but she replied, "Chris, they were murdered." Within a short while I heard it on the radio. I went straight home to my girlfriend. She knew Fran through me and we just sat there together, looking at each other in disbelief, crying our eyes out. We were devastated. I listened to the news every day and I didn't know who to blame. In the end, it didn't matter to me who was responsible. I just remember thinking, f**k them all, a plague on all their houses. For this country that had been through so much, killing the Miami was the real death of innocence ...'

And as he says the word 'innocence', Hudson suddenly inhales sharply and starts sobbing. He clutches his face, hiding the tears that are rolling down his cheeks. I'm astonished. For a moment, neither Stephen nor I know what to say. It's one of those remarkable moments, a reminder that, for many people, the pointless murder of the young musicians is still, after thirty-two years, impossible to understand.

It is obvious that Chris Hudson's memory of his friend-ship with Fran O'Toole is still fresh, a pain that runs deep, but is never far beneath the surface. 'It's still sore,' he says. 'I haven't talked about it for a long time and, suddenly, it all came back. It was just such a shock when it happened.'

While Chris composes himself, I reflect on how a twist of fate can bring together the strangest elements. Chris Hudson was an old friend of Fran O'Toole's, yet, over the years, he became closely involved with the organisation that had murdered him.

I ask him how he got to know Fran and he explains that he had been a fan of the singer since the days when Fran played with a rock outfit called The Chosen Few, based in Dún Laoghaire, in south Dublin. The 'in' crowd jokingly called it 'snob rock' because of all the well-to-do youngsters who had formed a clique that hung around the Caroline Club in the seaside town. 'I would get up on the stage in the middle of their set and make revolutionary speeches,' he recalls. 'It was, of course, nonsense, but we thought we could change the world. At that age, you feel you can do anything.'

Ironically, one member of the group would change the world a little. Bob Geldof was a familiar face on the scene and the soon-to-be-famous Boomtown Rats front man was a regular guest at Hudson's parents' home. 'It was a very cool scene, very fashionable and The Chosen Few had a select following,' Hudson recounts. 'We would hang out together all week, but the weekends were the highlight. I would finish work on Friday, change into my trendy gear and hitch a lift to Limerick if the lads were playing down there. We'd all pile into someone's van and travel to Cork or Galway, or wherever they were playing the following night. Even then, it was obvious that Fran O'Toole was a gigantic talent and that success was inevitable for him.'

The Chosen Few were not destined to become successful on the same scale as The Boomtown Rats, but it provided Fran with a platform to show the country that he was one of the most charismatic artists Ireland had ever produced.

Whilst Fran joined Ireland's most glamorous pop

band, Chris moved to England and they lost contact. Chris was on the road to becoming a committed socialist, joining the Communist Party in Britain and becoming involved in the trade union movement in Ireland in 1981, a few years after he returned. Working his way up through the ranks, Chris became one of the leaders in the Communication Workers Union, a position he held until he retired in 2005. It was through his work as a trade unionist that he would eventually find himself sitting across a table from the men who represented those who had killed his friend. And this is why Stephen and I are sitting with him today, in the plush surroundings of a Dublin hotel. We hope that Chris Hudson, through his contacts, will help us to meet with that very same organisation. We are well aware that a group as notoriously secretive as the UVF cannot be approached without a trusted introduction.

Initially, we had considered contacting directly the three men who had served time in prison in an attempt to get them to talk about their role in the Miami massacre. All three had been released long before their thirty-five-year recommended sentences expired, with Thomas Raymond Crozier the first to get out in March 1992, followed a year later by James Roderick McDowell, in March 1993. They were both freed under the 'tariff scheme' that awarded prisoners for 'cumulative good behaviour' while behind bars.

John James Somerville regained his freedom in November 1998, under the Life Sentence Review Scheme and not, as it has been thought, under the terms of the Good Friday agreement. Not much is known about Crozier and McDowell since they left prison, and we found it difficult to find out anything about them. Somerville, however, became a figure of controversy after his release, forming an alliance with a controversial preacher and ex-UVF man.

Due to our lack of knowledge as to the whereabouts of Crozier and McDowell and what we knew of Somerville's hardline views, Stephen and I thought we would get further in our efforts to talk to the UVF if we were guided by an intermediary, someone who would act as a go-between. However, as we would soon learn, even that approach was fraught with difficulty. Some individuals with previous access to the UVF flatly refused to assist us, saying it was a bad idea. We had been warned by others, such as Margaret Urwin of Justice for the Forgotten, to be careful. One journalist, who has been writing about the North for many years, told me in no uncertain terms that some of those we were seeking out were still very dangerous people. But we persisted. While we were aware that we might be accused of providing a platform for the organisation to justify murder, Stephen was steadfast in his resolve. He argued that even if the UVF agreed to talk to us, there was nothing they could say that would excuse what they had done. He was adamant that the story of the Miami massacre must include the cause and effects on all the players in the tragedy.

This could also be a unique opportunity for Chris Hudson to come to terms with the loss of one of his great heroes. If he agreed to help, he could provide us with a link to the loyalist paramilitary leadership and become the conduit through which we would finally come face-to-face with the architects of the incident.

Stephen was the first to mention Chris Hudson as a possible liaison. In the book *Loyalists*, by respected BBC journalist Peter Taylor, Chris is credited by one of the most senior UVF leaders with saving many lives through his clandestine work in bringing formerly bitterly entrenched parties to the table. In *Loyalists*, Taylor tells how Chris worked behind the scenes to create an avenue of dialogue between the various warring factions. The more I researched Chris' background, the more convinced I became that he was our man. When I telephoned the Communications Workers Union in Dublin, however, I was told he had retired and there was no forwarding number. I left my contact details, but the secretary was not very optimistic that he would get in touch. The trail appeared to have gone cold before we had even started. We were looking at other options when, out of the blue, Chris returned my call. After explaining why I had got in touch, we had a long conversation about his old friend.

He explained that recently, after his retirement, he had become a minister of the All Soul's Church in Belfast, a twin of the Unitarian Church on St Stephen's Green in Dublin. He agreed to meet with Stephen and me a few days later, saying that, in the meantime, he would pass on our request to his contacts in the UVF.

Chris received considerable attention during the 1980s because of his involvement in the famous Peace Train movement, which made front-page news across Europe. The Peace Train was a unique protest campaign aimed at highlighting the public's increasing frustration with the seemingly endless carnage in the North. Specifically, it was aimed at stopping the IRA's attempts to cut the Dublin–Belfast train service by planting explosives on the line. Chris eventually became joint-chairman of the Dublin Peace Train committee in 1988, and it was through this work that he met David Ervine. Chris was speaking at a meeting in Dublin and was introduced to Ervine, a fellow speaker, who was there in his capacity as a community worker. In fact, Ervine was a prominent member of the UVF.

Chris was enjoying a drink in a pub after the meeting when a friend pulled him aside to 'mark his cards', telling him that the man with the moustache was actually a loyalist paramilitary.

'Ervine must have realised that I knew who he was. He came over to my table and pulled me up over some remarks I had made on the radio criticising the loyalist paramilitaries. Ervine accused me of inaccuracies, but I dismissed his criticism, politely pointing out that I was entitled to my opinion. He said, "Well, why don't you come and meet them in Belfast and find out for yourself?" I had had a few pints by that stage and, in a fit of bravado, I agreed. Two weeks later, I got a phone call from Ervine to say the meeting was on. Coincidentally, I was in Belfast at a book launch and, despite very real considerations for my safety, found myself waiting outside the Duke of York Hotel. A car pulled up and a window was rolled down, then a voice demanded to know if I was Chris Hudson. I nodded and the man told me to get in. I climbed into the back seat and we took off. Ervine was sitting up front. He told me that I was being brought to meet these people in a house on the Shankill Road. Along the way, I reflected on the fact that, in the past, I had been outspoken about the UVF. I had even referred to them as murdering thugs on more than one occasion.

'We arrived and I was brought into a room that was decked out in all the UVF regalia. Flags, banners and standards lined the walls. I was kept waiting until two men came in. I would later discover that they were the two most senior commanders of the UVF. My initial impression was that they were not very friendly. Their handshake was cold and brief. As we sat down, I decided to lay my cards on the table. I said, "Look, I'm on my own, nobody knows I'm here except my wife. I'd like to take five minutes to say what I think about you because there's no point in me being here if I can't speak openly."

'They agreed and I immediately launched into a litany of their crimes. I accused them of slaughtering and killing innocent people in pubs, planting bombs in streets. I pointedly mentioned The Miami Showband. For those five minutes, I spoke non-stop about the unnecessary pain and suffering they had caused. I said, "I want to look into the faces of the leaders of the organisation that killed my friend and ask them why they did it." A man I would later get to know very well leaned across the table and said, "We regret we didn't do more." This was early 1993 and things were still very unstable. There had been talk of a loyalist ceasefire, but that wouldn't take place for another year. I asked him what he meant and he said, "We should have planted more bombs in Dublin, we should have stepped up our campaign in the South." "To what purpose?" I asked him. His response was that it had worked for the IRA – by bombing London they had forced the British establishment to listen. He said they should have done the same as the IRA to get the attention of the Irish government. He added, rather chillingly, that it was still a distinct possibility.

'I told him that planting bombs in Dublin would scupper any hope of dialogue with the Irish government. I don't think it cut much ice, their attitudes were hardened. We carried on talking for an hour and a half but, unfortunately, it was not a meeting of minds.'

The meeting ended and Chris remarked to Ervine as he left that they would probably dismiss him as 'some sort of lentil-eating peacenik from the South'.

'But I found out later from Ervine that this had in effect been a job interview. A week later, he phoned and told me that they wanted to meet me again. He explained that they needed a conduit between Belfast and Dublin. They wanted someone who, they felt, had some understanding of their issues, who would communicate their words exactly. They knew there were moves within the Republican movement toward peace talks. They had spoken with community leaders, such as Catholic priests, who told them there was a process there. They indicated their willingness to engage in that process.

'The next time I met them, they outlined their main points. "We understand that there is a process, we want to engage in this process. We want this conflict to end but, understand, we will target the enemy as long as the conflict continues." Certainly, that didn't exclude the South. They did continue the violence and, would later plant a bomb in the Widow Scanlon's pub in Dublin.'

Chris wrote down what the loyalists had to say on a piece of paper and gave it to Fergus Finlay, an aide to the Irish Foreign Minister, Dick Spring. Over the delicate period leading to the loyalist ceasefire of 1994, a trust was established between the UVF and their 'man in Dublin'. 'It took me a while to realise the role I had taken on,' Hudson says. 'I thought I was just doing my little bit, but they apparently had placed a greater emphasis on what I was doing on their behalf.'

Hudson found himself on the receiving end of angry phone calls from both sides when some incident threatened to derail the talks. Each one pointed the finger of blame.

'In the middle of our dialogue the Shankill Road bombing in 1993 happened. The IRA blew up a fish shop beneath the offices of a loyalist organisation. Ervine rang, screaming blue murder, as if I had something to do with it. I told him, "David, I'm trying my best here", but he actually shouted down the phone, "Well, try f**king harder!"'

As Chris battled to keep the lines of communication open, his role as an intermediary between the UVF leadership and Taoiseach Albert Reynolds necessitated numerous phone calls to and from Belfast. He devised a series of code names, which he used when discussing the various participants. As Peter Taylor outlined in *Loyalists*: 'The CLMC (Combined Loyalist Military Command) became the 'Full Cricket Team' and the UVF, 'Half the Cricket Team'; the Irish Foreign Minister, Dick Spring, was 'the Grocer' and his aide Fergus Finlay, 'the Grocer's Assistant'.

Ervine was called 'the Milkman' because he had once worked a milk round. The UVF second-in-command, who had been instrumental, along with Ervine, in pushing forward the peace process, was called 'the Craftsman'. Although the Milkman could decipher the politics, Chris knew it was the Craftsman who could deliver the ceasefire.

This was the man Chris now proposed we meet. He attributed the eventual moves toward peace and the continuing UVF ceasefire to him and still holds him in high regard for bringing the UVF in from the cold.

'I have always said that I could never accept what they did, but that I applaud their efforts towards a lasting peace. The Craftsman is officially second-in-command of the UVF, but many believe him to be the main figure. He has already been made aware of your desire to meet the men who were jailed for the Miami massacre, but has advised against it. When I spoke to the Craftsman, he indicated that Somerville is wired to the moon. He told me that while Somerville was in prison, even the other Volunteers would stay away from him. He is considered an extremist, a person who cannot be trusted. He doesn't know much about Crozier and McDowell. He said they went to ground following their release and didn't have much more to do with the organisation after that.'

However, the Craftsman had indicated that he might be prepared to meet Stephen in person.

'Is he accepting responsibility for the murders?' Stephen asked Chris.

'No, not at all. He would not think that way. In fact, when I first met him I thought he was a hardliner, probably one of the most extreme UVF men I've ever met. I remember speaking at a conference once and the Craftsman was there. I had brought along a friend of mine, a member of the IRA, and introduced them to one another. I asked this friend later what he thought of him and he described him as very cold and calculating. This hardened Provo said the Craftsman was a man he would not like to cross. Over the years, I've got to know him better and I don't see that in him anymore. He is very calm, never raises his voice. He's not necessarily an educated man, but he is well read and is well informed on Irish history. I think he must have read every book that has been written about the Northern conflict.

'He took up arms to defend Ulster against what he saw as a tidal wave of Irish Republicanism. Not so long ago, the twenty-six counties would have been seen as the breeding ground for the IRA. It is an attitude that is still apparent in some places today. You go into loyalist areas in Belfast and you will see the Israeli flag dotted around … they really associate the Six Counties in the province with the Israeli struggle in the Middle East. Like the Israelis, they feel they are totally surrounded by the enemy and that all it would take is one big battle and they would be annihilated.'

Despite coming from such an entrenched position,

Chris revealed that there are certain things about which the Craftsman feels uncomfortable. 'Many terrible things were done in the name of both causes. The Miami massacre is one such incident that the Craftsman would say the UVF is not proud of. He once told me that, on a personal level, he was sorry that one of my friends had been killed. I told him that I could not accept an apology.'

Chris explained that the Craftsman was just a foot-soldier in the UVF when the Miami incident took place; he actually served in the colour party at the funeral of one of the bombers. However, he tells us that in his current position as a leader of the UVF, the Craftsman is prepared to offer us an insight into what he understands of the events of that night. We agree to meet him. We shake hands with Chris and he tells us he'll be in contact. True to his word, a week later he calls to say the Craftsman is ready.

Stephen and I are sitting in the lounge of the Europa Hotel in Belfast, waiting for Chris Hudson to arrive. As I take in the ornate surroundings and classic design of this fantastic building, I reflect on the fact that it had once earned the dubious reputation as the most bombed hotel in Europe.

Today, Belfast is far removed from the grainy newsreel depictions of cordoned-off streets and gutted buildings that were broadcast on television news bulletins during my youth, though reminders of its history and divisions are never far away. As we approached the Europa, Stephen and I could not help but notice the massive Union Jack mural emblazoned on a gable end just around the corner.

Belfast is less than three hours' drive from Dublin, but as I contemplate our reasons for being here, I feel we are much farther from home. We have arranged to meet Chris before we are brought to the Craftsman. It had been agreed previously that the meeting would take place on neutral ground, as it were, so it has been decided that Chris' church will be the venue.

Stephen is quieter than usual, calm, but obviously deep in thought. This is a crucial moment for him. In less than an hour, he will come face-to-face with one of the leaders of the terrorist organisation that almost killed him. For the past thirty-one years, he has wanted to put a face to the group that carried out the Miami massacre. Now, we are about to do so, and I wonder if he is having second thoughts.

'No,' he says quietly. 'But I am apprehensive that, after thirty-one years, I'll be able to stand up for the lads. I want to represent them, my family and myself and, in a strange way, I'm aware that what is said today may also reflect on the unionist people.'

He admits he hasn't slept well. He had just two hours' rest before flying to Belfast from Cork and is concerned because his mind needs to be sharp today.

'I normally just lie down and fall asleep, but last night I kept thinking just how important today is. I spent the night running through all the various scenarios that may happen. I don't want to waste a second of it. There can be no small talk. I assume we are meeting somebody who is going to state their case and explain how they thought at the time. From our point of view, hopefully, we will learn what motivated people to join an organisation that sanctions murder in pursuit of a cause. Maybe they will be able to put some flesh on the bones of the people involved. But, most importantly, we will find out if they have learned any lessons from the incident. By tonight, we will know if their opinions and attitudes have softened over the years or if they have become more resistent. I would like to think that they would acknowledge the error of their ways and assure us that something like this will never happen again. That's probably the best thing I can hope for today. That they realise that continuing along the road of violence is futile.'

I ask him what he considers the best possible outcome.

'Well, I hope that they will learn something from meeting us today. We can't change them or their beliefs, but maybe there will be, at the very least, a mutual understanding, if not an appreciation of values. I'm under no illusions that the Miami holds any greater significance for them than any of their other atrocities, but if they can acknowledge their guilt, then who knows where today might lead? By this evening we will know.'

'When did you first want to meet these men, Stephen?' I ask him.

'1 August 1975, when I woke up in hospital, the day after the murders,' he replies firmly.

Somewhere in his mind, Stephen Travers has spent the past three decades waiting for this moment.

Chapter 21

Chris Hudson crosses the foyer to greet us. He is businesslike. The atmosphere is very different from our relaxed meeting in Dublin a week earlier. Stephen and I listen intently as he goes over a few ground rules for the meeting.

'First of all, the Craftsman wants you to understand that he is meeting you in a personal capacity. He will not speak as an official spokesperson of the UVF. He wants you to understand that he will advance his own opinion and not that of his organisation.'

He lists more conditions. I will not be allowed to record him during the meeting, but will be permitted to take notes. There is also one simple, but important, consideration – when they first meet, is Stephen prepared to shake his hand? It appears to be the most important protocol of all. Stephen nods his agreement. We are ready.

We stand up and walk briskly outside into the bright day and wait anxiously on the pavement while Chris hails one of Belfast's famous black taxies. It is eerily quiet on the streets and Chris makes a few jokes about how the city empties around the 12 July holidays. It helps to distract us from the increasing tension during a very long ten-minute journey to the university district of the city.

The sun comes out as we wind our way through the streets. By the time we arrive at the pretty suburb, the sunlight is streaming through the trees. We stop outside Chris' church. I am admiring the beautiful building when I notice a figure arriving at the same time as us. We get out of the taxi and I turn my head to get a better look. Chris ushers us ahead before he turns back to talk to the other man.

I quietly mention to Stephen that I think this is him. Chris joins us and, as he unlocks the church door, I ask him if that is the Craftsman. He confirms that it is. This is going to happen after all. The brightness outside is snuffed out by the cool, damp dark of the interior of the old church as we step inside. It feels ancient and peaceful, with the dust of ages settled on the flagstones. The altar is immediately to our left. There are raised pews and I notice some faded RAF emblems in a far corner.

Chris follows us inside and directs us to the sacristy,

where he unlocks a small, thick, oak door. We stoop and enter a miniature, star-shaped chamber. A round table dominates this stone enclosure. Massive wooden beams loom over us. The walls host anonymous pictures and old paintings. There is an imposed stillness in the room, which I feel certainly holds many secrets of its own. Chris takes his leave of us momentarily. We sit down at the table and wait. Silence.

Stephen asks if I am afraid. I tell him I'm not, but, in truth, I am getting increasingly uneasy. Just who are we meeting in this strange place? After months of preparation, we are here at last. But until this moment, I hadn't thought about the dangers of meeting a man who commands one of the world's most secretive and notorious terror organisations. While focusing on our efforts to make this day possible, I had neglected to consider our vulnerability. Are we safe here? It hadn't even occurred to me that we might be in danger. I cannot even begin to imagine what it must be like for Stephen. I don't get time to ponder any further. We hear steps coming and I turn.

'Stephen,' I whisper, 'if you feel angry, try to hold back.'

He doesn't reply.

The heavy door opens and Chris enters the room. Behind him walks the Craftsman. He is not as big as I had imagined, but looks fit and tanned. His head is shaved and he is a hard-looking man. He nods slightly during the introductions. In the brief moment of a handshake, Stephen appears to look into his soul. We now know his name, but for obvious reasons we will continue to refer to him by his code name.

As we sit, I take a closer look at him. I presume he is in his late fifties. Under strong glasses, his eyes are small and hooded. He is wearing a tweed jacket over a neat polo shirt. I catch a glimpse of some old tattoos on his forearm, but it is not possible to make out what they depict. Stephen, sitting on my right, faces him directly. Chris, as mediator, has taken up a position between them. The Craftsman opens a briefcase and removes a thin sheaf of papers. Without looking up, he launches immediately into what is obviously a prepared statement.

He speaks slowly and quietly. His accent is distinctly Northern, but clear and easy to understand. There is no discernible emotion in his voice. He begins by reminding us that he is here in a personal capacity. He states that this is not an official meeting and he has not been ordered to attend. He has, however, agreed to be here so that he can discuss several theories about 'what happened to you' – as he says this, his small, glinting eyes attempt to evade Stephen's. We can disregard these theories if we wish, he adds, that is our choice. He reiterates that this is simply his personal understanding of the event. He tells us that he has looked into the Miami incident and has tried to examine it in a 1975 context.

First, he offers a description of the men who were arrested and convicted for their participation in the massacre. He hopes to give us what he calls 'the broader picture of what was going on at the time'.

'Of the three men I knew John Somerville best. Crozier I knew only casually, and McDowell I didn't know at all.

'John Somerville is a man of extremes. He was always a bit strange. While in prison, he was meticulous in appearance and personal cleanliness. He showered all the time. He liked to exercise and would run around the yard every day. After each session, he would come back into his cell, take his trainers off and lay them on the ground. Then, he would wash them. He would remove the laces and clean them with a toothbrush. He was imprisoned in Long Kesh with other loyalist prisoners. Although they could visit each other in their cells to pass the time, nobody visited John. A man who shared his cell for many years told me later that even though he spoke to John every day, he felt he never got to know the real John Somerville.

'In prison, John found God and got into a religion that I personally find hard to understand. It's very intolerant of other beliefs or traditions. It's a persuasion that suits John's mentality. He was always right; somewhere in his head, John convinced himself that he was right and everyone else was wrong, to the extent that he fell out with many people, even with his close friends. Once, I got him a job in a shipyard. When it closed down or laid-off workers, he lost his job. He blamed me for that.'

The Craftsman then describes Somerville's behaviour in court when he went on trial for the murders of the Miami men and Patrick Falls.

'He spoke from the dock about how he never had any intention of killing anybody on the night the Miami was ambushed. In answer to the prosecution that he was responsible for the deaths of the musicians, he turned to the judge and said, "I did not kill anybody that night." He was making it clear to the judge that, as far as he was concerned, the accusations were lies. He insisted that while he was there that night, he had never set out to kill anyone. In prison, as he had in court, he would speak openly about the murder of Patrick Falls, for which he was sentenced and imprisoned. But during the ten years he served for that murder, nobody ever heard him talk about The Miami Showband. Maybe it was just too painful for him, perhaps it was the memory of his brother, who was blown to pieces, it may have even been remorse. I don't know, but whatever the reason, he never mentioned it.'

The Craftsman shuffles through his papers before he clears his throat to speak again. From our side of the table there is only silence.

'As for Crozier and McDowell, I cannot tell you much about them. And perhaps they might not tell you much more than I can about the events of that night. While I realise the importance of closure for you here today,' he glances up at Stephen for the first time, 'I'm telling you now that they were just foot-soldiers. They were given orders and told to bring their uniforms. They were handed a gun and told there was an operation on that night and to report for duty at a particular time and place.

'I only heard last week that Crozier is also a born-again Christian. I understand that when he left prison, he met up with another ex-loyalist, a woman, which is a rare thing in the UVF. This woman he took advantage of financially and became a person non-gratis among the UVF.

'Of Roddy McDowell there is very little known. He was sentenced and served his time quietly. When he came out, he kept his head down and there is very little known about him apart from that.

'There may have been other, more sinister people there that night that I'm not aware of. I don't know who they are but, most likely, the people who could tell what really happened that night either cannot or will not. They are more than likely dead or they are in prison for other things. Perhaps it can be assumed that people like Robin Jackson were there. I wouldn't doubt it. He was also a born again Christian.'

The Craftsman has been speaking with his head down for almost the entire time, reading carefully from the neatly handwritten notes in front of him. He pauses for a moment and looks up while he explains that within the UVF there is an understanding when it comes to discussing past events. 'Even today, it is difficult to speak of these things,' he says staring straight at Stephen. 'There is a code of honour. You don't discuss operations from the past. We have a saying, "Those who know, don't talk, and those who talk don't know …"

'You will not meet these men face-to-face and the organisation does not want to talk about them,' he adds. 'As far as the organisation is concerned, Gusty Spence issued an apology to all of the innocent victims of our campaign at Fernhill House in 1994. There will be no apologies made for individual cases because where then do you draw the line?'

There is no reaction from Stephen. I am furiously taking down notes. The Craftsman has not been talking particularly fast, but he is covering a lot of ground. From where I am sitting, I cannot see Stephen's face. He is only the width of the table away from the Craftsman, but there is no indication of what may be going through his mind. I look for hints. I glance at his hands on the table, but they are relaxed, with one thumb moving slowly and confidently over the other.

The Craftsman is now speaking directly to Stephen. It

appears, for the moment, that he has departed entirely from his notes.

'I'm proud of what I have done. I'm satisfied that everything I did or was involved in was right, but there have been incidents carried out in my name, or rather in the name of my organisation that we are not proud of – the Shankill butchers and The Miami Showband are right up there at the top of the list.'

The Craftsman has offered this snippet of information for no apparent reason. It is hard to decipher why he would suddenly steer away from his well-prepared speech to declare his feelings on this subject. Before I have a chance to consider his words further, he begins the next part of his statement. Having outlined his incredibly limited knowledge of the three men jailed for the Miami atrocity, he now embarks on an explanation of what may have happened on the night. First, though, there are a few theories he wants to dismiss.

'I cannot recall where I heard this or when it was first suggested, but there was a theory that the Miami was mistaken for another showband that night. There was a rumour that another showband playing in the province had an IRA member among them, but I have found no evidence whatsoever to support this.

'Perhaps the most ridiculous allegation was that the Miami was carrying the bomb that went off when they were pulled over that night. This was released in a statement that I think came from Belfast, in other words, from headquarters. I looked at the wording of the statement and I recognised who issued it from the language used. I was able to subsequently identify them. In effect, they were suggesting that the Miami was being used by the IRA to ferry bombs or weapons over the border. This was a ridiculous statement issued in the immediate aftermath and can be discounted entirely.

'Another theory was that they wanted to put the bomb in the van and between Newry and Dublin it would go off, killing the Miami and all witnesses, the intention being that people would think, well, who can you trust anymore? Initially, I dismissed this out of hand, but when I thought more about it, I decided to look at it again. It's an interesting theory, but one that I eventually realised held no weight. The people who were involved in the operation that night were only interested in the military results of their mission. They would not consider world opinion. They were not trying to play mind-games to fool the population into thinking a particular way about a pop group.'

At this point, the Craftsman launches into a detailed explanation of the methods the UVF employed when handling explosives.

'In the 1970s, bombs were very crude devices. They were dangerous to handle and very unstable. The timing devices used were alarm clocks. The minute hand was used as short-timers where the maximum amount of delay could be only fifty-nine minutes. The hour hand would afford anything from short to a maximum delay time of eleven hours and fifty-nine minutes and was used as a long-timer. One hand would be removed depending on the delay time required. In this case, I believe the big hand was removed, leaving the small, or hour, hand to activate the bomb.

'I do not believe that it was timed to go off soon after you left the roadblock. I don't believe they would risk using a short-timer. To do this, they would need to know the exact time you were to arrive in order to set the timer. There was no way of knowing this. Perhaps they would have known that the show would end at a particular time, but for all they knew you might have stopped for a sandwich or a cup of coffee. They would not take a chance that you would arrive and leave within fifty-nine minutes. My belief is that a long-timer was used, but due to the crudeness of the device the re-soldered hour hand may have fallen off while placing it in your van and triggered the device.

'After consideration, my belief is that this was an accident. They were killed by mistake while loading a bomb into the back of the van. Their intention, I would suggest, is that some time later, possibly many hours later, the bomb on a long-timer would go off when you were already back in Dublin and safe in your beds. The bomb would, of course, obliterate the bus and later the UVF would claim responsibility. It would have been a propaganda exercise, to prove to the Irish authorities that we could, and would, strike anywhere we chose. I believe this was the intention.'

By now, the Craftsman has put down his notes and is discussing the operation with the confidence of a lecturer. He claims that, over the past twelve years, he has discussed the Miami incident with the UVF leadership on three separate occasions and this is their conclusion. He reveals that the Miami operation was approved by the UVF high command as opposed to a renegade group operating with autonomy, discounting yet another myth surrounding the Miami massacre.

'You must understand, bombs were not used casually. People were terrified of them. Careful planning was always involved. My information is that the initial idea came from the local group. The group involved were big enough to have their own materials and guns, but they were obliged to ask the leadership for approval. They received this by describing the proposal as a propaganda exercise.

'I honestly believe this was a plan that went wrong. Both as a man and as a UVF member, I sincerely believe that nothing would have been gained by deliberately setting out to kill the Miami. The Miami was popular with both Protestant and Catholic communities, indeed I had seen them myself on a number of occasions. Trying to discredit them by killing them and saying they were carrying bombs could not outweigh the negative consequences.'

With that, he pauses, shuffles his papers and sits back. He crosses his arms defensively. For a moment, there is no reaction from anyone at the table. For the entire time that the Craftsman has been talking, nobody has interrupted him.

I'm trying to take in all that he has said, while glancing at Stephen to gauge his reaction. After thirty-one years, he has just been told that his friends were killed in a tragic accident by very considerate terrorists using a politically correct bomb. I wonder what he is feeling. How will he react? I have come to learn that anger is not an emotion associated with Stephen, but surely this would enrage a saint. He has just been offered an innocuous explanation that this was all just a terrible mistake. There are no apologies, only a blithe explan-ation. I am incredulous. I try to remain detached, but having shared experiences and mixed emotions with Stephen over the course of the past few months, I would understand if a rising tide of anger burst from him in a torrent of furious indignation.

Stephen knows only too well that Somerville intended to kill that night. His own brother, Wesley, was one of the men placing a huge bomb in the musicians' minibus.

John Somerville is a self-confessed murderer and during his trial was proven to be a consummate liar. The reference to 'another showband with an IRA member' is nothing more than a red herring. Stephen is already satisfied that the officer who arrived on the scene would have had every opportunity to prime the bomb with his cohorts at the well-documented nearby safe-house belonging to James Mitchell.

Lookouts monitored the movements of the band inside and outside the Castle Ballroom. The car, clearly seen by their road manager racing ahead of him, would have had ample time to announce the imminent arrival of the band. The mathematics of big- and small-timing devices were simple for Stephen, he can instantly work out all the possibilities. I know him well and he can easily tear these arguments apart. But, to my utter amazement, he is not drawn into, nor does he engage in, a debate on personalities or mechanics. He completely ignores the lecture on the psychology and modus operandi of the UVF. He appreciates the Craftsman's attempt to minimise the blame to his organisation; after all, that is his mission today. Stephen knows he has been subjected to a PR and damage-limitation exercise.

Unexpectedly, I witness one of those unique moments when the unimagined happens. With just one sentence, Stephen completely changes the atmosphere and disarms all present. He leans forward to address the Craftsman, not taking his eyes off him for a second. The Craftsman stares back, readying himself for the onslaught.

'Would you agree that the men who murdered my friends disgraced the noble cause of unionism?'

It is a remarkable opening shot. In a split-second, it annihilates completely any pre-planned strategy. The word 'noble' has changed everything. There is a palpable release of tension in the room. Even the Craftsman's hardened features take on the appearance of surprise. It is a case study in dignified composure and diplomacy. At a stroke, Stephen has condemned an act but shown respect for a people, their traditions and aspirations.

The Craftsman side-steps the question. 'What do you believe?' he asks. 'Do you believe the showband was deliberately targeted?'

'I believe there is no excuse for murder,' Stephen says.

'I think that once the bomb went off, they lost the plot,' the Craftsman says. 'They panicked and opened fire.'

'Trained soldiers … losing the plot … methodically checking that the musicians were all dead … kicking Brian's lifeless body … shooting Fran twenty-two times in the face …' Stephen counters.

The Craftsman sighs and says something I can't quite catch about people having their own way of seeing things.

'I know what I saw with my own eyes,' Stephen replies.

'You are the better judge,' the Craftsman acknowledges 'You were there, I wasn't. I am offering a reason here, not an excuse, just a reason. I believe they lost the plot when things went wrong.'

'I believe they set out to kill us all that night. There were to be no witnesses to the roadblock, no survivors to tell what happened. Everyone would die and the suspicion of an involvement in terrorism would hang over our heads, and that of our families, forever.'

'I cannot dismiss that,' the Craftsman nods, 'but it is just another theory.'

The planned thirty-minute meeting lasts for five hours. Both men are courteous to a fault. They discuss history, politics, economics and their own personal journeys arriving at this time and place. They explore common ground and find there is much of it. Stephen is forthright in his conviction that the Craftsman was engaged in a damage-limitation exercise for his organisation, but said he understood that to be necessary. 'If all we do is point out the negative, then we will remain in the mire,' he says.

Stephen tells the Craftsman, 'I was asked this morning what I thought the best outcome of this meeting might be, to which I replied, "I would like to be convinced that the violence is done with."'

'Hopefully you will be,' the Craftsman replies. 'We are now convinced that violence is not the way to achieve our aims. I regularly visit the historic First World War sites. When I go to France, I clearly see the futility of war.'

'Is your war over?'

'We are engaged in dialogue and that is very important, but we have to move carefully and slowly. It's like turning a big ocean liner, which must be done with great caution. I must give credit to the leadership of the IRA for their efforts to take their people down an alternative path. There is no point in running forward under a flag of peace if, when we look over our shoulder, nobody is following. We must take the focus of our young people away from violence as a solution to our problems. We show them that we have much to be proud of in our heritage. We encourage our young to join the Somme societies, and so on.

'It's important for loyalists that they can feel safe in their own space. But in 1969, when the nationalists viewed the attacks on their communities as a pogrom, we viewed what they were doing as an insurrection, a threat to our way of life. We felt we had to stand up and fight or go under.'

'From the beginning you silenced the voices of reason,' Stephen counters. 'Captain Terence O'Neill and later David Trimble in fact secured the union for you, but you supported the bigots who incessantly stoked the fires of sectarianism.'

The Craftsman furrows his brow and replies, 'We were often ill-served by our political leaders, who were happy to use us but ready to denounce us when it suited them. It took me a long time to understand that the events of

1969 had been a continuation of things that had been going on for a very long time. And until the Good Friday Agreement in 1998, that's how the loyalist community had always felt – like a community under siege from the nationalists who would have whittled them down had they not made a stand. The only way to lift a siege is to lift the siege mentality.'

I interject for a moment to ask why he personally became involved in the loyalists' armed struggle.

'I saw the UVF as a counter-balance to the IRA. I was a bit of a romantic when I joined the UVF in 1966 and I knew a bit about Irish history. They had their heroes, such as the men of 1916, and we had ours. I read about Tom Barry and the so-called glory days of the IRA and the UVF, but I learned that it is a myth – there is no such thing as glory when it comes to war. That's the reality and we have to get away from that mindset. I have had to accept that some of the arguments that I held for thirty years are not relevant any more. The South is no longer a priest-ridden society and it's not the bad economy it once was. I'm fifty-seven now,' the Craftsman adds wearily. 'I have children and I have to think about the future for them.'

Three hours into the meeting, my hand is aching from scribbling my unpractised shorthand. Chris, too, is anxious to avoid fatigue setting in and asks diplomatically if we would like to wind up the meeting. But neither Stephen nor the Craftsman wants to stop.

'This is good for me,' the Craftsman says, 'it is like therapy. To be honest, I knew this day would come. A long time ago, when I first met Chris and he mentioned that he knew Fran O'Toole, I knew then that some day I would have to sit down and answer these questions.'

'It is very heartening to hear you say that violence is wrong,' Stephen says.

'Look, I have had comrades die at my feet. I have had the blood of my enemies and my friends on my boots. At the end of the day, it makes little difference, blood is blood. Don't get me wrong, I'm not a pacifist. I believe I have a God-given right to defend myself, my family, my way of life and my country. That's my justification for being in the UVF. But the methods must change. Hard lessons were learned and an important one is that there is a better way than killing. No matter how just your cause, there will be others who feel differently and their views have to be tolerated.'

Stephen asks the Craftsman about his own background. He says he was born and grew up in the loyalist stronghold of the Shankill Road, in Belfast. He describes it as small, insular society where the children were well-versed in the sacrifices of the Somme and those made by their ancestors for the province. 'At the same time, there was nothing sectarian about my upbringing,' he says. 'I was not brought up in an atmosphere of hating Catholics. In fact, our family was seen as not quite typical of the area.

I remember street parties for the Queen, for example, and we were not invited. My father was a Labour man and that was not considered a respectable background for a unionist.'

He joined the UVF in 1966, against a backdrop of increasing tensions in Belfast with the anniversaries of the Battle of the Somme and the Easter Rising occurring in the same year. Across the province there were fears that the IRA was about to mount a major offensive to coincide with the anniversary and, like many young men, the Craftsman was willing to defend his homeland.

'I started off as a volunteer and then became an officer commanding a platoon of twenty-five to thirty-five people. It was similar to the structure of the army. There were no cells like those that came along later because the security forces had not got their act together at that point and there was no fear of infiltration. Later, I was assigned to battalion HQ staff. I trusted everyone I knew. I knew the names of their wives and their children and I was involved in their lives and their family's lives.'

'Families sometimes fall out,' Stephen remarks.

'I know, but it never happened to our unit. We were entirely self-sufficient. We were willing and able to defend ourselves. If we needed new guns or bombs, we went out and got them ourselves.'

Although the Craftsman admits to being arrested 'many times' over the years, he has never been charged with any offence. 'I've been lucky in that way. Paranoia for a man in my position is a valuable affliction. It has kept me alive. It's not a nice way to live, but that's why I'm sitting here today. People might say that my life is self-inflicted, because we come from violence that we created the way we live, but we are victims too. I didn't see my sons for the whole time I was on the run. Until the Good Friday Agreement, I couldn't lead a normal life. Only then could I attempt to pick up where I left off so many years before. I'm just telling it the way it was for me. I'm sitting here telling the truth because, for some strange reason, I believe today is good for the soul. Ultimately, there is only One who can forgive me any wrong I have done and he is not in this room ...'

Stephen pauses before replying, 'We possibly have a lot in common. If we knew each other under better circumstances, we probably would have liked similar music, the same bands. We might even have been friends.'

'I liked the showbands,' the Craftsman replies. 'I even saw the Miami play a few times. I feel British, but I've always been into traditional Irish music, for example. I have no problem with being an Irishman, but when I go to the South, as far as I'm concerned, I'm on holiday in a different country. I believe that, as a UVF man, I have tried to understand the Irish better than they have tried to understand me. Maybe they don't see it that way, but it's changing all the time, there is a sea change ...'

'At what point did we diverge?' Stephen asks him. 'When did our paths go off on tangents?'

'It's probably difficult for you understand, but I've drunk with guys who have tried to kill me. I got back into the building trade where some of those guys had been my friends.'

'Did you hate them then?'

'No, I did not. When we were young, they joined the IRA while I was doing what I was doing. One of them had been away in prison for many years for his IRA activities. When I met him after all that time I said to him, "Ah, you've been away for a while! What about ya?" and he said "Ah, ya know yourself", and we both laughed. You know, there are misconceptions that we were all a bunch of psychopaths, but nobody said to me, "Go kill a Catholic." Innocent people did get killed, but there is a big difference in fighting for what you believe in and being a psychopath.'

'What is your concept of a psychopath?'

'I have met those who enjoyed killing,' the Craftsman explains. 'I've seen guys hysterically laughing about killing until they got physically sick. I have never experienced that myself, I could never feel good about it. I could not possibly imagine feeling good about killing. If it is your duty, then you must kill – but kill with regret, even if the target is an enemy soldier.'

'Can you admit you got it wrong?' Stephen asks him.

'It's easy to do so with the benefit of hindsight.'

'Would you say it publicly?'

'We are working on it.'

'Is there hope for the future?'

'Times have changed. A lot of things are different across the North and South now. The South is not the priest-ridden society it once was and the economy has been a revelation. The UVF is in the process of going away, but there has to be a structure to that. There has to be a redirection and that is why we are creating more awareness among the young of our full history. I grew up on the Shankill Road with the sacrifices of the Somme never far away, but I didn't realise the scale of the killing until I went there myself and saw the endless rows of graves. Now when we take our children to the battlefields of Northern France, the first lesson they learn is the futility of war. We bring kids from both communities and it is a culture shock for some of them to find themselves on the bus with Catholics or Protestants. It's all part of the process ...'

'It's good that you are able to channel that energy into something else.'

'You're absolutely right. I'm also a great advocate of education. It has helped break down barriers that have been built up over forty years. I have a great interest in it and I want to become more involved. Just recently, I discovered that of the top-ten failure rates in schools in the province, four are on the loyalist Shankill Road.'

Stephen sighs and says, 'Ignorance is the great enemy of civilisation. Without an understanding of other traditions and cultures, there can be no co-operation. I want to live in a united Ireland, united in tolerance and respect. The Miami was a model for that. We are currently campaigning to erect a memorial to the memory of The Miami Showband. I have accused a government minister of attempting to airbrush sections of recent Irish history out of existence.'

The Craftsman replies, 'We have learned valuable lessons, too. I'm telling you that war is futile, but I am proud of the UVF and the Volunteers. If you ask me if my beliefs and aspirations have changed, I would say no, but my views on the methodology to safeguard and promote them have. Although any threat to the sovereignty of my country would force me back to war. We will always maintain a praetorian guard and if we feel that our sovereignty is under threat, we will take up arms again. The bottom line is that we signed up to the Good Friday Agreement and that agreement is like a business contract. If any one of the parties breaks its terms, then all bets are off as far as I'm concerned.'

'With regard to the British officer at the scene of the murders,' Stephen asks, 'was it Captain Robert Nairac?'

'I can't help you with that,' the Craftsman replies, 'but it is a possibility which I wouldn't rule out.'

'One final thing,' Stephen adds. 'I spoke to Helen

McCoy, Brian's widow, and asked if she would be able to forgive her husband's murderers. She said she could if she was sincerely asked. She made the point that Somerville was once asked by the BBC what he would say to the families of the Miami. His response was that he had family killed yet asked God to forgive them. To me, it sounds like an opportunity lost for a born-again Christian. What do you think forgiveness is?'

'I suppose, for me, forgiveness comes from being able to get past a difficult event in the past. A lot of people are trying to find a better way to do things. We have to look forward and not back, if that's what it takes for some people to move on then they should be prepared to forgive. Never forget what it has cost all of us, but forgive … Yes.'

Chapter 22

After the meeting, Stephen and I sat down to eat with Chris, our minds in overdrive trying to make sense of what we had just experienced. The Craftsman had given us a lot to think and talk about.

Stephen accepted that the Craftsman no longer believed in violence as a means to achieve his political aims. His attitude was that the Craftsman was engaged in a PR exercise for the UVF, and he fully understood the reasoning behind that.

'The dialogue between us felt like that of ordinary men caught up in extraordinary events. Not pretentious, accusatory, condescending or self-righteous. It was not for the sake of the book. I talked with him like Fran, Brian or Tony would have; curious, like a musician. I spoke for me and for them and, representing them, I felt the UVF didn't scare us now and we weren't afraid anymore. Perhaps there is hope for the future if such men can convince others that there's a better way forward. However, for all of our wishful thinking, we both know that it would be a dreadful mistake simply to agree to disagree with his account of the Miami incident. The Craftsman's assertion that the Miami was a tragic accident, an operation that went dreadfully wrong, just didn't ring true.'

Another intriguing meeting was to prove our instinct on that score to be correct.

I received a phone call from Stephen on New Year's Day 2007. He was in London on a business trip, so I knew it must be important.

'I've just received a contact number for one of the police officers who worked on the Miami murder case and I've been told that he will talk to us. It's very important that we meet him.'

Astounded by this latest development, I quickly scribbled down the details. For months I had made various efforts to contact any of the detectives who were involved in the Miami case. They all proved futile because the nature of their work meant that the people I had thought could help were reluctant to put me in touch with any of them. Now I had a number, a Northern one, and it belonged to James Patrick O'Neill. I told Stephen I would call the man the following day to arrange a meeting.

I looked at the information I'd hurriedly scrawled.

O'Neill. I was sure that was the name of a policeman we had already written about. I checked my notes. Sure enough, it was none other than the man who had been the Scene of Crime Officer (SOCO), one of the first at the scene after the Miami attack. This man could provide a clear perspective of the events of 31 July 1975 – it was imperative that we speak to him.

I called the following day and waited anxiously while his phone rang. Finally, he picked up. I asked to speak to James O'Neill, explained who I was and why I was calling and, to my relief, he agreed to see us.

The following Monday, Stephen and I walked into the Skylon Hotel in north Dublin, full of anticipation. There was no way of knowing what this man could tell us. But either way, we expected an interesting day.

We walked through the foyer and glanced around at various men sitting alone. We approached a couple of them and asked if they were James O'Neill. Some smiled, but all shook their heads. I was getting a little bit anxious, thinking he had perhaps changed his mind. The last table had a couple sitting at it, so we turned in the opposite direction and were walking towards the exit when a voice called out, 'Are you Stephen Travers?' A well-dressed, well-built man was following us.

'I am indeed,' Stephen said, and the man introduced himself as James O'Neill. We shook hands and went to the table where his wife, Adelaide, was sitting.

I would never have guessed that the couple at the table were the people we were looking for. Perhaps in my subconscious mind I was looking for a much older man, worn down with years of tough police work, but James O'Neill and his wife were relaxed, calm and very friendly. They looked like a middle-class couple, with an air of retirement from a successful business life. Over the course of the next few hours, I would learn just how wrong my first impressions were.

As we sat down, James recounted the strange tale that had led to this day. He explained that his daughter had presented him with tickets to a showband concert at the Waterfront Arena in Belfast on 29 December 2006, at which Des McAlea was performing. James and Adelaide both enjoyed the night out. There was another, more personal reason why they were anxious to attend that concert, however. For thirty-one years a small, non-descript plastic bag had lain in the back of James O'Neill's wardrobe. Now and again, when he went to look for a pair of shoes or a tie, he would come across it. It always made him frown. The bag and its mysterious contents remained locked away until the night of the concert. This, he thought, was the ideal opportunity to gain closure to a long and painful saga.

He and his wife brought the bag to the concert. At first, they were confused to learn that Stephen wasn't taking part in the show, but they waited patiently while the other musicians signed autographs in the foyer. Finally, they saw Des McAlea alone and James approached him and introduced himself. He explained that he had been one of the policemen at the scene of the Miami murders. He then took out the bag and opened it. In it was a brown leather belt that had belonged to Fran O'Toole; James wanted to give it back. The belt had been among the items taken from the bodies of the three Miami men. As the SOCO, it had been his job to send the ruined clothes and personal possessions taken from the bodies of the three Miami men to the forensic science laboratory for analysis.

'After a while, they were sent back with instructions to destroy them because of the risk of contamination. The only thing that could have been returned to the next-of-kin was Fran O'Toole's leather belt. I held on to it with the intention of giving it to his wife or her family. But time went on, and I later learned that she had gone to Canada. I never got the opportunity to give it back until the other night. I'm glad to say, Des was delighted to receive it and told me he would give it to Fran's children.'

James O'Neill had held on to that belt all those years. Perhaps, as time passed, it had taken on a greater significance. Maybe it had come to symbolise the trauma that he experienced during his thirty-three years as a policeman in Northern Ireland. The sheer scale of his workload as a young RUC officer in the mid-1970s can be gleaned from the pages of his well-kept police notes, which he brought with him to our meeting.

The Miami, he had recorded, was case number 250. Only three weeks later, when he attended the scene of the murder of the two GAA men near Altnamacken, that number had increased to 266. Over the course of his career he investigated seventy-five bombings. Then there were the shooting incidents, as well as the rapes, traffic accidents and non-terrorist-related homicides that a policeman expects to deal with in his day-to-day work.

Yet, for James O'Neill and his wife, the night of the Miami Showband massacre will remain with them forever. 'We actually heard the bang,' Adelaide recalls. 'We were living in Ashgrove Park, near Banbridge, not far from where the attack took place, and the noise of the explosion woke us up. I remember lying in the dark thinking, Oh God, not another one. Whenever I heard a bomb go off, I used to pray, "Please don't let the phone ring. Please don't let the phone ring." Jim was always on call and I knew he would have to go. Sure enough, ten minutes later, the phone rang.'

At 2.15am on 31 July 1975, Jim picked up the phone to hear the station officer for Newry RUC station at the other end, 'Jim, there's been a big one. We need you down here now.'

James dressed hurriedly in the dark, trying to reassure Adelaide, then drove the few miles to Newry police station to pick up his SOCO gear. As the SOCO officer attached to the station, he provided the link between the detectives on the ground and the forensic laboratories.

'I had various specialist equipment stored there. A forensics kit, dabs, special clothing and polythene self-sealing bags for collecting evidence. I briefly saw Des McAlea at the station, but I didn't pay much attention. He was already being questioned by other detectives. By the time I left, I was aware that it was The Miami Showband that had been caught up in some sort of incident.'

He arrived at the scene shortly after 4.00am.

'It was in almost complete darkness when I got there. The road was still blocked off by the army. There was some light from the moon, but it was difficult to make out the scene. I left my car headlights on and got out to talk to the detectives who were already there. There weren't many police present at that stage, just the regular patrol teams from Newry. I was the first official investigator there. They pointed out some of the weapons and the bodies in the field. We agreed we would not be able to carry out a full investigation until it got brighter.

'I made notes for the report that I would write up later. I can show them to you, I have them here with me now.'

He retrieves a blue notebook from a black briefcase

he has beside him. The front is emblazoned with a RUC stamp. He turns back each meticulously written page until he reaches one with the date of 31 July printed at the top. Beneath the entry is a series of neat, hand-written lines and a hand-drawn map outlining the drama of that night. After thirty-one years, the note-book is in perfect condition and we have no problem reading his notations.

'I went down into the field where that big tree is now,' he points to his drawing. He refers to his notes and indicates the places where the young musicians were found. 'One was twenty-eight feet from the hedge, one was twenty-four feet and the other was twenty-one feet away. They didn't get very far.' The three tiny outlines indicating where the three men fell reveals the pathetically short distance they covered in their desperate attempt to flee before they were slaughtered.

He points out on his hand-drawn map where the terrorists' car was found and where the berets and weapons were retrieved. By following his every careful indications, it is possible to see a vague outline of the route the killers took as they escaped. Then he points out where the two bombers' bodies were retrieved. One was lying not far from the front of the wreckage of the bus, on the roadway. 'This man here was found thirty feet away. I think it was Boyle. He had pieces of the battery lodged in the back of his neck. But his head had been cut off. He had no arms, no legs and no face. The only way we could identify him was by a tattoo on his left upper arm.'

The other bomber, Somerville, had been blown a clear ninety feet away into the field. 'When I went down into the field, I could see the torso of one man. There was no head, one leg and just a wee bit of his arm left.'

The former detective slowly shakes his head in amazement.

He delves back into his black briefcase and retrieves another RUC booklet. 'I have some pictures from the scene that morning that will give you a better idea of what we found,' he says, opening the book. We flick through the black-and-white pictures. He points out one, now famous, picture of the aftermath of the massacre and indicates a figure walking through the wreckage. 'That's me there,' he says. 'This picture was taken while I was talking to one of my colleagues. You can see he's carrying one of the forensics kits.'

He flicks through the pictures and both Stephen and I gasp at the images. They are taken from various angles and show the remains of the minibus, which had been cut neatly in half by the force of the explosion. One picture shows the taped-off road with army personnel in the background. There are pictures of unrecognisable debris from the bus that had rained down all across the motorway and into the field.

'This is taken from the Newry direction, further down

the road,' O'Neill says, explaining one picture. 'The markings on the road here indicate where bullets and guns were found. This one shows where we found one of the Sterling submachine guns. It still had a full magazine and the safety catch was on, which suggests it belonged to one of the bombers.' The spot where the gun was found is located beside a twisted and torn piece of rubber from the windscreen. They are so far away from the scene of the explosion that it is almost impossible to make out the carnage in the background.

'You can see that the bomb did a lot of damage, but there was very little sign of a crater. That's the engine at the back and that's the front section. You're a very lucky man, Stephen,' he adds. 'I think the fact that you were so close to the explosion is what probably saved your life. The van took the brunt of the blow, but for anybody to survive that at all is absolutely amazing.'

'Were all these pictures used as evidence in the case against the Miami killers?' I ask.

'Oh aye, yes, they would have been,' James says. 'And hair samples would have been taken from the berets. We also found McDowell's glasses around here. I was pleasantly surprised to find they had a particular significance given that the optician in Lurgan quickly recognised how rare the prescription was.'

Stephen asks him if he could gauge from his initial investigation what had happened at the roadside in Buskhill.

'I had a fair idea in a short time from looking at the situation that there had been a premature explosion that had killed two of the men. Later on, we learned how they had lined you all up and asked you questions while these two were placing the bomb under the driver's seat. They were going to say, "On your way lads", and set the bomb on a short timer. The bomb itself was made up of 10–15lbs of commercial gelignite – the type used to blow up quarries. It may have been small in size, but it was very lethal – much more powerful, for instance, than a 250lb bomb made from the usual home-produced ingredients. As they were priming the bomb, it went off.'

'The UVF have attempted to diminish their responsibility,' Stephen tells him, 'claiming that the bomb was meant to go off after we were safe in our beds. They explained that they used two types of timer – an alarm clock with one or other hand removed, depending on the timing required. The hour hand afforded them a longer delay time as it moved more slowly. The minute hand only gave them a maximum of fifty-nine minutes. It was suggested to us that they used the long-timer, which would go off hours later.'

'No, that's absolutely wrong,' O'Neill responds. 'They used a short-timer on the bomb. You would not have gone much further than Newry when you would all have been killed.'

'How did you know it was a short timer?' Stephen asks.

'We examined the remains found at the scene,' he says, reading directly from his notes again. 'There were pieces of a short-delay detonator found, parts of the battery and traces of a bomb consisting of 10–15lbs of commercial explosive.'

'So there was no way the Miami would have been back in Dublin by the time it went off?'

'Absolutely not,' he says firmly.

'What happened when they tried to put it the van?' I ask.

'I'd say they had already set the timing device. They would connect the leads and move the hand of the clock around and as soon as it made contact with the terminal, it would go off. In this case, they accidentally moved the hand and it touched the terminal.'

'We were told that they would not use a short delay in case they blew themselves up,' Stephen adds 'We've been led to understand that they would not risk having us delayed, even though they had seen men monitoring our movements earlier that night. But you're saying that they could prime it on the spot?'

'Every bomb that goes off has to be primed first,' O'Neill answers. 'Before it is primed, it is harmless. They could have had it in the boot of a car and, as soon as they saw you approaching, they could set the timer.'

What this police investigator was telling us was that the intention all along was to cause an explosion that would leave no survivors. A bomb of that size was capable of obliterating the Miami minibus and everyone in it. As far as James O'Neill was concerned, this had been the plan all along.

It's an astonishing insight, which leaves no doubt as to the intentions of the UVF. We are still trying to take in the possible significance of what we have been told when O'Neill shows us more photographs. There are pictures of the Ford Escort that the UVF had left behind in their panic to get away. I point out that the horrific images are set against the backdrop of a beautiful summer's day. The incongruity of the setting makes it all the more disturbing.

'That wouldn't have been the first time that I'd have spent a nice summer's day at a scene like that,' O'Neill says.

I ask him about the state of the men caught up in the Miami atrocity and whether they would have been in a similar condition.

'Well, the difference is that, in an explosion, there is a lot of dismemberment, with pieces blown in many directions, while at a shooting, yes, they can be badly disfigured, but it's not as grisly at a post mortem. Having said that, the Miami members were very badly shot up, in particular Fran O'Toole. He was hit at least twenty times.'

When the sun came up later that morning, O'Neill

made the grim trip to the mortuary, where the bodies had been brought.

'Where were they laid?' Stephen asks him.

'They would all have been placed on separate slabs,' O'Neill says.

'Were our lads and the terrorists together?' Stephens asks.

'Well, Daisy Hill was not the largest hospital so the bodies would have been put in the same room.'

'What condition were they in? You say Fran was particularly bad?'

'Aye, Fran was in a bad way. He was shot through the face, and most of his head was gone. I can see there from my notes that he was hit twenty times – eight times in the face, four in the neck, three in the right arm, once in the back and there were four hits in the right side of his chest.'

'That would suggest that he was shot as he tried to get away?' Stephen says.

'That's right.'

'Do you think he was still alive when he went down?'

'I don't know, it's difficult to say. He was killed with bullets from a Sterling submachine gun. It's a rapid firing weapon capable of loosing off many rounds in seconds.'

'There was no mercy then, James?' I say.

'Absolutely no mercy was shown whatsoever. Tony was shot in the back five times and in the back of the head twice. He was also hit in the right and left side and right arm. One of the bullets came out through his left eye. There was also a .45 bullet in his scrotum, fired from an old-style revolver. Again, he was possibly running away when he was hit in the back before they finished him off. Also, there are indications that he was putting his arms up to protect himself.'

'And Brian?'

'Brian McCoy was shot four times. He was hit in the right neck, right forearm, rear left hand and left shoulder. All three were shot in the field, having been blasted over the hedge by the force of the bomb.'

'I remember being thrown into the air by that blast,' Stephen says.

'It's incredible that you're alive,' O'Neill says again. 'It was an amazing escape.'

'Was it?'

'Absolutely, it's a story in itself. I have notes here that I received a blue sweater and grey trousers taken from Stephen Travers. I was also handed a bullet that had been found inside a jacket belonging to you. I don't know what kind of a bullet it was, but it could have been a low-velocity .45 bullet.'

'So it went in through my right side, exited under my left arm and ended up in my jacket?' Stephen asks incredulously.

'It's very possible,' O'Neill replies. 'Bullets sometimes

lose their velocity and are found in clothing, just like that.'

Stephen tells him that he heard one of the gunmen saying, 'Come on, I got those bastards with dum-dums.'

'If they were that meticulous about finishing off the lads, why didn't they fire another burst into me?' he asks.

'I think you were the first man shot,' O'Neill suggests. 'They probably thought you were a goner, so they went after the others. Des had been blasted into the hedge here. We call this type of hedge a 'shuck', and they are very thick on the ground. I've no doubt that he would have got the same as the others had they found him.'

'I saw Fran's hand,' Stephen remembers. 'I recognised his jacket. There was the neatest line of blood on his open palm.'

'Well, he was hit three times in the right arm and he was found on his back, so that would make sense,' O'Neill remarks.

'They tell me that I saw more, but my mind has blocked it out,' Stephen tells him.

'It was a grim scene that nature has mercifully blocked out for you,' O'Neill says.

Reading again from his notes, O'Neill states that he remained at the scene from 4.00am until about 12.00 midday. The first post mortem was carried out on Brian

McCoy. O'Neill, looking directly at me, says he has some photographs of the lads, but warns that they are 'not very pleasant'. I glance over at Stephen. This is not what we had expected. As the detective retrieves a small folder of photographs from his briefcase, I wonder if this is something we want to do. I've occasionally seen pictures of death and destruction in magazines and on television, but this is different. These are Stephen's friends. I honestly don't know how to respond.

'Stephen?' I ask him.

'I have to see them,' he says quietly, his gaze falling from me onto O'Neill's folder.

This is where it has all been leading. After all the talking, the interviews and the research, after all I've read and written about the Miami, this is the ultimate reality. This is the irrefutable proof of what we have been discussing for the past year. Stripped of the cold analysis and forensic detail, this is what it has all been about.

Unsure of what to expect, I offer to look at them first. O'Neill gingerly opens the first book of photographs. I think it is Brian McCoy. The pictures are in black-and-white, but unerringly sharp. The first few are not as bad as I had feared. They show close-ups of the bullet wounds to various parts of the body. Without any apparent emotion, O'Neill discusses the pictures. 'This is a portion of the small of the back. These are the forearms, where he appears to have defended himself …' Each picture shows a neat, black mark where the bullet entered. At each turn of the page, the pictures get worse. I begin to feel dizzy. By the time we get to Tony, I'm short of breath. I feel panicked.

In a dispassionate voice, O'Neill describes the various entry and exit wounds. There is a photograph of a skull with numerous bullet holes. A close-up of Tony's face shows an exit wound through his left eye. They are getting progressively worse. I feel increasingly uneasy and I am on the verge of asking him to stop. I can't even look at Stephen. Although I feel sick to my stomach, something forces me to focus as each page is turned. The last few are probably the worst. They are pictures of the lads lying naked on the cool slabs of the mortuary. They are spread-eagled across the table, their eyes open or half-closed, no expressions on their faces. No hint of what their final moments were like.

The very last images prove to be the breaking point. Tony is lying on his back. His long hair is stuck to the cold tile. He is fully clothed. The peculiar platform shoes that they wore are clearly identifiable in the picture. His jacket is splayed out around him. He looks like a bedraggled doll dragged from the sea. The heavy dew- and blood-soaked clothes form a dark pool around him. Trickles of blood seep from under him.

By the time O'Neill reaches for Fran's file, I can bear no more. I know what happened to Fran – shot repeatedly in the face. Even O'Neill warns me that they are even worse again than those I've just seen. I cannot do it. I've seen enough and I ask him to stop.

Stephen looks at me with a mixture of fear and a strange deliberation in his eyes. 'Stephen,' I tell him, my voice quavering. 'I don't think you should see these.'

'I glimpsed one as James was passing them to you,' he says in a soft voice. 'I have to see them, Neil. I can't leave here without looking at them.'

I look over at James. He is staring at his knees. I glance at Adelaide. She doesn't meet my eyes. I don't know what to do here. I'm out of my depth. I breathe in deeply and stand up uneasily. I have to get some fresh air.

'Stephen,' I say, 'I'm going to the toilet. Wait until I get back.'

He agrees and I walk unsteadily from the room. I feel like I'm moving through water. There are faces and people in the lobby. It is obviously a busy place and when I listen back on the dictaphone later, I am astonished to hear noises in the background. Music is playing, waiters are taking orders, glasses are clinking, people's voices are raised, but my memory of that moment is one of absolute silence. I don't recall hearing a sound. It's an astonishing experience.

In the toilet, I grab the washbasin and stare hard into the mirror. I exhale a stale breath that I feel I've had in my lungs for far too long. I stand there for endless minutes, repeatedly rubbing my hands and splashing water in my face.

By the time I return to the table, James is showing the pictures to Stephen. Adelaide stares at the floor. I can't look at them again. Nobody speaks. I glance again at Adelaide and her face is downcast. O'Neill is quietly going through the pictures with Stephen, offering the same running commentary. 'Straight though the stomach … in through the shoulder … we used wire to see the trajectory, to give us an idea where the gunman had been standing … struck in the arm as he tried to defend himself … his raised arm …'

Stephen looks dazed. Suddenly, I'm very, very worried. This is a mistake. This is all wrong. What are we doing here? The only audible reaction from Stephen is a sigh as he moves a hand up to his face, his eyes staring into another world. 'Oh my God,' he whispers softly.

Finally, they reach the end of the book and, thankfully, James puts the photos away. Nobody speaks for a moment. Without trying to be too dramatic, I honestly cannot remember whether it was seconds or minutes before somebody spoke, but it was Stephen who finally broke the silence.

'It's almost like a closure to see Tony's and Brian's faces. I've been told that they were dead, but I could only visualise them alive on stage. I found it difficult to believe that they were dead. It's like the curtain came down on a performance and I'm still waiting for the next act. I think if I hadn't seen them, I would be sorry. But I won't look at Fran because I know what happened to him and out of respect for him, it wouldn't be right to view the handi-work of the butchers.'

'Perhaps all this may bring some peace?' offers O'Neill.

'I had no idea a week ago that this would be brought back to me so vividly,' Stephen says, closing his eyes. 'This is a watershed in my life. For the rest of my days, I'll remember today.'

We all sit quietly for a moment. I am still reeling.

Stephen opens his eyes and says, 'It has not taken away the good memories, you know. I still remember them as they were, happy, smiling, laughing.'

'That's good, Stephen,' we console him. 'That's good. It's good that you can remember them the way you do.'

'I was told once that it could all come back some day. I took a chance today, it could all have come back, but it hasn't. It was like standing at the edge of a cliff and feeling that urge to jump. Today has made me realise how close I came to death.'

'You're a miracle man,' O'Neill says.

'Sometimes I feel that I'm dead. I once saw a movie called *The Sixth Sense*. Bruce Willis played a counsellor to a child who sees dead people. The twist is that he himself is a ghost, but he doesn't know it. Sometimes, I feel like that. I'll be sitting in a room on my own and I'll suddenly think, Where am I? Am I dead? It is at times like that that it is hard to make sense of your life – in fact, it's hard to make sense of anything.'

O'Neill nods very gently. From Adelaide's expression, I just know they've seen all this before.

'God bless you, Jim. I don't know how you did it,' Stephen adds.

'I tried to remain professional but at the same time I look at certain things, like these pictures, and I know so many things were not right,' he says, resignedly. 'After thirty-three years, I did the best I could. I never expected any thanks, I just did my job, and did it fair and square, and I'm content with that.'

'You and your family had to live with this every day,' Stephen says.

'Our children were very well shielded,' Adelaide says. 'And they grew up with a good attitude. All went to university and did well. But at the same time, it still haunts us. We are very lucky to have come out of it with Jim alive. But how many death threats have there been? It leaves its mark on you.'

'I'm sure you realised when you came home from work how important a good family background was,' Stephen says.

'That's what it was all about at the end of the day,' the policeman agrees.

'Anne, who was only twenty-one at the time, or I had never seen anything like this before,' Stephen tells him. 'We had been living in a small country town on the borders of Tipperary, Waterford and Kilkenny. It was a very close-knit community, quiet and peaceful.'

'I think that may explain a lot about your character and your ability to forgive,' O'Neill says.

'When we met the UVF commander, I thought I might hate him, but I couldn't. And now, if the men who did this sat down beside me, I'd still be incapable of hating them. I would not even raise my voice to them. I thought by looking at these pictures, I would finally feel some hatred. But I can't. It's something I have never been able to do. It's almost as if something is missing.'

'Well,' offers O'Neill, 'if you had been eaten up with hatred, wouldn't that have destroyed you? Aren't you really lucky, in many ways, that you have such a good outlook? I think that is what has pulled you through.'

Driving back that night, Stephen and I are both in what I can only describe as a state of shock. Listening back on the tape, I can hear us both babbling. I'm certainly not making much sense. Stephen, ironically, regained his composure sooner than me.

'Up until today, I had always thought of the men who did this as misguided foot-soldiers ordered to carry out a job. But the obvious savagery goes far beyond a man going out to fight for a cause. It took a psychopath to be able to stand over Fran and shoot him that many times in the face. They appear to have enjoyed their work. It's savagery not worthy of a human being. It was not out of fear that they shot them and then, as they lay dead, shot them again and again and again. Those photographs proved that to me today.'

He admits that he was affected very badly by the pictures, particularly those of the lads in their clothes.

'I could relate to them through the clothes they were wearing. When you see them lying naked you think, That is a dead body. They are in a clinical environment and they are being cared for. But seeing them with their clothes on … that's how I last remember them, wearing those same clothes … I remember Tony was very proud of that new jacket … those jeans and platform shoes.'

I admit to Stephen that I felt powerless and did not know what to do when James O'Neill took out the photographs.

'I'm a grown man,' he replies after a while. 'I had to do it for myself. Those images will be in my mind for a long time, but I'm glad I saw them. I have to say though, that I started to feel my heart race and my knees were shaking. Tony didn't look like himself at all. I don't ever remember him looking so serious. He always had a smile on his face. As for Brian, God, it looked like he was still alive.

That was the first time,' he adds after another silence, 'that I felt I was incredibly lucky.'

'You were, Stephen,' I tell him. 'James said so himself.

He must have seen a lot in his time and he still described you as a miracle man.'

'I know, you hear that, "He's a miracle man. He is so lucky to be alive", but it's hard to imagine, to really accept it until you live through a day like today. God knows what I saw that night.'

'It's impossible to know what was going on in your head back then,' I reflect.

'It's impossible to know what is going on in my head right now,' he answers. 'On one level, I'm this rational, normal human being, sitting here talking to you, but at the same time there are fourteen different universes swirling around in my head.'

'For what it's worth, Stephen, and it's probably little or no consolation, it knocked me for six as well,' I say.

'Today you've been thrown into the thick of it, Neil. Nobody should have to see that.'

'I just wasn't ready for it, that's all,' I say more to myself than anyone else. 'It just caught me by surprise. It really brought home to me what this book has all been about.'

'You found it hard?'

'It was upsetting, but we could not come all this way and back down at the last minute. I really don't think I could have done that either.'

'Here's the strange thing,' Stephen says after a while. 'I've been trying to figure this out since I looked at the pictures and put into words what I saw. And the best I can come up with is I've seen all this before … it wasn't new to me. When I saw them lying there, I thought, this is all familiar … somewhere, deep in my mind, I had seen those very images before. I'm lucky that it didn't trigger anything worse.'

'I think that's it, Stephen,' I say. 'Maybe you're over it now. Maybe there is nothing more to fear … maybe there is nothing more that can come back. Ever.'

'You know it's not the physical destruction that was the worst part. As I looked at the photographs, all I could think was – is that the best they could do? This great army? Though their history is contaminated by the murder of three beautiful people, it wasn't their greatest crime. No, they did worse by taking them away from their friends and families. Helen McCoy was left with two small children. She's had the rest of her life to contemplate the unnecessary murder of her husband while her two children grew up knowing that people from their own parents' birthplace, religion and political background murdered their father. Fran's wife and two children … Tony's fiancée, his parents, his siblings … the men who did this did a lot more than just kill three men. They caused a wave that destroyed everything in its path and disgusted an already hardened world. Even their own families were destroyed when they were sent to jail. They stigmatised their family names forever and no amount of murals or propaganda can cover up the shame they afflicted on the loyalist community that they so scurrilously claimed to represent. They were traitors to true Protestantism, a creed which holds such outrages in utter contempt. They were anathema to the great faith of my own grandmother. The consequences of their unbridled evil are an even worse crime. But they have failed to make me hate them.'

We've parked up where I left my car all those hours ago. I feel very different from how I felt then. Before I get out of the car, we talk about the lads for one last time.

'The biggest concern Brian had was painting his children's rooms,' Stephen says, laughing almost to himself. 'Tony, from the moment I met him, took nothing seriously except his music and Fran ... Fran, probably the deepest of them all, just loved his way through life. He adored the adulation of the fans, not in an egotistical way, but he revelled in the happiness he created.'

'And what about you?'

'It's an ill wind that blows no good ... I hope I've become a better person.'

Epilogue

Under the headline 'We Must Learn from History', the editorial in Dublin's *Evening Herald* on Thursday, 30 November 2006 ran as follows:

'Young people might question why the government keeps revisiting events of the past like the latest report on the Miami Showband atrocity in 1975. To put it in context, the gunning down of three members of the Miami band was the equivalent, in its day, of the British security forces colluding to shoot members of Westlife. The deep shock felt by everyone in the 1970s is still remembered thirty years later. We can always learn lessons from the events of the past. Unless we deal with the residual anger, change attitudes and acknowledge wrongdoing, we cannot move confidently into a peaceful future.'

'We cannot move confidently into a peaceful future.' The last phrase keeps running through my mind. That editorial could have been written by Stephen Travers; it sums up perfectly what he has been saying for the past thirty-one years.

Over the eighteen months we've spent together on this project, Stephen has impressed on me how the Miami Showband incident serves as a reminder of what can happen when society slips into complacency. Judging from the editorials written at the end of 2006, it would appear that most of the country would agree with him.

On the surface, it feels that the worst of the Troubles are long gone, but, as we learned from the Craftsman, while there is a genuine desire to keep it that way, there is always a risk that things could flare up again if the politicians get it wrong. 'Neither side has gone away, you know.'

And now the Miami is back in the news, thirty-one years after they innocently stopped their bus and stepped out into history. I glance over the headlines on the pile of newspapers in front of me as I wait for Stephen to emerge from his meeting with An Taoiseach, Bertie Ahern.

'Butchered by the British' in the Irish *Daily Mail*; 'London must Co-operate on Collusion Inquiries – Ahern' in *The Irish Times*; 'I Don't Need a Massacre Probe' in the Irish *Sun*; 'The Day the Music Stopped' in the *Irish*

Independent; 'Government backs Report on Collusion in Northern Ireland' in the *Irish Examiner* – the news has made the front pages of almost every national newspaper. Inside, there are larger news features examining the astonishing revelations in more depth.

The media is reporting the findings of a high-level government subcommittee, which studied various atrocities that resulted in eighteen deaths during the mid-1970s, including those of Fran, Brian and Tony. The subcommittee had examined the earlier findings of Justice Henry Barron and concluded that there was, as has always been suspected, widespread collusion between loyalist terror groups and British security forces in Northern Ireland. The joint Oireachtas Committee on Justice stated that it was 'horrified' that people employed by the British administration to preserve peace and to protect citizens were 'engaged in the creation of violence and the butchering of innocent victims'.

And the buck does not stop there. According to the latest investigations, the identities of the killers of The Miami Showband were known within weeks at the highest levels in the British government. The subcommittee also referred to a 1975 meeting between then Labour British Prime Minister Harold Wilson, Secretary of State for Northern Ireland Merlyn Rees, the leader of the Conservative opposition and future British Prime Minister, Margaret Thatcher, and Airey Neave, the

Conservative party's spokesperson on Northern Ireland, who was murdered by Republicans four years later. From the minutes of this meeting, it appears the British government was 'more worried about sectarian murders than bombings in Belfast'. However, the British failed to do anything about the fact that their army considered the UDR to be 'heavily infiltrated by extremist Protestants who could not be relied upon in a crisis'.

In almost all of the newspapers, the reports are accompanied by the now familiar black-and-white photographs of the Miami in their heyday ... the smiling musicians lined up in the park, the six strapping lads in their smart 1970s clothes and hair, Stephen, the latest addition, proudly taking his place at the end of the line-up, all grinning at the camera. 'This is fun, lads,' they are laughing. 'We're going to have a ball,' they seem to be saying.

Under these pictures are other images now associated with the band – the shaded motorway strewn with debris; the Miami band card lying among shards of torn metal on the road; the remains of the minibus torn in two by the powerful explosion. Now, the first photographs take on a different meaning, they become a mass card, images of remembrance. As I look at the photographs, a few lines of a poem run through my head – ironically, it is one associated with the fallen heroes of the British forces:

'They shall grow not old, as we that are left grow old;
Age shall not weary them, nor the years condemn.
At the going down of the sun and in the morning
We will remember them.'

I sip my coffee and wait for Stephen, glancing at my watch and wondering what's keeping them. The meeting at Government Buildings this morning was supposed to take half-an-hour, but it is now late afternoon and there is still no sign of him.

With the publication of the report, the focus has now turned on Taoiseach Bertie Ahern and his response to the findings. Speaking to reporters before the meeting, accompanied by some of the victims' families, Ahern said it was 'deeply troubling' to learn that the British authorities had aided and assisted loyalist paramilitaries.

'It is absolutely essential that the British government examines the findings of all these reports, as well as the forthcoming MacEntee Report into the 1974 Dublin and Monaghan bombings, and that it fully co-operates with all investigations into the serious issues that have arisen.'

Finally, the phone rings. It is Stephen. He has left Government Buildings, and has just finished with the media scrum outside the huge gates. He had dashed through the reporters and photographers, stopped long enough to give a quick comment, but did not linger.

What he said to them will be broadcast by radio stations and TV studios late into the night.

'While I'm grateful for this report, I didn't need it to tell me what I already knew, that there was a British army officer on the scene in charge of the operation that night. This was not a bogus checkpoint or a set-up. It was a British army operation.'

I walk out of the hotel and stand in the rain until he pulls up in his car. As we slip into the traffic, I ask him how the meeting went with Bertie Ahern.

'He seemed genuinely concerned that the British should stop ignoring the evidence of such highly respected inquiries and he made a commitment to do his best to get their co-operation. He knows how we feel. We trust him to keep his promise. He has to ask the British for the co-operation they have so long refused.'

I ask him how he feels now that it is out in the open, after all these years.

'I think it was pretty obvious all along that there was collusion, but now there is no question in anyone's mind that it took place. However, it now depends on whether the British government has the courage to acknowledge it. I can understand the reluctance of Whitehall to accept this insurmountable evidence as they may face huge compensation claims.'

I mention to Stephen that it has taken a long time for the bubble to burst.

'It has, and it seems that the longer the conspiracy of silence went on, the bigger the bubble. I've always believed that both the British and Irish governments co-operated with each other at that time against what they saw as their common enemy – the IRA. The Irish authorities didn't ask the questions that needed to be asked because they didn't want to rock the boat. Burying their heads in the sand simply put off the day of reckoning. Today, the chickens have officially come home to roost in the reports of widespread collusion, deep infiltration of the forces of law and order and state-sponsored death and destruction.'

As we drive though the rain-soaked streets, we talk about where writing this book has led us. We reflect on that day we spent with James and Adelaide O'Neill and I ask him if he feels that, finally, he is getting some closure on the events of the past.

'I'm not looking for closure here, Neil. I never have been. I've been forced to open and close all sorts of doors through the writing of this book. One reporter asked me today if I've been forced to relive some bad experiences, but some I'm only recognising for the first time. The truth is that I've been in denial for a long time. Rather than closure, this is a beginning. I have recalled with terror getting out of the bus that night. That has come back with frightening force. In my mind, that's the moment when everything changed. I saw more than I realise that night, but my mind had gone into protection mode. All I could think about as I lay in the field was that we were going to be off the road for the weekend. I can see now that I immediately refused to accept the reality of the situation.

'My doctor recently said that I had compartmentalised all these issues. It's an Americanism for neatly filing away issues that I didn't wish to confront. But, eventually, you have to deal with them and this book and the memorial campaign have forced me to do that. I have to admit though, sometimes the gravity of it all really gets to me. It really hit me after seeing those pictures, and now we are in a situation that involves the highest echelons of two governments. I felt all along that what happened to the Miami was important, but it's only now that it has all been brought home to me. Before I left the house this morning to meet the Taoiseach, my fourteen-year-old daughter asked me to tell him that schoolbags are too heavy for Irish children. Thirty-one years ago, my political agenda would not have been far removed from that level of innocence. My major concerns would have been with car tax or street lighting. All I ever wanted to do was play a bass guitar. Now, I find myself engaged in events that are part of history. It's overwhelming at times.'

I ask him if he feels he has become a standard-bearer for peace, justice and reconciliation.

'I don't think so, I wouldn't be worthy to represent those great aspirations. But I do have a responsibility. I survived and was given a second chance to enjoy all the things in life denied to my friends. But there is a price to be paid for that. I was left alive to tell the truth.

'My main concern now, as I said to the Taoiseach, is that this never happens again. We must learn lessons from the past. The only way I can hope for a good future for my child is to avoid the mistakes of the past. My parents must have felt that way, too. They had just come through the Second World War and must have thought that it couldn't happen again. Then their own son gets shot and almost killed by someone with a political agenda. I don't want that to happen to anyone's child. If we continue to sweep things under the carpet and not recognise that these things were all too possible only recently, then chances are it will happen again. If it does, I want my government to have the right structures in place to deal with it properly. I told the Taoiseach that we cannot afford to live in a country that is content to turn a blind eye to murder and collusion and all the other things that are anathema to civilised societies.

I believe the only way forward is through education. The Craftsman acknowledged this. He now admits that the best thing he can do for his community, after the abject failure of violence by all the protagonists, is to educate his people. I feel we met a man for whom reality has hit home. Whatever his agenda on the day of our meeting, I don't doubt for a second that he loves his people. Though he was misguided in his thinking, I believe he has learned some valuable lessons which he can now pass on to all of us.

It was reassuring to hear him admit that violence is wrong. I believe him to be a man genuinely concerned for the future of his people. I believe that he wants what I want – a better country for our children, just as our parents wanted for us.'

We have left the outskirts of Dublin and are now on the motorway, heading north. The rain has stopped, but the sky is darkening steadily. It will be another hour before we get there. We talk about Stephen's return from England, when he plunged himself into a new career. I have seen him play with Johnny Fean, guitarist with the legendary Horslips. It is a collaboration that gives him much joy. He also runs a successful music agency. He has been honoured at Áras an Uachtaráin by President Mary McAleese for his services to the Irish music industry. His other great passion is the campaign for a memorial to his fallen Miami friends. Dublin City Council has, to date, conditionally offered the families of Tony, Fran and Brian a site, and at today's meeting the Taoiseach offered his full support for the project.

We are getting closer to where this story all began. It has been several months since we were in this place. Then, it was also in the bleak depths of winter. Now, we are back again for one last visit. We get out of the car and walk towards the field. On our previous visit, I had only a vague idea of what had happened here. Now, having been immersed in the story for the best part of a year, having seen James O'Neill's photographs of the scene, it is incredibly moving to be standing at the same spot.

Stephen breaks the silence.

'The only bright lights in this part of the world during the 1970s were bands like the Miami. They were totally blind to sectarianism. They could sit together in a van and not know or care what religion or political persuasion each other was. Nor did they care about the religion or political persuasion of their audience. They were good, young men. They ran the gauntlet to bring happiness to ordinary folk. They loved being loved. They brought people of all traditions together. Only good people do that, but they died for their innocence. If there are memorials to be erected, let them be to good people. That's how they should be remembered, as icons of happiness and decency, as a light that shone through the darkness of the Troubles.'

'Do you feel you have a duty to achieve that for them, Stephen?' I ask.

'People from the North and the South have already honoured their unique sacrifice. The families and friends of Tony, Fran and Brian are deeply appreciative of that.'

'Who do you think bears the ultimate responsibility for the Miami massacre?' I ask him.

'I would like to feel that the tragedy was due to ignorance, intolerance, sectarianism, evil or some other abstract condition. It was the work of bad people. Sometimes, bad people are in authority. We can't control renegades, we can't reason with psychopaths, but we can demand that a neighbouring government act in a lawful, civilised manner. British soldiers were sent out to murder innocent people. We have to stand up for ourselves. We were slaves to injustice for far too long. We should not sell our freedom. This may not be on the forefront of everyone's minds in a country that is booming, but history shows just how costly our freedom has been. We must demand that Britain act like the civilised nation she claims to be. It has been accepted by our government that collusion between the security forces and terrorists did take place and has been verified by irrefutable international reports. When such investigations unambiguously find that Britain colluded in murder and is, therefore, guilty of murder, she must answer the charges. Every day, the British government accuses Syria or Iran or some other far-flung place of aiding terrorists – they should examine their own consciences. How can we watch the news and nod our heads in agreement with them as they accuse other countries of sponsoring terrorism. They sent their trained soldiers out to murder a pop group on their way home from a concert. We cannot be complacent and believe that it could never happen again.'

'What do we have to do?' I ask him.

'Edmund Burke once said, "All that is required for evil to prevail is for good men to do nothing." I believe we should never take our freedom or our safety for granted. We must make sure that this part of our history never repeats itself. To safeguard the future, it is necessary to understand the past.'

The last of the winter sun is setting over the cold fields. The scene has not changed. The same trees still stand mute, having borne silent witness to the horror of 31 July 1975.

We take some photographs and walk back to the car. We stand still for a moment, looking back into the field, saying our last goodbyes. Stephen opens the car door.

'God bless them. If only we had been allowed to go on our way that night.'

Postscript

Just before this book first went to print in the summer of 2007, another astonishing development occurred.

On Sunday 29 July, 2007 the *Irish Mail on Sunday* stated that Thomas Raymond Crozier had offered to meet with Stephen. Under the headline 'Sorry for the Miami', Crozier was quoted as saying: 'It couldn't be justified at the time or since and I am sorry it happened. There were victims on both sides who should never have been touched and the band were among those. I totally and absolutely regret it.'

Stephen was also quoted in the article: 'It makes me very happy if Thomas has moved away from violence. It's great news to us and for our communities generally. If Thomas and others are sorry, then it will stop others suffering.'

At the time of this book going to press, no effort had been made to contact Stephen. However, in the light of the news of Crozier's willingness to meet, Stephen and I made the journey to Crozier's home in the hope of talking to him, but to no avail. Stephen remains open to a meeting taking place; only time will tell whether it ever will.

10 April 2008

Following the publication of this book, the story of The Miami Showband garnered renewed widespread interest.

The official launch of the book by the former Taoiseach Albert Reynolds in Eason Hanna's on Dawson Street on 11 September 2007 was quickly followed by a whirlwind tour of most of the country's media outlets. Stephen embarked on a punishing schedule of radio and newspaper interviews as the book created a surge of fresh curiosity about the group and the fate that befell them. Once again, Stephen found himself under the spotlight as a new generation of awestruck journalists quizzed him about the awful events that have been indelibly written into modern Irish history.

More often than not, he was obliged to recall the incident in all its terrible detail. He found the process an exercise in forbearance, explaining to print journalists and radio and TV reporters the happenings and consequences of the events on the morning of 31 July 1975. At times, he attempted to steer the line of questioning away from the events of the night and on to broader subjects but invariably younger writers, unfamiliar with the tragedy, were curious to learn what had happened on the night of the massacre. It was a trial he readily accepted in order to bring the story and, more importantly, the lessons to be learned from it, to as wide an audience as possible.

As the dust settled, he found himself taking stock of his achievements. His greatest wish remains to be that the world will realise the futility of violence and the bankruptcy and disgrace it visits on any cause regardless of how firmly it is believed in. However, a sense of relief that the book was published and well received was replaced with the realisation that this was not quite the end of the Miami Showband story.

The success of the book leant a new immediacy to the efforts to commemorate his three friends and the momentum would carry him to the steps of the former National Ballroom on Dublin's Parnell Square on an unseasonably bright day in December 2007. There, in front of hundreds of well wishers An Taoiseach Bertie Ahern unveiled a permanent memorial to Fran O'Toole, Tony Geraghty and Brian McCoy.

The event was more a celebration than a sombre

remembrance ceremony and numerous celebrities and dignitaries enthusiastically supported what turned out to be a very joyful occasion.

Former MEP and Eurovision Song Contest winner Dana Rosemary Scallon, with the help her talented brother Gerry Brown, sang the beautiful touching song penned by Fran O'Toole and Des (Lee) McAlea ,'Love Is'. Afterwards, at a reception hosted by Dublin City Council at the Hugh Lane Gallery, there were smiles all round and a warm feeling of friendship among the families and friends of The Miami Showband. Fran's daughter Rachel had travelled from Canada with her sister Kelly's young son to attend the event. Helen McCoy was accompanied by her son, Keith. The Geraghty family too was represented. Former RUC detective Jim O'Neill and his wife Adelaide rubbed shoulders with Ray Millar, Des Lee and Chris Hudson, the man whose contacts led us to the UVF leadership.

After the unveiling ceremony, as I shook his hand to take my leave, Stephen casually mentioned another development in the Miami Showband story.

The previous month Des McAlea met with Stephen at his home in Cork where both men discussed the Miami Showband incident for the very first time. Understandably, the details of the discussion remain private, but Stephen said he now had a clearer insight into the mindset of his fellow survivor in the days, months and years since the terrible massacre of their colleagues. Amazingly, the seeds of a Miami Showband reunion tour, involving Stephen, Des, Ray Millar and former Miami Showband member Paul Ashford, together with guitar legend Johnny Fean and Gerry Brown were sown on that day.

The prospect of a reformed Miami, featuring the surviving members of the line up that last took to the stage on that fateful night thirty-three years earlier would became a reality two months after the unveiling ceremony when I accompanied Stephen to London to accept a literary award for this book.

The UK-based *Irish World* newspaper awarded us the *Irish World* Literary Prize for 2008 and at the prestigious black-tie affair, and to thunderous applause, Stephen and I walked onto the stage to collect the prize.

Later that evening, the newly reformed Miami Showband launched into a stirring medley of their hit songs. But when they played 'Clap Your Hands, Stomp Your Feet', the hall erupted with wild cheering and applause. Everyone was on their feet. From my position on the balcony, I had a sense of what it must have been like to witness the excitement of the Miami all those years ago. I looked at a woman beside me and although she was smiling and clapping her hands to the beat I could see tears streaming down her face.

After an emotional night, we arrived back in Dublin

where the Miami is now in rehearsal for a tour that is being scheduled for autumn 2008. The proceeds of the Belfast and Dublin concerts will go to the charity Children in Crossfire.

Stephen has recently accepted an invitation from the charity founder, Richard Moore, to accompany him to Africa to witness the great work of the foundation. On 4 May 1972, at the age of ten, while innocently making his way home from school in Derry city, Richard Moore was permanently blinded by a rubber bullet. He had since made contact with the British army captain that fired the bullet and they have become firm friends.

Stephen reflected that it would be wonderful if out of two such terrible events, something positive could be achieved on the other side of the world.

It would appear that it will be yet another chapter in the story of Stephen Travers and The Miami Showband.

Acknowledgements

In her book *Orlando: City of Dreams*, Joy Wallace Dickinson quotes the Reverend Jerry Girley, a founder of The West Orange (County) Reconciliation Task Force:

> The idea is 'let sleeping dogs lie'. 'What's the point in digging up a painful past?' people ask. Girley is ready with a response. 'When you visit a doctor for the first time, you don't just start with a physical exam," he says. "You answer a clipboard full of questions; you give your medical history. That's because there's a predictive value in knowing your history. [Then] there's a path to greater understanding.'

I owe a great debt of gratitude to all those who helped me rebuild my life following the incident of 31 July 1975 and to those who inspired and fortified me by their example before and after the event.

Most of all to the love of my life, my wife and best friend, Anne Travers, for her unconditional love, patience and sacrifice and for giving me my greatest treasure, our daughter Sean.

My parents, Patrick and Mary Travers, for their love and inspiration.

Our immediate and extended families.

Des Lee, Ray Millar and Brian Maguire.

Helen and Keith McCoy for their courage.

The Geraghty family for their dignity.

The O'Toole family, especially Fran's brother, Michael.

James Blundell, Tony Treacy and everyone at Daisy Hill Hospital in 1975, especially Belle.

All at Elm Park in 1975.

Billy and Maria Byrne for being our family in 1975.

Marie and Bertie Murphy for their love and kindness.

My great friend Johnny Fean for restoring my confidence as a musician.

Liam O'Dwyer for his loyalty and friendship.

Arthur Walters for his gentleness and dignity.

My friend Joe Carroll, I miss him very much!

Mary Feehan for her encouragement.

Ronan Collins for remembering.

Margaret Urwin for her great kindness and energy.

Ken Murray and all in the media for their constant support.

Peter Taylor and Julia Hannis.

The President of Ireland, Mary McAleese.

An Taoiseach, Bertie Ahern.

Former Taoiseach Albert Reynolds.

The Mayor of London, Ken Livingstone.

Dublin City Manager, John Tierney.

Dublin City Arts Officer, Jack Gilligan.

Alan Brecknell of the Pat Finucane Centre.

John Matthias Murphy, Paul Ashford, Mike Hanrahan, Jim Aiken, David Hull, George Jones, Julie Price, Gerry Brown, Mick Rowley, Alan Murphy, Dana, Maggie

Fean, Kieran McClure, Barry McLeavy, Eamonn Delaney, Chris Browne, Eddie Pierce, Finbar Holian, Richard Hennessy, Nick Kenny, Marty Walsh, the Fagan family, Paddy Cowan, Maurice McElroy, Jim Millar, Jim Bradford, Wishey Patterson, Liamie Doherty, Nicky Cahill, Jesse Walsh, Clem Walsh, Don and Eleanor Weldon, Brian D'Arcy, John O'Rourke, Brian Hurley, Jimmy Magee for 'that remark', Mick Crowley, Cranston King, Jackie McAuley, Mitch Palmer, Tommy Lundy, Frank Hayes and Henry McCullough, for being an icon and an inspiration.

All my colleagues past and present in the UK and Ireland – the artists, agents, managers and promoters who continue to sponsor and support live entertainment.

All the artists, friends and media who took part in and supported the Miami Showband 30th Anniversary Memorial Concert at Vicar Street.

During the thirty-one years between the incident and starting to write this book, I had blown hot and cold about the idea of publishing my story. Some people advised, some encouraged and some even demanded that it be written. Others warned me about the negative consequences of revisiting my past and/or of opening old wounds. I'm thankful now for my past inertia. The truth is, I wasn't ready. The two years spent writing this book have been among the most testing of my life. I would never have done it on my own. From the very beginning, I believed the story should be viewed and related from two separate perspectives. I was, understandably, emotionally involved and, at times, too close to the event. Sometimes, I took it for granted that my viewpoint was a universal one. I needed a younger co-writer with no preconceived ideas on the subject, with no political axe to grind or no great expertise on Northern Ireland political affairs and, unlike me, no baggage – just an insatiable curiosity, a sharp, independent mind and plenty of energy and enthusiasm. Throughout our journey, Neil Fetherstonhaugh supported, challenged and accompanied me every step of the way. He brought a professionalism, discipline and experience to this project for which I am truly grateful.

'Though we have walked through the valley of the shadow of death', we have survived and returned as friends.

Stephen Travers

May 2007

Neil Fetherstonhaugh would like to thank:

His mum, Dot.

Paul Howard for his friendship, brilliant advice and clever insights.

Sue Bolger, Robin 'Bob' Eklund, Carl 'Burner' and Karen Byrne, Tony 'Gally' Gallagher, Fiachra 'Fod' O'Donoghue, Knuttle and Fiona, Damo and Suzy, Raghnall O'Donoghue, Imedla 'Meel' Huggins, Derek and Yvonne, Gav, Ronan 'Rozy' O'Brien, Johnny and Aido, for the beers.

Faraway friends Pat Coyler and Suzanne Blaney and Kev Sheehy.

The Perrem family.

Steve Travers for the journey; Tony McCullagh and Ray O'Neill of the Dublin People group.

And, finally, Elizabeth 'Liz' Perrem … for saying yes!

The authors would like to thank:

Producer Jonathan Golden of Doubleband Films for getting the ball rolling.

Faith O'Grady for picking it up.

Breda Purdue of Hodder Headline Ireland for running with it.

Claire Rourke and Ciara Doorley of Hodder Headline Ireland for making it what it is – it is customary for authors to thank their editors, but in this case a particular note of genuine thanks and appreciation must be acknowledged for the work that Claire and Ciara put into this book.

Kieran Kelly.

Chris Hudson for making it happen.

James O'Neill and Adelaide for their bravery.

Permission Acknowledgements

Extract from 'For The Fallen' by Laurence Binyon (1914). Reproduced with kind permission of the Society of Authors as the literary representative of the Estate of Laurence Binyon.

The publishers would like to thank the *Belfast Telegraph* and James O'Neill for their kind permission to use images in the book. Every effort has been made with regard to reproducing copyright material. The author and publisher will be glad to rectify any omissions at the earliest possible opportunity.